DEVELOPMENT CENTRE STUDIES

# TECHNOLOGY AND GLOBAL COMPETITION

## THE CHALLENGE FOR NEWLY INDUSTRIALISING ECONOMIES

BY
DIETER ERNST
AND
DAVID O'CONNOR

DEVELOPMENT CENTRE
OF THE ORGANISATION FOR ECONOMIC CO-OPERATION AND DEVELOPMENT

Pursuant to article 1 of the Convention signed in Paris on 14th December 1960, and which came into force on 30th September 1961, the Organisation for Economic Co-operation and Development (OECD) shall promote policies designed:

- to achieve the highest sustainable economic growth and employment and a rising standard of living in Member countries, while maintaining financial stability, and thus to contribute to the development of the world economy;
- to contribute to sound economic expansion in Member as well as non-member countries in the process of economic development; and
- to contribute to the expansion of world trade on a multilateral, non-discriminatory basis in accordance with international obligations.

The original Member countries of the OECD are Austria, Belgium, Canada, Denmark, France, the Federal Republic of Germany, Greece, Iceland, Ireland, Italy, Luxembourg, the Netherlands, Norway, Portugal, Spain, Sweden, Switzerland, Turkey, the United Kingdom and the United States. The following countries became Members subsequently through accession at the dates indicated hereafter: Japan (28th April 1964), Finland (28th January 1969), Australia (7th June 1971) and New Zealand (29th May 1973).

The Socialist Federal Republic of Yugoslavia takes part in some of the work of the OECD (agreement of 28th October 1961).

*The Development Centre of the Organisation for Economic Co-operation and Development was established by decision of the OECD Council on 23rd October 1962.*

*The purpose of the Centre is to bring together the knowledge and experience available in Member countries of both economic development and the formulation and execution of general economic policies; to adapt such knowledge and experience to the actual needs of countries or regions in the process of development and to put the results at the disposal of the countries by appropriate means.*

*The Centre has a special and autonomous position within the OECD which enables it to enjoy scientific independence in the execution of its task. Nevertheless, the Centre can draw upon the experience and knowledge available in the OECD in the development field.*

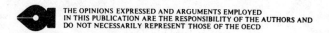

THE OPINIONS EXPRESSED AND ARGUMENTS EMPLOYED IN THIS PUBLICATION ARE THE RESPONSIBILITY OF THE AUTHORS AND DO NOT NECESSARILY REPRESENT THOSE OF THE OECD

Publié en français sous le titre :

TECHNOLOGIE ET COMPÉTITION MONDIALE
Un défi pour les nouvelles économies
industrialisées

This study forms part of the Development Centre's research programme on comparative advantages in new technology, industry and trade. It is partly based on a high-level experts meeting organised under the auspices of the Centre at Dourdan, France, in February 1989.

*Also available*

"Development Center Studies"

FINANCIAL POLICIES AND DEVELOPMENT by Jacques J. Polak (1989)
(41 89 01 1) ISBN 92-64-13187-6   234 pages                    £17.00  US$29.50  FF140.00  DM58.00

RECYCLING JAPAN'S SURPLUSES FOR DEVELOPING COUNTRIES by T. Ozawa (1989)
(41 88 05 1) ISBN 92-64-13177-9   114 pages                    £11.00  US$19.00  FF90.00  DM37.00

NEW FORMS OF INVESTMENT IN DEVELOPING COUNTRIES: Mining, Petrochemicals, Automobiles, Textiles, Food (1989)
(41 89 02 1) ISBN 92-64-13188-4   368 pages                    £28.00  US$48.50  FF230.00  DM95.00

THE WORLD ECONOMY IN THE 20th CENTURY by Angus Maddison (1989)
(41 89 05 1) ISBN 92-64-13274-0   160 pages                    £17.00  US$30.00  FF140.00  DM58.00

"Development Center Seminars"

ONE WORLD OR SEVERAL? Edited by Louis Emmerij (1989)
(41 89 04 1) ISBN 92-64-13249-X   320 pages                    £19.50  US$34.00  FF160.00  DM66.00

*Prices charged at the OECD Bookshop.*

*THE OECD CATALOGUE OF PUBLICATIONS and supplements will be sent free of charge
on request addressed either to OECD Publications Service,
2, rue André-Pascal, 75775 PARIS CEDEX 16, or to the OECD Distributor in your country.*

# TABLE OF CONTENTS

*Part Three*
# AN AGENDA FOR THE 1990s

# ACKNOWLEDGEMENTS

The views expressed are solely the authors' and do not represent an OECD Secretariat position. For stimulating discussions and helpful criticism, we are grateful in particular to Manuel Castells, François Chesnais, Daniel Chudnovsky, Carlos Correa, Michel Delapierre, Chris Freeman, Kotaro Horisaka, Ken-Ichi Imai, Henry Kelly, Dave Mowery, Lynn Mytelka, Ashok Parthasarathi, Francisco Sercovich, Jon Sigurdson, Dennis Simon, Constatine Vaitsos, and Graham Vickery.

We would also like to thank our colleagues and friends Antonio Botelho and Richard Conroy for their invaluable help throughout the preparation of this study, and for the information they have provided on Latin America and China. We have been lucky to have two dedicated and efficient research assistants, Maud Bruce and Halvor Nafstadt, who provided us in time with statistics and other background information. A special debt of gratitude goes to Christine Johnson for her tremendous efficiency and patience in organising the Dourdan expert group meeting at short notice and for co-ordinating the production of this study, and to Sandra Lloyd for her strong and good-humoured support in typing numerous drafts and revisions.

# PREFACE

The world economy is in a state of flux. Powerful economic globalization trends are confronted with a growing "politicisation" of international trade and investment, and these two fundamental trends are to a very large degree shaping a transformation of the international economy. Today, oligopolistic competition and strategic interaction rather than the "invisible hand" of market forces condition comparative advantage and the international division of labour.

The introduction of new technologies plays an important role in this process. Firms as much as states are striving to utilize technology as an instrument of global competition, and are rushing to modernize their industrial structures, particularly at the high value-added end of the industrial spectrum. Major technological breakthroughs, particularly in the fields of information technology, biotechnology, new materials and renewable energies, are currently reshaping the basic parameters of industrial manufacturing. As a result, both the direction and the composition of international trade and investment are rapidly changing. This has important implications for economic relations between OECD Member countries and an increasingly important group of actors on the world economic scene which are commonly subsumed under the heading of Newly Industrialising Economies (NIEs).

In this important book, Dieter Ernst and David O'Connor analyse how these basic transformations of the international economy affect the future scope for industrialisation and industrial policies in different groupings of NIEs and what this implies for their integration into the world economy. In terms of the new technologies, the focus is on microelectronics and related computer-based automation and information technologies. Based on a sophisticated classification of NIEs, the authors show that global economic security depends on the fate of such economies in a threefold sense:

> *i)* NIEs are potential new competitors which are determined to compete for markets and technology in a growing number of industrial markets and service activities;

> *ii)* As important potential future growth markets, NIEs could arrest the recessionary demand conditions that are likely to confront most of the OECD region's high tech industries in the years to come; and

> *iii)* Lastly, but probably of greatest importance in the longer term, NIEs could become partners to a growing variety of technological co-operation schemes ranging from subcontracting and so-called OEM (original equipment manufacturer) relations, to more complementary forms of joint production and technology sourcing.

So far, most of the debate has concentrated on the "competitive threat", and this for quite understandable reasons. Yet, as the book convincingly argues, the second and third issues are of at least equal importance, if we want to sustain a stable world economy. More energy should be spent on identifying new possibilities for selective, and increasingly complementary North-South industrial and technological co-operation, with a view to expanding mutual flows of trade and investment. This, in turn, requires a clear understanding of the commonalities and diversity of growth and industrialisation patterns in NIEs, and of the constraints and strategic options with which such countries are currently confronted. Probably the most important contribution of this book is its discussion in Chapter V of the policy agenda for the 1990s, and its analysis of some basic prerequisites for a reversal of today's intensifying technological protectionism.

This study deserves wide circulation because it yields important lessons for policy makers both in NIEs and in OECD Member countries. At the same time, the book could broaden our debates on how technological change affects the international distribution of competitive advantages.

I hope that the present study will be seen as a contribution clarifying the important, but complex, area of the relationship between technology, international trade and competition, and export patterns of nations.

Louis Emmerij
President, OECD
Development Centre
July 1989

# EXECUTIVE SUMMARY

## The issue

This study deals with the role of technology in the worldwide restructuring of industrial manufacturing and trade. It is based, at least to some degree, on the rich and often quite spirited debates which took place during a high-level expert group meeting that one of the authors convened for the OECD Development Centre[1]. The purpose of this study is to contribute to a better understanding of how new technologies influence the international distribution of competitive advantages, and what this implies for strategies of latecomer industrialisation, pursued in a number of newly industrialising economies (NIEs). In addition, the study addresses some emerging issues related to international trade and investment and the industrial and trade policy agenda of the 1990s.

Apart from presenting a "state-of-the-art" review of what we know about this complex issue, the study will also suggest some priority areas for future research and make a few policy recommendations. In particular, an attempt will be made to assess how the above basic transformations affect industrial and trade policy options in NIEs, and what this implies for economic rivalries and industrial co-operation between OECD Member countries and NIEs.

## Basic definitions

The terms "latecomer industrialisation" and "newly industrialising economies" are heavily charged and open to all kinds of misunderstanding. For lack of better alternatives, however, we have decided to stick to them.

The term latecomer industrialisation is used in order to highlight three specific features of such industrialisation patterns[2]: their still quite recent historical origins; their weak foundations, in terms of low international competitiveness of their capital goods industries and of the related support services; and, finally, their very high, if not overwhelming dependence on generic technologies and product standards developed in the United States, Japan and Western Europe[3].

As for the NIEs, we have used the analytical concept of "structural competitiveness"[4] as a guideline for our classification. The criteria used include: the size and structure of demand (both domestic and exports) for industrial products and related services; the share of industrial manufacturing (output or value-added) in gross national product (GNP); industrial structure and firm size; the breadth and intensity of linkages, both forward and backward[5], and the existence of user-producer and subcontracting networks; the sources of technology and the constraints to its diffusion and adaptation; the role of the state in fostering industrial and technological development; and, lastly, some microeconomic indicators of international competitiveness (in terms of price, performance and market shares)[6]. Based on these criteria, we have chosen to focus on the following five country groupings[7]:

*i)* First-tier Asian NIEs: Hong Kong, Singapore, South Korea and Taiwan;

*ii)* Second-tier Asia: Malaysia, Philippines and Thailand;

*iii)* Large Latin American economies: Argentina[8]; Brazil and Mexico;

*iv)* Next-tier Latin America: Chile, Colombia, Uruguay and Venezuela; and

*v)* The two quasi-continental economies in Asia: China and India.

Obviously, there are substantial differences between each of these country groupings, as much in their patterns and strategies of industrialisation, as in the challenges and constraints confronting the individual latecomer industrialisation attempts of each. Such differences have tended to increase rather than decrease over the last decade — powerful differentiation trends among Third World societies, after all, do not stop at higher levels of industrial development. We will discuss the reasons for this divergence later on in detail, when we analyse the diversity of growth patterns and industrialisation strategies, and assess the strategic options open to each of these NIEs[9].


**Focus, key questions and contents**

This study focuses on one particular set of new technologies, microelectronics; and the new generations of computer-based automation and information technologies which have emerged from it. For reasons of research economy, we could not deal in this study with three other important new technologies: biotechnology, new materials, and renewable energies; all of which are likely to have a profound impact on the development and world market integration of developing countries[10].

Due to its vast potential for unlocking new technology combinations, the implications of microelectronics transcend by far the narrow confines of nation states. Its international diffusion has already imposed quite drastic changes on international trade and investment, and on the patterns of conflict and co-operation prevailing between different countries and regions. In essence, this is due to the convergence of computer, communication and control technologies, which would have been impossible without recent developments in microelectronic hardware and software and in complementary interface technologies, such as sensor and transmission technologies. This convergence has opened up vast new possibilities for rationalising economic activities, within a firm, and for changing its interactions with suppliers and customers, through the establishment of increasingly sophisticated "networking" strategies[11]. New information technologies have also led to a radical restructuring of whole sectors and to a realignment of geographic allocation patters. In other words, substantial changes are taking place in the economics of spatial location, both within countries, and increasingly also across national boundaries.

Two technological trends are of particular importance for the purposes of this study: the transition towards computer-based or programmable automation and the establishment of captive worldwide information networks. Both developments, in a very fundamental sense, are likely to affect the scope for internationalising economic activities and institution.

Programmable automation (PA)[12], across all kinds of industrial sectors, is perceived as a key to international competitiveness. While automation traditionally was geared to achieving savings of labour and, to some degree, capital, by sacrificing product-line flexibility to economies of scale, PA is expected to allow companies to reconcile these conflicting objectives and thus to open up new paths to regain competitiveness.

In addition, the convergence of computer, communication and control technologies has made it technically feasible today for multinational corporations, banks as much as industrial firms, to install captive worldwide information networks, through which headquarters' management can link together production facilities around the world, as if they were divisions within one factory. Thus it has become possible today to synchronise, on a worldwide scale, decentralised production with a strictly centralised control over strategic assets. Such global information networks in fact enable corporate management to control affiliates around the world, to put them under pressure if need be, and even to force them into ruthless mutual competition. In short, there are many ways in which current market leaders can utilise new information technologies in order to retain their grip on strategic assets.

Yet, at the same time, new information technologies can also open up new windows of opportunity for NIEs which would allow them to imporve their competitive position and to expand their market share. Our study discusses various instances where new information technologies, for limited periods at least, have led to a reduction of barriers to entry, and thus to a destabilisation of established market structures. In other words, new information technologies can strengthen both decentralisation and reconsolidation trends of the world economy.

Which of these two developments will prevail, depends as much on technology as on industrial, market and organisational structures, and on the strategies and policies pursued by private firms and governments. It is safe to say, however, that under the impact of rapid technological change, both the direction and composition of international trade and investment are rapidly changing.

This is bound to have important implications for the distribution of wealth and income as much as of economic and political power, both within and among nations. These are complex issues which do not lend themselves easily to quantitative analysis. As a result, they are all too easy to ignore. Yet, given their enormous importance not only for latecomers but for OECD governments as well, there is a compelling need for clear thinking about what the new opportunities and challenges may be. It is in this context that we will address the following key questions:

*i)* Will microelectronics-based new information technologies open up new possibilities for NIEs to modernise their industrial structures and to improve their international competitiveness? Or, rather, will they increase the barriers to latecomer industrialisation? How will this affect the exports of manufactured products and of services, originating from such countries, and their import capacity? And what changes are likely to occur in the cross investment links between OECD Member countries and NIEs?

*ii)* Furthermore, under what conditions could NIEs secure access to these new technologies, in the context of an increasingly restrictive international technology system? What scope is there for enlightened and mutually beneficial industrial co-operation between OECD Member countries and NIEs?

*iii)* Which factors condition the application and diffusion of such technologies, given the specific features of industrial supply and demand prevailing in different groups of these countries? What are the basic prerequisites — in terms of public policies, company strategies, and basic and R&D infrastructures — which a latecomer society would have to realise, in order to acquire, adapt, reproduce and redesign the new technologies successfully? Finally, will production systems built around new generations of information technology open new opportunities for latecomer development that are based more heavily on internal or regional markets instead of on markets in the OECD region, in particular in the United States?

Our answers to these questions are by no means straightforward and simple. The reader at times may find that we vacillate between an optimistic and pessimistic assessment of future perspectives for international technology diffusion and for the distribution of competitive advantages. To a certain degree, this ambiguity is deliberate and reflects some basic contradictions which we are currently witnessing in the restructuring of the world economy. Our way of sorting out this basic dilemma is that in Chapter V ("Emerging Policy Issues"), we explicitly confront a pessimistic scenario ("Intensifying Technological Protectionism") with a somewhat more optimistic one ("Barriers to International Technology Diffusion Decline"). We use these two scenarios in order to identify some basic conditions required for reducing the current unevenness of international technology diffusion.

The study consists of three parts. In Part One, we set out a conceptual and normative framework for analysing how new technologies, global competition and latecomer industrialisation interact. In Part Two, we develop a classification of NIEs, based on the diversity of their growth patterns and industrialisation strategies, and we spell out in quite some detail the specific constraints and strategic options, which confront each of these different groupings of NIEs. It is on this basis that in Part Three, we identify emerging potential conflicts and policy issues which, we feel, should be addressed in our current policy debates. We conclude by spelling out a research agenda for those areas where lack of sound knowledge has been particularly harmful for policy formulation and implementation.

## Policy implications

The dynamics of technological change and global competition have far-reaching policy implications, both for OECD Member countries and for the NIEs, and this applies as much to government policies as to the strategies and organisational structures of private firms. In both groups of countries, established industrial and trade policy regimes and competitive strategies are currently under tremendous strain. There is widespread experimentation with new approaches towards industrial transformation and a restructuring of international trade and investment. In our study, we have focused primarily on how firms and governments in NIEs have had to rethink accustomed strategies and policies, and the possible implications for future economic interactions between these societies and OECD Member countries.

New barriers to industrial transformation have emerged in nearly all NIEs. In the first-tier Asian NIEs, export-led strategies, which once seemed to be unbeatable, have run up against stiff and escalating protectionist barriers in many OECD countries. At the same time, the more inward-looking strategies of some large Latin American economies and of the quasi-continental economies of Asia have confronted equally severe structural constraints. Thus, without exception, NIE governments have been searching for alternative strategies and policy instruments which would enable them to respond more effectively to the changing global economic (and political) environment. Strategies for gaining, or maintaining, access to new technologies are vital to a successful strategic response.

A number of important policy issues with regard to technology acquisition are emerging. First, NIEs must engage in a more active search for alternative technology sources to diminish the vulnerability that comes with over-reliance on a single or a few sources, especially when those sources may fear the so-called "boomerang" effect. There are limits, however, to the possibilities for diversification of technology sources, since long-standing relationships with particular technology suppliers may be necessary to the acquisition of certain key technological know-how.

The NIEs have also had to reconsider traditional approaches to technology acquisition in the light of intensifying efforts by OECD governments and firms to tighten intellectual property regimes. Extensive reliance on technology licensing and "reverse engineering" has become increasingly problematic. While new channels have emerged for the transfer of technology, only a small minority of the most advanced NIE companies can make use of them. This is true as much for strategic partnering between OECD and NIE firms, and for foreign direct investment by NIE companies in OECD countries. Countries without capital surpluses and where few firms possess strategic assets which could complement those of OECD companies, are per definition excluded from such new approaches. Those with large domestic markets, on the other hand, may trade strategic market access for technologies. Some NIEs have discovered that the development of indigenous technological capabilities can constitute a double-edged sword which, on the one hand, enhances the efficiency of technology absorption while, on the other, makes potential technology suppliers more wary of transferring their know-how.

As for intellectual property rights (IPR), in recent years there has been an escalation, led by the United States, of punitive measures against countries not willing to conform to its expectations of what constitutes an "appropriate" intellectual property regime. A particularly disturbing feature is the increasing use of bilateral trade retaliation as a means of imposing demands for IPR protection. The situation remains fluid — due in particular to considerable disagreement even within the United States on the appropriate form of protection for different types of intellectual property. Yet NIEs, as much as other developing countries, can no longer avoid confronting the crucial issue of what sort of IPR regime they should adopt. There may be good reasons why each country should choose a somewhat different approach, depending on: i) the level of development of its indigenous technological capabilities; ii) the multiple trade-offs between producer and user needs; and iii) the perceived interests between private and public sectors.

Technology diffusion and generation are also the object of policy initiatives by NIEs, though until now too little attention has been devoted to policies for promoting the effective diffusion of new technologies. User requirements, in terms of information, organisational change and skill formation, need to be studied more carefully, in order to identify and address the main deficiencies. The creation of an effective and increasingly sophisticated demand for new technologies often requires the selective use of government procurement markets, subsidies to small and medium-sized firms which are first-time users of new technologies. Especially where demand is highly price-elastic, there is also need for additional measures designed to lower the costs to local users of equipment embodying the new technologies — with state-funded equipment leasing of computers being just one example.

Of equal importance to technology diffusion is the overall macro-economic environment. Countries which are forced by massive debt servicing obligations to become major capital exporters are severly constrained in their ability to finance investment in new technologies. The same applies to the destructive inflationary effects of foreign debt and trade deficits which discourage long-term investment by domestic firms in productivity enhancing new technologies, not to mention investment by foreign firms which might introduce such technologies.

Industrial policies in the NIEs must be designed to confront the conflicting pressures on the existing structure of various industries exerted by rapid technological change and global competitive shifts. In addition, political initiatives — by, for example, the United States to revalue currencies and liberalise domestic markets of the more successful NIEs — have compounded pressures towards industrial restructuring. These pressures have posed a serious policy dilemma for such NIEs. Should the state intervene to try to save troubled firms in those industries which are no longer competitive or should it let them die? This poses the issue in the starkest terms. There is also the possibility of course that the state adopts a "carrot-and-stick" approach to get firms to restructure gradually away from declining sectors without the disruptive effects of bankruptcy. Still another dilemma faced in particular by first-tier NIEs, relates to the role of outward-bound foreign direct investment (FDI). While in terms of securing future access to key markets and technologies, FDI is bound to gain in importance, it could also retard the upgrading of domestic production capabilities and the restructuring of domestic capacity towards higher value-added product market segments. Second-tier NIEs in turn may be inclined to move too rapidly into more technology-intensive production, when domestic technological capabilities are not yet sufficiently developed. Timing is crucial since excessive delay in making necessary product and process adjustments would render the second-tier countries vulnerable to the loss of competitive advantage to still other countries which, while starting from a much lower industrialisation base, are rapidly expanding their manufacturing capacities for standardised, low-technology products.

Futhermore, industrial policies require close co-operation with the existing trade policy regime. For example, in some countries the trade regime has resulted in an incentive structure which encouraged very high degrees of vertical integration by individual firms at the expense of scale economies; in other countries, the result has been the excessive entry by small companies, fragmenting production structures with similar outcomes. Such NIEs face the question of how to foster selective liberalisation without jeopardizing the substantial accumulated technological and skill base in the liberalised sectors. Moreover, liberalisation is by no means an advisable policy for all sectors. As we show in our study, strong economic arguments apply for the selective protection of key sectors at an early stage, in order to consolidate learning effects and industry linkages.

Each country's industrial structure is unique, and so must be its attempt to reshape its structure. Yet, certain broad issues cut across the great variety of NIEs with which we are dealing in our study. Some of our sample countries, for instance, have an abundance of small and medium-scale speciality firms, but few large, diversified companies. Others have a top-heavy structure with very high concentration of industrial activity in a few very large conglomerates. Each structure has its distinctive strengths and weaknesses, and leads to different policy implications. In the second case, for instance, the issue is how the government can strengthen small- and medium-sized firms, so that the large conglomerates have access to versatile supplier networks. Where such small firms predominate, the issue becomes the government's helping these firms to realize economies of scale and of scope, for example in R&D, basic support services, marketing and distribution. Furthermore, without some sort of government assistance, such firms could hardly overcome the very high investment thresholds to entry and the huge fixed capital cost burdens which are typical today for relatively technology-intensive forms of industrial manufacturing.

A final set of policy issues confronting the governments of NIEs relates to the prospects for increasing international technological co-operation, both South-South and North-South. The first sort of co-operation is rendered urgent by the growing constraints to competitive export strategies focused on increasingly protected OECD markets. Export market diversification has become imperative, as has an increased focus on domestic demand growth — at least in the more dynamic Asian NIEs not saddled with the severe barriers to short-term expansion in domestic demand of the Latin American NIEs. Increased trade flows within regional groupings of NIEs, as well as between them and other developing countries, could become an important counterweight to slower export growth to the OECD region. Moreover, similar income levels and consumer preferences could serve as the basis for specialisation and trade patterns that would involve considerable product differentiation without sacrificing economies of scale. Complementarities in technological assets could also serve as an inducement to greater intra-regional technology flows, not only through trade but through foreign direct investment and strategic partnerships among NIE firms. The opportunities for such innovative forms of South-South technological co-operation remain largely unexplored. This is hardly surprising, given the enormous historical weight of failed attempts at South-South regional co-operation. In its future research on technology, globalisation and regionalisation, the Development Centre will address this crucial issue[13]. Will new technologies make possible new forms of co-operation with a somewhat higher probability of success? Clearly, political factors will still play a crucial role, but in this field alliances between firms across countries may have to take the initiative from overly cautious governments.

Finally, with regard to technological co-operation between OECD Member countries and the NIEs, a number of important policy implications are emerging. OECD countries may have to take some bold measures to reverse the policy drift towards rising protectionism against NIE exports. For example, the spectre of heavy local content requirements being imposed on non-EC companies to qualify as European vendors after 1992 haunts NIE exporters. Given the increasing internationalisation of European firms, such policies may well be self-defeating and may even claim some of those firms among their victims. Policy-makers in the OECD region also would do well to ponder the implications for their own capital goods exporting sectors of neo-mercantilist policies which would substantially weaken the investment and import capacities of NIE firms.

The NIEs in turn must adopt industrial and trade strategies and policies that are conducive for technological co-operation between them and OECD Member countries. This may involve some accommodation of the legitimate concerns of OECD countries to lessen their adjustment costs in the face of international trade realignments. At the same time, there can be no denying of the fact that the NIEs are in an extremely weak bargaining position vis-à-vis OECD countries to ensure that they do not bear the lion's share of such adjustment costs. Co-operation among NIEs and developing countries as a whole is still a valuable means of strengthening their bargaining position in international forums on trade and in attempts to ensure a favourable environment for continued international technology flows.

16

# NOTES AND REFERENCES

1.  This meeting, which took place from 20th to 25th February 1989 at Dourdan, France, has greatly influenced our thoughts on this topic. This does not, however, imply that the participants of the meeting would necessarily endorse the thrust of our argument and the research and policy implications that we have drawn in this study. For a list of participants see Appendix; for further background information see D. Ernst, "Issue Paper: New Technologies, Global Competition and Latecomer Industrialisation — Implications for International Trade and Structural Adjustment", OECD Development Centre, Paris, 15th February 1989.

2.  For details, see Chapters II and III.

3.  See Chapter III.

4.  Developed by the French regulation school (see, e.g. Mistral 1983), this concept refers to key features of the economic, institutional, social and political framework within which firms have to pursue their competitive strategies. See the excellent synthesis by François Chesnais in this study "Science, Technology and Competitiveness", *STI Review, No. 1*, Autumn, 1986, pp. 88-92. For an interesting application of this concept to small OECD countries, see Vivien Walsh, "Technology, Competitiveness and the Special Problems of Small Countries", *STI Review, No. 2*, September 1987.

5.  The concept of linkages goes back to Albert O. Hirschman's pioneering study, *The Strategy of Economic Development*, New Haven, 1958.

6.  See Chapter III, "A Classification of NIEs".

7.  For reasons of research economy, we had to leave out three important country groupings which follow-on research however should definitely include: the EEC Mediterranean Periphery (Greece, Portugal and Spain); four non-EEC Mediterranean countries (Egypt, Israel, Turkey and Yugoslavia); the socialist economies of Eastern Europe (Bulgaria, Czechoslovakia, the German Democratic Republic, Hungary, Poland and Romania); and, finally, the Soviet Union.

8.  Due to the extended period of de-industrialisation during the military dictatorship, Argentina has become somewhat of a border case between the third and fourth country category.

9.  See Chapters III and V.

10. Biotechnology, in developing countries, so far mainly affects the agricultural sector. These issues are addressed in the Development Centre's research programme "Changing Comparative Advantages in Food and Agriculture". New materials and energy technologies however are already drastically changing the economics of industrial manufacturing and the distribution of competitive advantages. They thus should be dealt with in the Development Centre's future work on "New Technologies, Industry and Trade".

11. From the rich body of literature on this topic see in particular: Child 1987; Imai and Bata 1989; and Aoki 1989.

12. PA is still a hazy concept. At the very least, it would involve computer-aided design (CAD) and computer-aided engineering (CAE), linked to separate numerically controlled machines, such as handling equipment, robotics, automated production tools, inspection instruments and test equipment. Full-fledged integrated PA systems would involve not just connecting CAD/E terminal to computer-controlled machines, but thoroughly computerising a plant's or a company's manufacturing operations, including control of the flow of parts and materials and the movement of products through the various stages of manufacture. In its most sophisticated form, i.e. computer-integrated manufacturing (CIM), PA is a corporate strategy of long-range integration of

all the key corporate functions that support manufacturing operations. PA, in other words, refers to the automation and integration of industrial manufacturing and related services, such as design, engineering, testing, inventory, maintenance, subcontracting, marketing and finance. For details, see Ernst, 1987.

13. See Chapter VI, "A Research Agenda".

*Part One*

# A CONCEPTUAL AND NORMATIVE FRAMEWORK

*Chapter I*

# NEW TECHNOLOGIES, GLOBAL COMPETITION AND INTERNATIONAL TECHNOLOGY DIFFUSION

## THE CONCEPT OF TECHNOLOGY

It is important to clarify from the beginning, the concept of technology that we intend to use in this study. In our view, technology cannot be reduced to machines. It has to do with certain kinds of knowledge, which allow the adaptation of means to ends. Part of this knowledge is embodied in machines, but most of it is not. It is embodied elsewhere — in the brains of people, in organisational structures and in behavioural patterns, which in turn are conditioned by the strategies of different social factors and their patterns of conflict and co-operation. Understood in this broader sense, technological change cannot be separated from market structures, patterns of competition and social regulation, and from the quality of the educational system and of the labour force.

Technological change, that is, the generation and diffusion of new technologies, does not occur in a vacuum. It is driven, to a very large degree, by the fundamental requirements of competition. This is also increasingly the case with scientific discoveries. More than ever before, unequal access to basic science, innovative capacities and to key technologies is used today by the leading players of the world economy as a leverage for improving their position in a ruthless global technology race. This applies as much to the triangular relations between the United States, Japan and Western Europe, as to the those between the developed North and the developing South.

In short, we would strongly argue that one cannot expect to understand the nature of international technology diffusion, and the chances of different actors to gain access to key technologies, if one doesn't analyse explicitly the driving forces behind global competition and the restructuring of production and markets.

Let us add a further point which, we believe, is of crucial importance. For any industry, diffusion patterns of technology cannot be theorised and hence known in advance, but must be discovered empirically. In other words, identifying specificities and historical contingencies rather than premature generalisations should deserve high priority, and this requires in-depth case studies of particular technologies, at a sectoral, product and firm level. The need for such a research agenda has been aptly described by Nathan Rosenberg:

> "It is not possible to come to grips with the complexities of technology, its interrelations with other components of the social system, and its social and economic consequences, without a willingness to move from highly aggregated to

highly disaggregated modes of thinking. One must move from the general to the specific, from technology to technologies. One must even be prepared to "dirty one's hands" in acquiring a familiarity with the relevant details of the technology itself"[1].

## HOW TECHNOLOGICAL CHANGE AFFECTS COMPETITIVE POSITIONS

In relation to competition, technological change (TC) acts as a double-edged sword. On the one hand, it can be a great equaliser, eroding the competitive advantages of even well-entrenched countries and firms and propelling others to the forefront. Under certain circumstances, TC might even give rise to the emergence of new competitors, so-called latecomers, which until then had been excluded from a particular market[2].

On the other hand however — and this has been its historically predominant role — TC is a powerful instrument for consolidating oligopolistic structures. While, for specific sectors or regions, entry barriers may be lowered — during limited periods of transition at least — the most fundamental development is towards increasing concentration.

Let us take the case of advanced electronics (semiconductors, computers and telecommunications). With the exception so far of telecommunications, this has certainly been an industry where new start-up companies continuously have been able to enter the game. In addition, quite extensive product differentiation and market segmentation have led to a situation where mutual poaching of each other's established market turfs has become established industry practice. This, however, does not mean that we have experienced a decreasing concentration in this industry. On the contrary — concentration has increased, in fact, quite substantially.

Increasing concentration in the electronics industry has been documented by means of three indicators: the share of the largest ten companies in the sales volume of a particular branch or market segment[3]; the share of intra-firm trade in a country's foreign trade[4]; and the share of R&D outlays in relation to firm size[5].

It is hypothesised that, if the same three indicators are used, concentration can be shown to have increased over the last twenty-five years or so in most industrial sectors, and that this increase will be particularly significant in the high-tech industries.

As for the electronics industry, it has been shown elsewhere[6] that increasing concentration has been due primarily to three factors: the growing fixed capital cost burden of R&D, capital equipment and distribution networks, the acceleration of technological obsolescence and cash flow problems resulting from a general slow-down of demand growth.

Obviously, it is of great importance to understand the conditions under which either of these two effects of TC will prevail. This requires, first and foremost, an analysis of how TC interacts over time and space with barriers to entry and how these interactions differ, depending on the sectors, geographic regions and the actors involved.

## NEW TECHNOLOGIES AND BARRIERS TO ENTRY

New technologies are commonly defined as major technological breakthroughs recently achieved in the OECD region. Most discussions focus on four of them, that is, microelectronics, biotechnology, new materials and renewable energies. Common to all of them is a vast potential for unlocking new technological combinations — hence the term "generic technologies". Such technologies have a pervasive application potential and they drastically improve possibilities for upgrading existing technologies and for extending the range of organisational innovations required to improve the "structural competitiveness" of an economy.

By radically changing product design, production technology and system engineering, all of which have far-reaching effects on the economics of production, generic technologies can lead to substantial changes in industrial structure and in the rules of competition. Thus, control over generic technologies is a key instrument of any competitive strategy.

## Towards increasing barriers to entry

At first sight, some of the intrinsic characteristics of new technologies appear to offer a gloomy prospect for latecomers to industrialisation, especially when other global and social factors such as the burden of debt in many countries are taken into account. In what follows, we will focus on the following basic features of the new "techno-economic paradigm"[7] which and to increase barriers to entry[8].

### A new relationship between supply and demand

The increased flexibility of supply, economies of scope, the integration of design and production, and just-in-time systems allow companies to reply more rapidly and sensitively to changing patterns of demand. Some firms, particularly in Japan, but also in other OECD countries, have begun to exploit this possibility to shorten lead times and product life cycles and to widen the range of product and service differentiation. This confronts the slower-moving enterprises, wherever they may be located, with a new type of competitive challenge.

### Scale economies continue to be important

With the advent of computer-based production equipment, there have been strong expectations that the innate flexibility of such advanced manufacturing technologies and associated management methods would lead to reductions in the scale of production in many industries, particularly in "replication industries" where production equipment consists essentially of a number of identical units working in parallel — a characteristic of most handling and assembly industries.

However, applications to date suggest that the impact of computer-based automation has been much more complex, and that investment thresholds due to economies of scale remain important and, in many cases, continue to increase. The following impacts have been identified in particular[9]:

*i)* Reductions in the physical size of production, the number of workers, and in raw material and energy requirements per unit of output;

*ii)* Increase in the diversity of products from the same production unit;

*iii)* Greater volumes of production of different products from the same production unit; and *iv)* Closer integration between the central production unit or enterprise, and a reduced number of sub-contractors and suppliers who are increasingly responsible for design, quality and delivery schedules.

The overall result has been a change in the structure of production with more output from fewer, more efficient operating units. While advanced manufacturing technologies have improved the scope for factor cost reduction and product differentiation, economies of scale still matter and so do threshold barriers. In addition, compared to the once predominant paradigm of "mass production", the variety of possible approaches to factory automation has substantially increased, which for latecomers implies that the choice of appropriate entry strategies has become much more complex and risky.

## *The systemic nature of technology*

The capacity of some innovating firms to dominate a market by controlling a system also generates new forms of competitive challenge. A capacity for efficient production is often not enough to gain leverage in the system. Design capability, systems engineering and marketing networks become increasingly important, and their integration with production depends on management information and control systems.

## *Science-intensity*

The new technologies are increasingly science-dependent. Access to basic research has become a crucial prerequisite for the progress of technology, and the race is on to exploit basic research for commercial purposes. Developments in technology are also stimulating new advances in basic research. The growing importance of this interaction has induced corporate management, particularly in Japan, but also in Europe and the United States, to experiment with new strategies for more direct access to basic research, including strategic partnering with public domain research laboratories. As a result, equality of access to basic research, which once was taken for granted, is no longer guaranteed. Attempts to restrict access of "foreign" researchers to supposedly strategic areas of basic research, such as super-conductivity, are indicative of this trend.

## *Complexity of technology*

The simultaneous development and interaction of several new generic technologies confronts all actors in global competition with major problems and risks. Autarky is impossible and all have to rely, at least to some degree, on external sourcing of scientific and technical inputs through a combination of joint ventures, contract R&D, consultancies, licensing and know-how agreements, collaboration with university laboratories, technology "scanning" and so forth. But the effectiveness, cost and speed of this external sourcing depends on the company's in-house technical capability as much as on the scientific and technical infrastructure accessible to the firm. Improving the efficiency of internal knowledge accumulation in fact has become a major concern for corporate strategies, as it determines the effectiveness, scope and speed of external technology sourcing. In turn, this has added substantially to the investment thresholds required for successful industrial manufacturing.

*Threshold barriers*

The combination of points above has created quite formidable thresholds for R&D outlays and for investment in production facilities and in worldwide marketing networks. Extreme cases are very large-scale integrated circuits (in particular 1 mega-bit D-RAMs)[10] and large telephone exchanges, but there are many other areas where systems leverage depends on crossing rather high thresholds.

*The "lock-out" effect of dominant standards*

In addition to the threshold barriers mentioned before, there are other factors which may tend to limit the scope for latecomers and new entrants and to create competitive problems. As any technology develops and matures, standards are set either *de facto* by dominant suppliers or *de jure* by national or international standards organisations, or by a combination of the two. Software and telecommunication networks are two areas where the search for competitive advantage may lead to standards which tend to lock out alternative systems[11].

**New windows of opportunity**[12]

The picture, however, is not one of unrelieved gloom. There are also new possibilities and opportunities for latecomers, as for all other competitors. The range of possibilities and opportunities opened up by new technologies is so wide that no country and no oligopoly can possibly close off all the options or monopolise all the potential innovations. Whilst thresholds in some areas are high for both R&D and investment, this is by no means universally true. There are relatively low threshold costs in a number of software applications and in many specialised areas of instrumentation and machinery. While traditional manufacturing skills primarily required extensive "learning by doing", the new skills are in some ways more easily acquired through formal education and training systems. Lastly, but probably of greatest importance, competition between technology suppliers gives new opportunities for shrewd bargaining for access to technology[13].

In the case of the electronics industry, for instance, there are numerous examples of how barriers to entry have been reduced — at least for a particular period of time. Take, for example, mini-computers. Only a few years ago, minimum entry requirements for developing a new mini-computer system were $25 million and a five-year lead time. Since then, however, changes in design and production technology, the broadening of technology diffusion and the proliferation of standards have drastically reduced the entry fee. Latecomers today can do it for $3 to $5 million, in slightly less than one year[14].

Other examples include the "cloning" of IBM PCs, which has allowed both Taiwanese and South Korean computer companies to obtain, for some time at least, substantial market shares in the United States. Similar developments could result from the current paradigm shift in circuit design (to multi-project chip on wafer design) and from the emergence of "silicon foundry" activities which, together, allow the separation of circuit design from wafer fabrication. In the last case, however, there are strong indications that the leading firms, both captive and merchant integrated circuit producers, are already recapturing these activities, erecting even more powerful barriers to entry for latecomers.

So the real issue to be addressed today by latecomers to industrialisation is whether or not such examples can be repeated. And, if so, how long will be the transitional periods, during which latecomers can effectively enter a market and build up market shares large enough to reap economies of scale and to increase learning and experience economies? Under what conditions will latecomers be able to shoulder the increasing cost burden of continuous competitive battles? And, finally, how will countervailing strategies, developed by the dominant oligopolists, affect the latecomers' policies of "managing the technology gap"?

Before we can address these question, we have to review two basic transformations of the international economy which, to a very large degree, shape the scope for latecomer strategies. We are referring, on the one hand, to an increasingly pervasive globalisation of competition and, on the other hand, to a growing "politicisation" of international trade and investment. Identifying realistic options for latecomer strategies requires, first and foremost, an analysis of the forces shaping globalisation and politicisation trends.


## THE CONCEPT OF GLOBAL COMPETITION

We need to avoid reductionist concepts of competition which continue to claim that comparative advantage drives competition. As a number of economists have observed, the international economy is characterised by oligopolistic competition and strategic interaction[15]. We are living in a "... world in which comparative advantage, international competitiveness, and the international division of labor results in large measure from corporate strategies and national policies rather than from natural endowments"[16].

The scope for competition is no longer limited by national boundaries nor by the definition of a particular industrial sector — hence the term *global*. In essence, competition is about internalising on a worldwide scale key assets such as knowledge, finance, production experience and market access, that can lead to the development and to the effective commercialisation of a wide variety of products and services.

While huge, vertically integrated multinational corporations still are a dominant form of business organisation, new forms of inter-firm co-operation have emerged which are commonly subsumed under the headline of "strategic alliances". While the classical forms of inter-company co-operation, the joint venture and the licensing agreement, were primarily driven by tactical motivations related to ownership and control, strategic alliances are a reflection of quite different concerns. Apart from shifting the increasing cost burden of R&D and investment onto a greater number of shoulders, strategic partnering is primarily driven by the need to have access to pools of scarce qualified personnel, particularly for R&D and engineering. The same applies to access to knowledge, which is crucial for mastering the convergence between major technologies, but which is not available in-house. Finally, joint demand generation and market access have also been an important concern.

In short, strategic alliances are nothing but the continuation of competition by other means, admittedly often quite unusual ones. They constitute an important organisational innovation, whose importance for global competition we are only just beginning to understand. In essence, we are talking about new intermediate forms of organising the "economic institutions of capitalism"[17], which fall between the two poles of arms'-length market transactions and corporate strategies geared to an increase of vertical integration.

The desire to consolidate established oligopolies probably has been the main driving force behind the current wave of strategic partnering. It would be premature, however, to exclude the possibility that strategic partnering can be used as a sophisticated weapon to reduce barriers to entry and to improve the chances for latecomer strategies.

# THE PROLIFERATION OF "HIGH-TECH NEO-MERCANTILISM"

Global competition is more than just rivalry among firms. Competition among private companies is only its most visible manifestation. The concept of "structural competitiveness" helps to clarify this important point. In the final analysis, global competition leads to a continuous confrontation "... between different production systems, institutional schemes and social organisations in which business enterprises figure prominently but are nonetheless only one component of a network that links them with the educational system, the technological infrastructure, management/labour relations, the relationship between the public and private sectors, and the financial system"[18].

As a result, governments are playing an increasingly important role in international competition. A new industrial policy doctrine is currently emerging, both within and outside the OECD region. We are talking about an increasingly aggressive high-tech neo-mercantilism[19] which treats science and technology primarily as weapons in international competition.

Following the pioneering role of Japan, erstwhile champions of "free trade", like the United States, are among the most active proponents of such policies today. And Europe has rapidly learned this lesson, as current developments in ESPRIT, EUREKA, and in the European Airbus programme have shown. Violating GATT principles of non-discrimination, multilateralism and reciprocity of concessions has become everybody's favourite game.

We use the term "neo-mercantilism" in order to indicate that global competition has become increasingly politicised. Heavy state involvement is geared to an improvement, not only of the balance of payments, but to a strengthening of so-called "strategic" industries, that is, industries producing generic technologies such as advanced electronics. In short, we are talking about an increasing convergence between industrial and trade policies whose aim is the rapid and worldwide commercialisation of temporary technology leadership positions. Two main aspects are involved:

i) First, a far-reaching promotion and protection of industries which generate or heavily rely on generic technologies — such as microelectronics, computer-based information technologies, biotechnology, new materials, and renewable energies — by means of non-tariff barriers, investment regulations, government procurement policies, funding of basic and applied research, and an increasingly tough intellectual property right protection[20]. Such non-tariff barriers to trade have been increasing nearly everywhere. According to one estimate for the US economy, 35 per cent of US imports in 1983 were subject to non-tariff restrictions, an increase from around 20 per cent in 1980[21].

ii) Second, at at the same time, aggressive policies to open up (liberalise) foreign markets, in particular some potential future growth markets in Asian and Latin American NIEs, by means of a vicious "beggar-my-neighbour export promotion" and the insistence on "reciprocal market access".

But neo-mercantilism is not restricted any longer to national policies. Bilateral and even multilateral arrangements to restrict access to key technologies seem to have recently increased quite substantially in importance. We have already mentioned the European Communities' sectoral research consortia. Some would argue that the still quite pervasive restrictions to the international dissemination of so-called "dual-use technologies", as codified in the current COCOM lists, are basically an instrument of such neo-mercantilism. Finally, the US-Japanese trade agreement on semiconductors, concluded in September 1986, has probably been the most far-reaching attempt so far to create a bilateral, cartel-like "managed trade" agreement[22].

The success of neo-mercantilist policies is far from assured however, historical experience has shown that ironclad technology protection is the exception rather than the rule. Particularly in the fields of microelectronics and new information technologies, there is a great variety of possibilities for latecomers to copy, reverse engineer and upgrade proprietary technology of innovators. The issue is one of capital cost, cash flow and speed to market rather than of access to technology *per se*. And even the US legal community, despite all its sophistication and lavish salaries, is unable to erect an impenetrable thicket of patents and copyrights which could effectively prevent such latecomer technology sourcing. A recent survey of R&D strategies by US companies supports this argument: "Generally, lead time, learning curves, and sales or service efforts were regarded as substantially more effective than patents in protecting products"[23]. While patent protection was quite effective in the chemicals and pharmaceuticals industries, this was not the case in industries where marketing or production engineering were crucial assets. In short, there may be substantial limitations to the current US strategy of enforcing more restrictive intellectual property regimes!

Furthermore, many of the neo-mercantilist policies, pursued in the United States, Japan and Western Europe seem to have quite unexpected, perverse effects. As Mowery has shown for US companies[24], non-tariff and other restrictions to market access has encouraged the growth of transnational "quasi-firms" (joint ventures, strategic alliances, etc.) that accelerate international technology diffusion and increasingly blur national origins of high-technology products.


CAN NEW ACTORS ENTER THE GAME?


Global competition is still predominantly shaped by rivalries between the United States, Japan and Westen Eurpoe. They are the ones who can define product standards and paradigms for technological and organisational innovations and thus can set the rules of competition. Until quite recently, it seemed impossible that any outsider could ever make it into this exclusive club of privileged actors on the world economic scene. Yet, at least in a few industrial sectors, new actors are entering the game who are determined to compete for market share and technology. Confronted with fundamental constraints to their traditional growth models, these new competitors are convinced that they do not have much to lose by pursuing such strategies with a vengeance. As a matter of fact, some of these countries have already left their mark on international trade and investment in industries such as textiles and garments, steel, shipbuilding and consumer electronics, leading to new trade conflicts and some realignments of competitive frontiers.

Add to this current developments in the electronics industry. In consumer electronics, for instance, Korean and Taiwanese exports, as much as their out-going direct investment flows, have become an important concern, both in the United States and in the EC, leading to a panoply of countervailing protectionist measures. Similar developments can be discerned for personal computers and related peripheral equipment.

In semiconductors, finally, the massive push of Korean conglomerates into computer memories (in particular 256 K, and now also 1 M D-RAMs) is posing a challenge even to the leading Japanese producers who dominate this largest segment of the semiconductor industry. From practically zero in 1985, Korea has increased its share in the world market for

256 D-RAMs to 6 per cent in 1986 and 9 per cent in 1987[25]. And during 1988, Korea's D-RAM sales to the United States were projected to be four times larger than in 1987[26] — with most of this growth being at the expense of Japanese companies[27].

It remains to be seen whether such early cases of success can be sustained, or whether they will just be ephemeral aberrations from the predominant trend towards increasing concentration. Will it be possible, furthermore, to add new success cases, particularly in higher value-added segments of the market which would enable Korean and Taiwanese companies to escape the increasingly severe constraints of their traditional low-end market segment strategies?

It is in this context that the following questions need to be addressed:

i) Will there be an increasing concentration or rather a multipolarisation of global competition with new actors entering the scene? And will some of these new actors not only be able to adapt to but also to change the rules of competition to their advantage?

ii) Furthermore, will geographic decentralisation of investment and of access to key assets continue to prevail, and to what degree will it transcend the OECD region? Or, are we rather to experience a consolidation of key production and complementary support activities (such as R&D and marketing) close to a small group of major growth markets in the United States, Japan and Western Europe?

iii) Llast, but not least, what will all this imply for international trade? Can we expect a continuation of previous trends, where successful latecomers have been increasingly integrated into intra-industry trade flows, based on a growing complementarity of production factors and industrial structures? To what degree will the current shift towards "managed trade" counteract or even block such developments? Or will a radical break with the past occur, with international trade being increasingly segmented into regional power blocks, with a minimum of interaction among them?

## INTERNATIONAL TECHNOLOGY DIFFUSION IN THE CONTEXT OF GLOBAL COMPETITION: THE HISTORICAL EXPERIENCE

While, in principle, international technology flows can take many different forms, for the most part they are linked to international investment. Investment is defined in a broad sense to include equity investment such as affiliates and joint ventures, as well as non-equity investment such as technology licensing.

### Developments till the mid-1970s

Throughout most of the post-war period, international investment and technology flows have been highly skewed in terms of the actors involved and the sources of supply. At least up till the mid-1970s, large US multinational corporations played an overwhelmingly dominant role, with European and Japanese companies lagging quite far behind. Other actors, from the so-called ROW rest of the world, that is, CMEA (Council for Mutual Economic Assistance) countries, China and the Third World) played at best a very marginal role.

As for foreign direct investment, the United States has been by far its single largest source and the main home country for multinational coroporations.

In the case of international technology flows, we have to use an admittedly imperfect statistical indicator: the national technological balance of payments (TBPs), as collected by the OECD, which covers only part of international technology flows, that is, the sale of patents, licensing agreements, provision of know-how, and technical assistance. The available TBP data show that, since the early 1970s, about two-thirds of the international supply of disembodied proprietary technology has been of US origin, with the UK a distant second. Even more important, we can see that at least 80 per cent of measured international payments for technology stem from exchanges occurring *within* group structures of multinationals, most of them of US origin[28].

In terms of the destination of the international technology flows, the picture is a much more complex one. In historical terms, there has been a considerable decentralisation of international investment and technology flows, which contrasts quite a lot with the highly concentrated supply structure.

Most of the American foreign direct investment (FDI) during this period went to Western Europe, which also received the largest share of technology exports. While Japan hardly allowed any FDI, it managed to acquire a substantial and increasing share of international technology flows, particuarly through judicious forms of technology licensing. As for the ROW, a select group of "growth poles" in CMEA countries, Latin America and Asia, experienced considerable and, for some time at least, increasing inflows of technology. In the case of CMEA countries, it should be added however that European rather than US companies were the dominant sources of technology supply.

International investment, up till the mid-1970s has certainly been an important vehicle for the international diffusion of technology. While most of these technology flows remained confined to the OECD region and, to a lesser degree to CMEA countries, at least some of them ended up in Third World growth poles. US multinationals were under tremendous pressure to expand their technology exports, for at least three reasons[29]:

i) They needed to extend the life cycle of mature technologies by means of global strategies or "planned obsolescence";

ii) They were desperately searching for ways and means to recuperate the enormous cost burden of R&D, for instance through highly sophisticated transfer-pricing techniques; and

iii) Finally, they realised that technology exports would allow them to penetrate markets which were closed to their products.

The international diffusion of technology, nevertheless, has been selective and unequally distributed. This has been due primarily to the lack of finance, limited capacities of the so-called "host countries" to monitor, unpackage and absorb foreign technologies, and to the tremendous economic and social follow-on costs involved in the transfer of "inappropriate" technologies. Restrictions on the supply of technology have not been a major factor behind the spread of international technology flows.

**Current changes**

Since the mid-1970s, major changes have taken place in international investment patterns[30], and we are only beginning to understand their implications for international technology diffusion[31]:

— There has been a decline, later followed by a severe reduction, in the flow of FDI towards developing countries, with two exceptions: China and the Asian NIEs;

— The flow of FDI within the OECD region has experienced a radical restructuring. As European and later Japanese multinationals have developed their investment in the US market, the US economy became as much a "host" as a "home" country for multinational corporations. Of at least equal importance, Japan has emerged as a major home country for multinationals and a large source of FDI directed towards the United States, East and Southeast Asia and Western Europe.

Sound empirical evidence of what this implies for international technology diffusion is still lacking. Yet it is safe to say that with the exception of Asian NIEs and China, the dissemination of technologies to developing countries has substantially declined. Some of the least developed countries in sub-Saharan Africa and South Asia, for all practical purposes have dropped out of the international technology circuit.

The Asian NIEs, on the other hand, have received large inflows of technology. This is well reflected in their changing patterns of exports to the OECD region. In 1985, "... nearly 40 per cent of OECD imports from [Asian] NIEs were not in labour or resource-intensive products, but in products characterised by significant scale economies or extensive product differentiation. And intra-industry trade — which had been a marginal factor in OECD trade with developing countries in the late 1960s — accounted for fully 31 per cent of the NIEs' manufacturing trade with the OECD area in 1985"[32].

**Assessment**

Overall, there has been a growing multipolarisation of the sources of technology which, in principle, could signal an improved scope for latecomer strategies. A closer look, however, reveals two fundamental yet conflicting trends:

i) Among the core countries of the OECD region, there has been a certain convergence of technological capabilities, reflected in the relative decline of US technological supremacy relative to Japan and Western Europe;

ii) In the rest of the world, and in particular in developing countries, the diversity of technological capabilities has drastically increased. A few first-tier Asian NIEs (South Korea, Taiwan, Hong Kong and Singapore) and less than a handful of quasi-continental countries (Brazil, India and China) have consolidated or even slightly improved their position relative to the leading OECD countries. For the great majority of developing countries, however, the gap in terms of access to and the spread of new generic technologies has drastically increased, leading to a significant deterioration of their growth potential and international competitiveness.

In short, while technology diffusion has continued to expand its geographic spread, it has become even more uneven than before. A growing number of Third World societies are at best marginally integrated today into international technology flows.

# NOTES AND REFERENCES

1. Rosenberg, 1982, p. 17.

2. Ample historical examples can be found in: T. Veblen, *Imperial Germany and the Industrial Revolution,*, London, The Macmillan Company, 1915; A. Gerschenkron, *Economic Backwardness in Historical Perspective. A Book of Essays*, Cambridge, Mass., The Belknap Press, 1962, D. Landes, The Unbound Prometheus. Technological Change and Industrial Development in Western Europe from 1750 to the Present, Cambridge University Press, 1969; F. Braudel, *Civilisation matérielle, économie et capitalisme, XVe-XVIII siècle. Le temps du monde*, Paris, Librairie Armand Colin, 1979.

3. UNCTC, "Transnational Corporations in World Development. Trends and Prospects", New York, 1988, pp. 46 and 47.

4. J.S. Little, "Intra-Firm Trade and US Protectionism — Thoughts Based on a Small Survey", *New England Economic Review* January/February 1986, pp. 42-51, and "Intra-Firm Trade: An Update", *ibid.*, May/June 1987, pp. 46-51.

5. Annual BMFT (Ministry of Science and Technology, Bonn) statistics.

6. D. Ernst, *The Global Race in Microelectronics. Innovation and Corporate Strategies in a Period of Crisis*, Campus, Frankfurt am Main and New York, 1983, Chapter 4, "The Interaction between Recent Technological Breakthroughs and Industrial Restructuring". For similar evidence and conclusions see M. Borrus, *Competing for Control. Americans' Stake in Microelectronics*, Cambridge, Mass., Ballinger Publishers, 1988 and Ferguson, *Harvard Business Review*, April 1988.

7. Freeman and Perez, 1988, in particular pp. 47-61.

8. The following draws on the proceedings of a working group (chaired by Professor Chris Freeman) during an expert group meeting on "New Technologies, Global Competition and Latecomer Industrialisation — Implications for International Trade and Structural Adjustment" (Dourdan, 20th-24th February 1989) which one of the authors convened for the OECD Development Centre.

9. OECD, "Technology, Flexibility of Manufacturing and Industrial Relations", Paris, 18th October 1988.

10. Dynamic random access memories.

11. Arthur 1988.

12. For a detailed discussion, see Chapter V, "'Forced'" Industrial Restructuring: Constraints and Strategic Options".

13. The internal market in any country offers advantages to local suppliers of applications software and systems management, because they tend to have a better knowledge of the specific requirements. It also gives them bargaining power to obtain access to new technology. Obviously, this is particularly important for large economies such as Brazil, China and India.

14. Woodard 1987.

15. Among others see: G. Dosi and L. Soete, "Technical Change and International Trade", in G. Dosi et al., (eds.), *Technical Change and Economic Theory*, London and New York, 1988; Henry K. Kierzkowski (ed.), *Monopolistic Competition and International Trade*, Oxford, Clarendon Press, 1984.

16. Robert G. Gilpin, "Implications of the Changing Trade Regime for US-Japanese Relations", in Inoguchi et al., (eds.), *The Political Economy of Japan. The Changing International Context*, Volume 2, Stanford University Press, 1988, p. 164.

17. Williamson 1985.

18. F. Fajnzylber, "Technical Change and Economic Development — Issues for a Research Agenda", Santiago de Chile, November 1988, p. 2.

19. The term "neo-mercantilism" goes back to an article written by the late Joan Robinson in 1965, where she was trying to debunk the myth of *laissez-faire,* nearly 40 years after Keynes" famous lecture on "The End of *Laissez-Faire*" in 1926. According to Robinson, international competition throughout most of the 20th century has been increasingly politicised, with heavy state involvement geared to an improvement of the national balance of payments.

20. Today's arsenal of policy instruments, available to such "high-tech neo-mercantilism" is impressive indeed: "... subsidies for investment or research, restrictions on access to the domestic market by similar goods from foreign producers, restrictions on direct investment in the domestic market by foreign firms, or procurement policies that favour the domestic producer of a high-technology good", D. Mowery and N. Rosenberg, "New Developments in US Technology Policy — Implications for Competitiveness and International Trade Policy", mimeo, January 1989, p. 18.

21. Estimate by Laura Tyson, "Making Policy for National Competitiveness in a Changing World", in A. Furino, (ed.), *Co-operation and Competition in the Global Economy,* Cambridge, Mass., Ballinger Publishers, 1988, as quoted by Mowery and Rosenberg, Janaury 1989, p. 22.

22. Similar agreements exist in a number of important industries, such as the auto, steel and textiles industries.

23. R.C. Levin, A.K. Klevorick, R. Nelson and S.G. Winter, "Appropriating the Returns from Industrial Research and Development", *Brookings Papers on Economic Activity,* 1987, p. 794.

24. D. Mowery, (ed.,) *International Collaborative Ventures in U.S. Manufacturing,*Cambridge, Mass., Ballinger Publishers, 1988.

25. D. Ernst, interviews in the Korean semiconductor industry, May/June 1988.

26. May 1988 projection by ICE Corp., the leading US semiconductor consultancy firm, as quoted in author's interviews in the Korean semiconductor industry, May/June 1988.

27. At least up till June 1988, Japanese semiconductor producers have been unable to cope with the current demand boom for D-RAMs for three reasons: a reduction of investment in plant and equipment after the 1984-85 semiconductor industry recession; production restrictions imposed by MITI as a result of the July 1986 US-Japanese semiconductor agreement; and unexpectedly severe technical teething problems in the introduction of "next generation" 1 Mb D-RAMs (with the exception of Toshiba).

28. Figures quoted in Vickery, 1986, pp. 50-67.

29. For a detailed treatment, see Ernst, 1981.

30. See UNCTC, 1988, in particular Chapters IV-VI, X and XI.

31. See UNCTAD, 1987, Part Two, "Technology, Growth and Trade", Chapter II.

32. OECD, 1987, p. 287.

*Chapter II*

# NEW TECHNOLOGIES AND LATECOMER INDUSTRIALISATION: KEY ISSUES

The development of new technologies is primarily driven by a process of intensifying competition and shifting competitive advantages among American, Japanese and European firms. To some degree, the introduction of new technologies is also a response to the growing market penetration of imports from a number of newly industrialising economies[1]. The rapid pace of change is presenting growing challenges for NIEs at a time when they are struggling to sustain the process of latecomer industrialisation. One presumed advantage of being a latecomer is the ability to borrow technologies developed in the more advanced economies and thereby economise on their development costs as well as achieve high productivity levels. The pace of technological innovation, however, is arguably more rapid today than at almost any previous time, so that the technological frontier is rapidly receding. Product life cycles are being dramatically compressed. Under such circumstances, NIEs require a dramatic acceleration in learning processes to "catch-up" technologically. Even a strategy of "creative imitation" requires very substantial investments, extreme flexibility, and very rapid responses to market shifts. Such challenges are not restricted to NIEs. Many OECD countries today find it increasingly difficult to maintain a technological edge in any more than a few key areas. The critical issue facing the NIEs is whether they can muster the human, financial and other resources needed to maintain continued access to the new technologies and complementary assets that are so essential to sustained industrial development in an increasingly competitive global economy.

## THE CONCEPT OF LATECOMER INDUSTRIALISATION

The term "latecomer" industrialisation goes back to a debate among economic historians on how "relative economic backwardness", in the 19th century, has shaped the patterns and strategies of industrialisation of countries such as the United States, Germany and Russia[2]. Later versions focused on the experience and technological and growth performance of Japan or the USSR in the 1870-1920 and 1920-50 periods respectively[3]. It was argued that, under certain conditions, economic advantages are conferred on countries which are latecomers to industrial development. In one of its more sophisticated versions, this argument contends that, since the cost of changing to each more advanced level of technology progressively increases, latecomers do have a chance of bypassing industrial early starters[4].

Whatever this argument was worth at its time, it is hardly sufficient as a guideline for assessing current attempts of latecomer industrialisation. As Parthasarathi has argued "... there are numerous distinctive features of the total — political, economic, technological, sociological and cultural — predicament of the post WW-II developing countries which put them in a different category from Japan or the USSR"[5]. Furthermore, in the technological environment of the late 20th century, the conditions for latecomer industrialisation have drastically changed.

## ITS DYNAMICS TODAY

### Goals

Common to all newly industrialising economies is that they have succeeded in getting off the ground a process of development in which their industrial sectors have played a prominent role. Virtually without exception, those economies face increasing difficulties in sustaining that process. There are a variety of constraints involved, including severe balance-of-payments constraints for some countries and growing protectionism against the exports of others. All the NIEs then share a concern for how to prevent serious setbacks (or in some cases, further setbacks) to their industrialisation efforts.

New technologies figure prominently in shaping the future outlook for the NIEs. The ability to sustain the momentum built up in the Asian NIEs, or to restart the engines of growth in the Latin American NIEs, will depend greatly upon the ability to gain access to and effectively tap the potential of those new technologies. They can use these technologies to upgrade traditional industries and to seize new market opportunities spawned by those technologies. If a country fails to gain market shares in the dynamic growth industries while it loses market shares due to declining competitiveness in traditional industries, all hopes for latecomer industrialisation are bound to be frustrated.

Different NIEs may, however, place different priority on the revitalisation of traditional industries versus the development of new ones. Countries that have severe labour constraints, may favour the promotion of less labour-intensive activities. Countries with sizeable labour surpluses and with traditional industries that have absorbed large numbers of workers, may face strong pressures to keep such industries alive by upgrading them technologically, even if in the process they become less labour intensive. The quasi-continental economies may see more reason to keep a more highly diversified industrial structure than do certain of the smaller Asian NIEs. As capital and R&D investment requirements escalate in some high technology industries such as advanced electronics[6], the NIEs active in those industries face tighter financial constraints. They must consider the trade-offs between continuing to invest in traditional capital-intensive industries such as steel and chemicals and redirecting that investment to the new R&D and increasingly capital-intensive sectors. In the former they may already be well established and highly competitive, whereas in the latter they are newcomers and are still trying to catch up technologically under extremely strong competitive pressures.

**Trade-offs involved in latecomer industrialisation strategies**

The aforementioned trade-off is only one of a number the NIEs must face as they seek to adapt flexibly to the new competitive environment. Another is the appropriate balance between economies of scale (which in many NIEs, with the possible exception of the quasicontinental economies, means a small number of large-scale producers in a given industry) and the need to maintain a competitive market environment. This amounts to achieving a proper mix of firm sizes within the industrial structure. Of course, *that* mix will change as industries evolve, but NIEs must prevent concentration tendencies from proceeding too fast, as they may lead to "premature oligopolisation" with attendant rigidities and barriers to new competition[7].

A further trade-off latecomers must address is that between timely access to new technologies and ability to develop such technologies indigenously. Given the sizeable technology gap in most industries between technology leaders in OECD countries and the NIEs, relying principally on their own R&D capabilities, might well condemn the latter to using relatively obsolete technologies[8]. Importing the technologies would provide readier access to the latest vintages but at the expense of perpetuating an external dependence. While every NIE has had to make use of imported technologies, some have been more successful than others in integrating foreign technology procurement with the strengthening of domestic R&D capabilities. The crux is to minimise the incompatibility between the two ways of acquiring technological competence and to enhance their complementarities.

There is also a trade-off involved in industrial capital formation. The NIEs vary substantially in the extent to which they rely on foreign capital to fuel the investment process. In countries with relatively high domestic savings rates, foreign capital has been a less prominent source of financing. In countries with well developed capital goods sectors, it has been of limited importance in terms of physical capital formation. In almost all countries, its main contribution has been to provide organisational and technical know-how. The reliance on foreign investment may increase as investment thresholds rise in many industries, as capital equipment becomes more complex in design, and as technical expertise becomes more critical to competitiveness. This may be especially the case in high technology sectors.

The increasing technological competence of several of the NIEs suggests, moreover, that they are far better placed today to absorb the technological and organisational innovations accompanying foreign capital investment than they were a decade or two ago. Thus NIE firms have come to view joint ventures with foreign firms as a way of complementing their own strengths, along with technology agreements and other contractual arrangements. "Go-it-alone" strategies are as rare among NIE firms seeking to establish themselves in high technology markets as they are among OECD firms.

A final set of trade-offs faced by latecomer industrialisers relates to the balance between state and private initiatives in industrial development. This dilemma is a longstanding one and there are no clear-cut rules for deciding the proper role of the state in industrialisation. All that can be said at present is that both the naïve *laisser-faire* position and the equally naïve "Big Brother knows best" position have been consigned to the "dustbin of history". Undoubtedly, state industrial policy has played a prominent role in some of the more successful recent cases of rapid industrialisation. Yet, it has done so not by interfering with but rather by focusing private sector initiatives. Its major contribution, it would seem, has been to enhance the "structural competitiveness" of a particular economy. Still, what sorts of government policies and practices are most conducive to that end remains an area of considerable debate and uncertainty. The answer will greatly depend on a country's historical, social, cultural, political and other particularities.

## TRANSLATING THE VAST APPLICATION POTENTIAL INTO EFFECTIVE DEMAND FOR NEW TECHNOLOGIES

The diffusion of new technologies throughout the industrial structure of the OECD countries, though still highly uneven across sectors and across countries, has demonstrated their vast applications potential. The rate of diffusion, however, has been slower than originally expected. In the case of NIEs, the spread of new technologies has been far more limited. Take the case of advanced manufacturing technology (AMT), defined to include CAD equipment, computer numerical control (CNC) machine tools, flexible machining centres or other automated transport systems and automated storage and retrieval systems[9]. In the early 1980s, huge differences in the density of AMT have been shown to exist between OECD countries and NIEs[10]: the ratios between the density of these two groups of countries (where the value of the OECD countries accounts for the numerator) were 8.5 for numerically controlled machine tools, 8.3 for CAD and 43.0 for robots.

Once again, the experience is uneven across countries and sectors but the effective demand for new technologies in the NIEs as a whole is a mere fraction of what it is in the OECD countries. A number of factors underlie this discrepancy. First, the NIEs have much lower per capita incomes, so they are less able to afford new technologies, despite their declining cost. Further, because domestic demand is not yet very sophisticated or highly differentiated, it can be adequately met without resort to the flexible production technologies more suited to the differentiated demand patterns of OECD countries.

Moreover, firms are not as yet sophisticated users of new technologies in their production processes. After all, factor endowments and relative factor costs are vastly different in the NIEs from the OECD countries. The relatively low costs of labour in the former tend to slow the rate of adoption of labour saving innovations. While some of the new technologies appear to be skill-saving — and thus presumably suited to the many developing countries where skilled labour is scarce — in reality they simply substitute one sort of skilled labour for another. Often, the new skills are even more difficult to acquire than the old ones[11]. Moreover, given the order of magnitude difference in the investment required for a CNC lathe versus a conventional lathe, the costs of downtime while awaiting repair are vastly greater for the former than the latter.

As labour costs rise in certain of the NIEs (Singapore, Taiwan and South Korea), the incentives for adopting new technologies also increase. Still, it is arguable that the major inducement to the adoption of new technologies in the production systems of the NIEs until now has arisen not from cost but from quality considerations. One of the clear-cut advantages of the new production technologies is that they allow for the repetition of highly precise operations at high speed and with a low rate of error. They also enable companies to respond faster to changing customer requirements. NIE firms seeking to penetrate higher value added OECD markets, often must adopt new production technologies in order to meet the standards of quality and reliability, as well as the short turnaround times required.

The application potential for the new technologies extends far beyond the manufacturing sector. Agriculture and services are also potentially large users of the new technologies, though, in many developing countries they are far more labour intensive than

36

manufacturing. Only in those NIEs where labour costs are rising relatively rapidly may there be strong cost pressures to introduce new labour saving technologies. Certain segments however, of the service sector that are information-intensive and transaction-intensive (e.g. financial services) and for whom quality is important, have introduced new information technologies. Many such services are non-tradables, so the effective demand for upgraded services is likely to be concentrated among higher income groups. For example, urban hospitals are generally equipped with more advanced computer-based diagnostic, monitoring, and therapeutic equipment than rural hospitals, and private hospitals with more advanced technology than public hospitals.12

Of course, lack of new technologies may not be the only, or even the major, cause of poor quality of services in a particular sector or country. Institutional and organisational weaknesses may be serious problems which new technologies may ameliorate but may also exacerbate. Frequently, the effective introduction of new technologies requires major organisational and institutional changes which are often resisted. Financial constraints faced by many NIE governments — particularly those saddled with large external debts — also substantially hamper their ability to upgrade public services, especially when the equipment has to be imported.

The governments of NIEs need to devise more effective policy measures to promote effective demand for new technologies. More progressive income distribution policies in an environment of rising real incomes would strengthen consumer demand for a more highly differentiated product mix, as well as for higher quality products in general. This in turn would force suppliers to upgrade products and processes. Measures designed to make local firms more aware of the availabilities and characteristics of new product/process technologies would also enhance effective demand[13].


### NEW TECHNOLOGIES AND "CORE INDUSTRIES"

Historic debates on industrialisation have focused, among other things, on the question of which industries are critical to sustaining the industrialisation process. The criteria for selecting a core industry include the contribution to industrial sector value added; the extent of inter-industry linkages between a given industry and others (especially forward linkages to user industries, as for example in the case of steel); and technological and other positive externalities generated by that industry. In recent debates, attention has focused on certain industries that are associated with the new techno-economic paradigm, in particular, those producing goods and services incorporating new information technologies. Those technologies have a generic character: they are potentially widely applicable as inputs across a broad spectrum of industries. In OECD countries at least, it is difficult to find an industry where computers, for example, are not employed in some aspect of firm operations. In many industries, they are used in a wide range of activities from the control of processess, and machines inventories to accounting and payroll, and, to projecting market demand. The question that has confronted the NIEs and would-be NIEs is the extent to which a country must possess a strong information technology base to be able to industrialise. If the answer to this is that it must, then what sort of base? Must it be able to produce certain hardware to develop software or both? If so, what kind of hardware and software systems capabilities are indispensable?

## APPLICATION VERSUS PRODUCTION: A FALSE DICHOTOMY

Some might say the debate on this matter is closed, that it is obvious that a country must be able to master information technologies to sustain industrialisation in the present era. This does not go far enough however, since it leaves unanswered the question of the degree of mastery. If a country must possess an information industry on a par with those, say, of Japan or the United States, then industrialisation would no longer be on the agenda for the NIEs. What is increasingly clear is that to be an efficient user of new information technologies, a country must possess a degree of familiarity with the design and development of the hardware components (e.g. ASICs) and software which determine the basic functionality of various information-based systems or subsystems. It must also be knowledgeable about the interface between the new information technologies and other (e.g. mechanical) technologies to be able to combine them effectively. Learning-by-doing and learning-by-using are to a large extent complementary activities, which means that the interactions among hardware, software and systems suppliers and users are an important element in the learning process. Without a supplier sector, not only is one agent of the learning process missing, but the synergies arising from the user-producer interaction are lost as well.

## BUILDING UP VIABLE USER-PRODUCER LINKS

The diffusion of new technologies in the NIEs is retarded by weak linkages between users and producers of the products which incorporate those technologies. In some cases this is because there are few if any domestic producers, with almost all technologies being imported. If a given NIE market represents a small portion of the technology supplier's worldwide market, there is a high probability that the supplier will provide limited support for local users. For example, NIE users of computer systems may face a problem of inadequate software and services if they depend too heavily on foreign equipment vendors to support their customised requirements. They may also face difficulties in maintaining hardware due to unavailability of specialised components. As the market for a particular type of hardware or software grows sufficiently large, local firms may emerge to fill the vacuum. Even they, however, must have access to certain specialised components, in the case of hardware, or to details of the operating system, in the case of software, if they are to meet user requirements.

Producer firms in the NIEs also face an analogous problem in trying to export new technology-based products to OECD countries. As products become more tailored to specific user requirements, they need to have ready access to users in order to know and respond to those requirements. Many of those users are themselves firms whose requirements are rapidly changing in response to competitive pressures. The supplier must have a close communication link with the customer, a very quick response time, hence a very flexible production system to accommodate changing demands. A classic example of this would be application specific integrated circuits (ASICs), where engineers from user firms may design new ASICs interactively with circuit designers from IC design houses, which are in turn linked closely to silicon foundries which are able to produce prototype devices with very short turnaround times. While the foundry need not be co-located with the user firm, the two design teams must maintain close links for the duration of the task. Clearly, the whole field of computerised information systems, especially large ones using customised software and databases, is one where close producer-user links are critical. India has faced this constraint in its attempt to raise exports of software. For customised applications, constant feedback is required from the customer as well as frequent trial runs on the equipment for which the software is designed. Normally this means working on the customer's premises, unless communications links are sufficiently reliable to conduct tests by remote transmission. The NIE technology suppliers have thus far been unable to forge strong links with foreign users, beyond a few cases involving joint ventures with foreign firms, and thus remain confined to markets for more standardised products where such links are not critical[14]. Even then, products which were once standard commodity items are incorporating more customised elements, largely as a result of advancements in CAD/CAE technologies. For example, computer memory ICs are increasingly customised to the requirements of particular equipment vendors or market niches. Thus, the South Korean *chaebol*, for example, which entered the mass memory market at the time when memories were still standard "off-the-shelf" items, may have to establish closer user links — as well as stronger design capabilities — in order to remain competitive as the market becomes more highly differentiated.

New communications technologies may diminish the importance of close geographical proximity in fostering user-producer links. As suggested above, however, this is likely to be of benefit only to those NIEs with a highly developed telecommunications infrastructure which permits interactive data transmission between user and "producer". This is sufficient only in those instances where all of the relevant information is codified, which is very seldom the case with the development and application of new technologies, especially process technologies. That is why, for example, in the case of advanced manufacturing technologies (AMTs), equipment suppliers which provide strong customer support and maintain close user links are more competitive than those who sell at a distance. After all, much of the process refinement and improvement in equipment design occurs only as a result of constant interaction between the capital goods supplier and users. Process innovations hardly ever appear full-blown.

## "TECHNOLOGY LEAP-FROGGING" AND ALL THAT

Concerned with the prospect that the technology gap between OECD countries and the NIEs may widen into a chasm, some have suggested that the best hope for catching up is to leap-frog over an existing technology, by entering early into the one expected to replace it[15]. The term has been used in various contexts and there is considerable ambiguity about its meaning. It is useful to consider some of the more common ways in which it has been employed, so as to assess whether there are any senses in which leap-frogging may represent a realistic option for certain NIEs.

In its most common use, it refers to the effort to surpass the existing state of the art in the development of a new technology which is still in its prestandardisation (or preparadigmatic) stage. OECD firms and governments are frequently vying to "upstage" their rivals in a promising new technology system. The current race to establish a lead and define standards in high definition television (HDTV) is a good example[16]. One line of reasoning would suggest that, despite the high risks, certain NIE firms and states have a higher probability of catching up if they tried to enter the new technology system at this early stage than if they waited until it has been standardised and commercialised. The argument is that, at this stage, the principal entry requirement is a country's or firm's scientific and technical expertise, and that such expertise is more evenly distributed or readily accessible than the assets required for later entry[17]. The argument is not persuasive, since even in the preparadigmatic stage, very substantial stocks of complementary assets are likely to be critical to success. For instance, in the HDTV case advanced semiconductor design capabilities are essential, as is expertise in advanced display technology, to name but two. These capabilities were built up over extended periods of heavy investments in R&D, involve very significant elements of firm-specific know-how, and are not simply a part of the stock of scientific knowledge in the public domain. Moreover, it would be a mistake to overemphasize the availability of high level scientific and technical personnel in the NIEs. Even in the most advanced ones the scientific infrastructure may not be adequate to support such a leap.

A somewhat more extreme case of leap-frogging would be the effort to enter a new technology system when it is at an even more fundamental exploratory level — that is, when the area is scientifically and technically rich but the commercial potential is largely unknown. Here the risks are even higher than in the previous case, where the commercial potential was clear and the timeframe for commercial developments fairly short. An example might be superconductivity. Some NIEs — for example, China — have attempted to develop strong research capabilities in this area. Other NIEs with a pool of scientists specialised in this field — for example, Argentina — have also considered whether leap-frogging might be possible. Here again the main constraint (even if a NIE should achieve a major technological breakthrough) would be mobilising the complementary assets to be able to exploit its commercial potential; for example, advanced material handling and fabrication technology, process engineering know-how, product design and development capabilities.

The concept of leap-frogging is also used in another context where it is an outright misnomer. The entry of certain South Korean firms into the fabrication of large computer memories (D-RAMs) has been called an instance of leap-frogging[18]. Yet, when those firms entered, they did not do so at an early, prestandardisation phase of the product's development. The D-RAM market was already mature, the technology and its future path well defined, and product design standardised. Moreover, the South Korean firms did not even skip the existing generation of devices to introduce state-of-the-art chips. Thus, the only sense in which the strategy could be called leap-frogging is that the Korean firms had not gradually progressed from small-scale memories through medium-scale before entering production of large-scale ones. Still, it would be incorrect to suggest that they possessed no previous experience with semiconductor fabrication technology, since they had operated a joint facility with a government research institute. There were indeed high barriers to entry, namely, the large capital requirements, which the *chaebol* were perhaps uniquely situated among NIE firms to scale. Fortunate timing played a very large part in their commercial success but they now face escalating R&D requirements if they expect to out-leap-frog their Japanese and US competitors. The likelihood of that is probably small, given the heavy investments required in new process equipment (for example, synchrotrons). Thus, they are still forced to pursue a "close follower" strategy at best, but even to do that will become more problematical[19].

## TRADE AS AN ENGINE OF GROWTH: HOW LONG CAN IT LAST?

The Asian NIEs have been especially effective in utilising trade as a vehicle, not only to accelerate growth, but to accelerate technological learning. High volume production for export markets has permitted Asian NIE firms to reap economies of scale as well as to move rather quickly down learning curves. The sort of learning involved, however, is localised to a limited set of activities associated with low cost manufacturing of standardised products.

Continued reliance on such activities to sustain export growth is becoming increasingly unviable. To be able to move to a different sort of competitive advantage based on product enhancement, if not basic design, capabilities will require a new set of skills. To an extent their acquisition is rendered easier by the accumulated experience of producing for export. Still, considerable additional investments in foreign technology as well as in complementary R&D activities are required; likewise, they need to make substantial investments in marketing and distribution assets, which in some cases may even exceed investments in R&D.

Even then, there is no guarantee of success, as the international environment is far less favourable at present to continued strong export expansion than it was in the 1960s, when the first-tier Asian NIEs first embarked on this growth path. The rising protectionism makes it increasingly difficult for other NIEs to follow a similar course. As soon as a country becomes a sizeable manufactures exporter to the United States, for example, it immediately becomes the object of various forms of trade "harrassment", including threats of countervailing duties, "graduation" from GSP, etc. The NIE exporters are seeking to diversify markets so as to reduce their vulnerability to such bilateral retaliation, but the process is a gradual one at best and there are few markets that can compensate for declining export growth to the US market. Ironically, at the very time that the external environment for an export-led growth strategy is turning ever less hospitable, a growing number of NIEs and would-be NIEs are adopting such a strategy, frequently with the encouragement of international financial institutions. Thus competition among developing countries to attract export-oriented investments is intensifying, thereby diminishing whatever benefits the NIEs might be able to capture from such activities. The same applies to competition for market share in major OECD markets among those NIEs which have sizeable export sectors.

Traditionally, the export-led growth strategy rested heavily on the comparative advantages of the NIEs in labour-intensive assembly and simple manufacturing. In recent years the first-tier NIEs have begun to upgrade their skills and know-how so as to be able to add more value in such export industries. At the same time, the techniques of assembly and manufacturing have been radically altered by the diffusion of new microelectronic technologies. In many industries and product lines automation has substantially reduced unskilled labour content and undermined competitive advantages based on low labour costs alone. As skilled labour becomes more crucial to competitiveness, countries with already developed pools of such labour gain in competitiveness relative to those with a largely unskilled labour force. Thus potential new entrants into export manufacturing face increasing barriers. For all but a few relatively advanced second-tier NIEs, the barriers in more skill-intensive sectors may well be insurmountable. In those remaining areas where low cost labour still strongly affects competitiveness, countries like China and Indonesia are making inroads, but growth prospects in those markets will not accommodate many large players beyond those.


## REFOCUSING GROWTH ON DOMESTIC AND REGIONAL MARKETS

The first-tier Asian NIEs are beginning to enjoy per capita income levels which make possible a substantial expansion of the domestic market. Even if those NIEs were to achieve income levels comparable to those of OECD countries however, the largest of them, South Korea, would still have a market smaller than that of France. Thus production for the domestic market could not adequately substitute for export production as an engine for sustained industrial growth, especially for industries in which scale economies remain important.

The quasi-continental economies do not face the same constraint in the long run, but in the shorter term per capita income levels remain well below those of the Asian first-tier NIEs. Thus for many types of consumer goods effective demand is still quite limited, although in China demand for consumer durables has been strongly stimulated in recent years. In the Latin American NIEs demand has been stagnating due to macroeconomic constraints. As a result, even the investment goods sector has shrunk and firms have not been able to make the needed investments in upgrading productive capacity to remain competitive.

The second tier NIEs have per capita incomes somewhere between those of the first-tier NIEs and the quasi-continental economies of Asia. Still, their markets are quite small and income disparities are generally greater than in the first-tier Asian NIEs. Thus refocusing growth on domestic demand is especially difficult at present. Nevertheless, incomes are rising quite steeply in some of those countries (i.e. in Thailand and Malaysia) so domestic markets can be expected to assume greater importance over time.

Of perhaps greater potential for the NIEs than reliance on internal markets alone would be to develop stronger regional market links. Until recently, most NIEs have viewed neighbours principally as competitors for market shares in the major OECD markets. As the latter become less accessible, and as the NIEs seek to diversify their markets, regional trade becomes more attractive. The East and Southeast Asian region, for example, has a potentially huge market which soon could equal in size that of Japan. A process of integration is occurring *de facto* in that region as Japanese companies move segments of their manufacturing bases to other countries in East and South East Asia in response to the strong yen appreciation and escalating labour and other domestic production costs[20]. An intra-regional, intra-firm division of labour seems to be taking shape in which different countries become production bases for different components and/or final products and intra-firm trade takes place among countries in the region. The advantages to the firms are in terms of ability to achieve economies of scale through specialisation of production by location. The countries which have been drawn into this global sourcing network remain ambivalent since the linkages created are no longer solely within a given country but with neighbouring countries. Moreover, the linkages are largely intra-firm and thus do not substantially promote the growth of independent supplier networks[21]. Finally, some countries are concerned that, within the regional division of labour, they may be allocated the most labour-intensive, least technology-intensive operations and thus enjoy few opportunities for technological learning[22].

This sort of intra-firm regional trade does not, however, exhaust the possibilities. Since income levels within a region like Southeast Asia or Latin America are far more similar than income levels across regions (the NIEs on the one hand and the OECD countries on the other), demand patterns are also apt to be fairly similar across countries in the same region. Thus there would appear to be potential for intra-regional specialisation and trade based upon economies of scale combined with product differentiation rather than along lines of relative factor endowments. Given that income levels are rising in the Asian NIEs (and pending a resolution of the debt crisis can be expected to rise once more in the Latin American NIEs) at least demand patterns should become more differentiated. At the same time, economies of scale will remain relatively more important in the NIEs than in OECD countries, since consumers are likely to be more price sensitive and less willing or able to pay a premium for differentiated product characteristics. Thus regionally specialised production structures that reduce the severity of the trade-off between economies of scale and degree of product differentiation could be especially well suited to NIE requirements. The difficulty is that to achieve such complementary production structures may require a degree of regional policy co-ordination that has proven elusive in the past. Market forces might tend to generate some such pattern, but only if the countries in a given region were first forced — presumably by external circumstances like growing protectionism in OECD countries — to refocus demand on the regional (and of course the domestic) market. The advantage of this sort of strategy over the OECD-focused export strategy is that domestic market growth is no longer in potential conflict but is in actual harmony with growth in external (for example, regional) markets.

An example of such a process of regional integration is the recent economic agreement between Brazil and Argentina. The agreement covers, in its first stage, trade in a number of finished capital goods (excluding electronics and components thereof). Eventually, co-operation in aerospace, nuclear and biotechnology R&D is anticipated. Thus far, there has been a surge in trade in capital goods, accompanied by a pattern of intra-industry specialisation. Argentina exports mostly capital goods made in small batches with skilled labour, while Brazil produces capital goods in long production runs where economies of scale are important. Complementary technology agreements have been made between Brazilian and Argentinian firms[23].

# NOTES AND REFERENCES

1. OECD, 1988:69.
2. Habakkuk, H.J., *American and British Technology in the Nineteenth Century,* Cambridge, 1962; Gerschenkron, A., *Economic Backwardness in Historical Perspective,* Cambridge, Mass., 1962; Ames, E. and Rosenberg, N., "Changing Technological Leadership and Industrial Growth", *Economic Journal,* March 1963.
3. See e.g., Landes, D., "Japan and Europe: Contrasts in Industrialization", in Lockwood, W.W. ed., *The State and Economic Enterprise in Japan,* Princeton, 1965; and Carr, E.H., "Some Random Reflections on Soviet Industrialization" in Feinstein, C.H., ed., *Socialism, Capitalism and Economic Growth,* Cambridge, 1967.
4. Ames and Rosenberg, March 1963, pp. 29-30.
5. Parthasarathi, A., "Some Aspects of the Development of Poor Countries and the Role of International Scientific Co-operation in that Process", paper prepared for Pugwash Symposium on "What Can Scientists Do for Development?", held at Stanford University, USA, August 1970.
6. For example, Goldstar of South Korea is constructing a new wafer fabrication facility, due to be completed in 1996, which will cost $2.2 billion (A.M. Hayashi, "Hyundai Headache", *Electronic Business,* 6th February 1989, pp. 25-32).
7. Merhav, 1969
8. India's self-reliance policy is a case in point.
9. OECD, *Technology, Flexibility of Manufacturing and Industrial Relations,* 18th October 1988, p. 4.
10. C. Edquist and S. Jacobsson, 1988, p. 174. The density measure used is the installed number of AMT divided by millions of employees in the engineering sector.
11. For example, CNC machine tools eliminate the need for skilled machinists but at the same time create demands for skilled technicians for maintenance and repair of the computerised machinery (C. Edquist and S. Jacobsson, 1988).
12. Obviously, the extent of such disparities depends greatly on the overall social structure and income distribution in a particular country.
13. Lundvall, 1988:352.
14. A case in point would be Taiwan's exports of standard numerical control machine tools.
15. Soete, 1985.
16. For details, see "HDTV: Can the U.S. get its act together?", cover story, *Electronics,* March 1989, pp. 70-107.
17. Perez and Soete, 1988, pp. 472-74.
18. See the otherwise extremely stimulating article by Perez and Soete, 1988, p. 475.
19. Based on information gathered by one of the authors in interviews in the South Korean semiconductor industry, May, June and November 1988.
20. The Bank of Japan, "Greater Role of Asian Economies in the World and Growing Interdependence Among Asia, the United States and Japan", Special Paper No. 166, August 1988 and report on "Internationalization Strategies of Japanese Electronics Companies — Implications for Newly Industrializing Economies", to be prepared for the OECD Development Centre project

"Technological Change and the Electronics Sector — Perspectives and Policy Options for North-South Industrial Co-operation".

21. While in South Korea intra-firm linkages have played a much less prominent role, the predominance of huge, vertically integrated conglomerates has been an important constraint to the emergence of independent supplier networks.

22. This is certainly a concern of China, for example, but others share it.

23. Chudnovsky, 1988.

*Part Two*

# THE CHALLENGE AHEAD FOR NEWLY INDUSTRIALISING ECONOMIES

*Chapter III*

# GROWTH PATTERNS AND INDUSTRIALISATION STRATEGIES IN NEWLY INDUSTRIALISING ECONOMIES: COMMONALITIES AND DIVERSITY

## A CLASSIFICATION OF THE NIEs

Recent patterns of differential development in what has commonly been referred to as the "Third World" suggest the need for a more refined set of categories for analysing their problems and prospects. Any attempt at classification faces the problem that their economies are highly diverse and any grouping according to certain perceived commonalities must necessarily overlook other important differences. Moreover, choosing an appropriate set of criteria by which to classify these economies must depend in large measure on the purpose for which the classification is made. In this context, our primary concern is to understand why different NIEs have different degrees of access to the new technologies they need to upgrade their production structures; why, once they have access, they differ in terms of their abilities to absorb and exploit effectively the potentials of those technologies; why they differ in their abilities to adapt the technologies creatively, modify their designs, and even originate new designs and engage in local product development.

A complex array of factors combines to explain different countries' potentials along these several dimensions of technology development. For the purpose of this study the countries which enjoy very limited prospects — at least in the foreseeable future — of reaping substantial economic benefits from the new technologies in terms of latecomer industrialisation are excluded. Any judgement of which countries to include and which to exclude is to a degree arbitrary. For those countries which are included, rough geographical proximity emerges as a first classificatory principle. This is only valid because, for historical and other reasons, countries within a certain region exhibit certain commonalities along other relevant dimensions. The main factors to be considered in classifying countries are:

  *i)* Key markets, including the size and structure of markets and the relative focus on internal versus external markets;

 *ii)* Production structures, including industry structure and firm size, extent of inter-industry linkages, and "core industries";

*iii)* Degree and form of reliance on foreign technologies;

*iv)* Role of the state in industrial and technological development; and

 *v)* State of development of indigenous scientific and technological capabilities. Another set of considerations are *vi)* Institutional, social, cultural and political factors, which are often specific to a single economy but nonetheless may have an important bearing on technological capabilities.

All of these six sets of characteristics combine in complex ways within a particular national setting to shape what has come to be described as an economy's structural competitiveness[1].

The more extended treatment of how the different groups of NIEs compare according to the aforementioned criteria awaits the discussion below of the diversity of growth patterns and industrialisation strategies. Throughout the study, our analysis is weighted toward the experiences of the Asian NIEs, with far less detailed treatment of the Latin American NIEs or the quasi-continental economies. Among Latin American NIEs, Brazil receives more attention than the rest.

**First-tier Asian NIEs (South Korea, Taiwan, Singapore and Hong Kong)**

*i)* These countries have followed heavily export-oriented growth strategies targeted on dynamic market segments and have capitalised on their low production costs. Increasingly they are competing on the basis of low-cost skilled engineering and technical labour. Rapid per capita income growth is expanding their internal markets including demand for more differentiated products.

*ii)* Production structures vary quite widely within the group. At one end of the industrial structure are South Korea's large conglomerates, or *chaebol*, at the other end the small- and medium-scale businesses of Taiwan, Hong Kong and Singapore, where the largest firms are mostly multinational enterprises. All have domestic engineering sectors which foster inter-industry linkages, but only in South Korea and Taiwan is capital goods production well developed. Perhaps most importantly, whatever the industrial structure, intense competition has prevailed among the major producers in a given industry.

*iii)* Foreign technologies continue to play a critical role in all four countries, but South Korea relies much more on licensing and unbundled technology, while Singapore would be at the other extreme where foreign direct investment is a major technology source.

*iv)* With the exception of Hong Kong, the government has played an active role in encouraging industrial capital accumulation and, especially, private sector risk-taking in pursuit of export market opportunities created by new technologies. It has also actively promoted the strengthening of indigenous R&D capabilities.

*v)* The populations of the first-tier Asian NIEs have very high average educational levels, and education is widely accessible and quite evenly distributed. Likewise, they have relatively large numbers of scientists and engineers in proportion to their populations. Many have been educated and trained abroad but standards in domestic universities and training institutions are also rising. Research and development effort is quite high and growing rapidly, with commercial applications absorbing the bulk of R&D resources.

**Second-tier Asian NIEs (Malaysia, Thailand, Philippines)**

*i)* Unlike their first-tier neighbours, these countries are resource-rich and thus have traditionally relied heavily on commodity exports. Only recently have they become major exporters of manufactures. Per capita incomes (with the exception of Malaysia) are still fairly low, though in Thailand they are rising rapidly. Domestic market demand is thus still quite homogeneous and price sensitive.

*ii)* Their industrial bases are much narrower than those of the first-tier, especially their export sectors, which still produce mainly labour-intensive, low-value-added products. Linkages to local component sources are weak and the capital goods sector (with the exception of transport equipment and some farm machinery) is very small.

*iii)* All depend very heavily on foreign direct investment and have limited absorptive capabilities for unbundled technologies, especially highly sophisticated ones. In the more technology-intensive export sectors (e.g. electronics), foreign firms predominate. Technology access is also a problem since they lack the leverage of large economies or the relatively more advanced first-tier Asian NIEs in negotiating favourable transfer agreements.

*iv)* The state has played a more passive role in these countries than in the first-tier NIEs, especially in terms of developing the local R&D infrastructure. It has been effective mainly in creating favourable conditions for FDI, except in the Philippines where political conditions have tended to discourage sizeable investments in recent years.

*v)* Educational levels are relatively high, but below those in the first-tier NIEs and far less evenly distributed. Rural populations remain large in the Philippines and Thailand and have limited educational opportunities. Scientists and engineers in proportion to total population are also low by first-tier NIE standards, but there are still fairly large numbers of engineers and technicians in absolute terms and the quality of their training is adequate[2]. R&D activity related to manufacturing is very limited, either in public institutions or in the private sector, reflecting the heavy presence of foreign firms in the more technology-intensive sectors.

**First-tier Latin American NIEs (Brazil, Mexico, and Argentina)**

*i)* The main feature of these countries is their heavy reliance on import-substitution growth strategies focused predominantly on the domestic market. Their combined GDP is roughly three times larger than the combined GDP of the first-tier Asian NIEs. Average per capita incomes are comparable to those in the first-tier Asian NIEs, but income is quite unevenly distributed[3]. This has limited the effectiveness of their growth strategies. Since 1981/82, the debt crisis has led to still another round of import substitution in a period of shrinking domestic markets. The untenability of this approach has forced firms to search more determinedly for potential export markets.

*ii)* Production structures vary within the group[4]. In Brazil and Argentina, foreign firms account for about one-fourth of industrial value added. In all three, the most dynamic industrial sectors have oligopolistic structures. The small- and medium-scale enterprise sector is quite large, but the debt crisis has had particularly adverse effects on this sector. Linkages between this sector and the large oligopolistic enterprises are relatively weak. The capital goods sector is well developed in Brazil, with growing exports and a diversified product line. It is less well so in Mexico, and in Argentina it has recently been declining. The foreign-dominated transport equipment sectors in Brazil and Mexico are highly developed and exports have been growing rapidly.

iii) To perhaps a greater degree than most Asian first-tier NIEs, the Latin American first-tier has relied on foreign direct investment (FDI) for technology acquisition[5]. Given high degrees of protection, however, joint ventures with foreign capital have been relatively insulated from import competition and have had little incentive to introduce new technologies to upgrade their operations. Licensing and technical consultancy arrangements have been limited as compared with countries like South Korea. The severe foreign exchange shortages of recent years have reduced technology imports, and even FDI has virtually stagnated as a result of the crisis[6].

iv) The state has been highly interventionist in industrial and technology policy-making in all three countries[7]. At one end, Brazil's state intervention has been widest in scope, reflected in the relatively large weight of state enterprises in the economy. At the other end, state intervention in Argentina, which was already low, has been further reduced in recent years. Brazil's R&D effort is the largest, followed by that of Mexico[8]. Much of these outlays, however, have been concentrated on defence-related applications, nuclear energy and agricultural research. In all countries, R&D spending on new technologies is still a small share of total R&D expenditures. Meanwhile, Brazil's policy of market reserve, while stimulating private R&D investment in informatics, appears to have fostered an industrial structure comparable to that noted above in other industries, with attendant fragmentation of R&D efforts, whose scale remains well below that of certain Asian first-tier NIEs. More importantly, state regulation of trade and investment in new technologies has been less focused than in the Asian first-tier[9].

v) Secondary educational levels are on average one-third lower than in the more advanced first-tier Asian NIEs[10]. On the other hand, the average for higher education is close to that of South Korea. Density of scientists and engineers for Brazil is higher than in countries like South Korea. Overall, including technicians, however, Brazil's density is about one-fourth smaller than that of South Korea. The proportion of tertiary students in engineering in these countries is roughly one-half the proportion in South Korea[11]. The fact that the first-tier Latin American NIEs send a lower proportion of post-secondary students for training abroad than first-tier Asian NIEs partially reflects their higher level of development of educational structures and partially the debt constraints.

## Second-tier Latin American NIEs (Chile, Colombia, Uruguay, Venezuela)[12]

i) These countries all have relatively small markets and a fairly good income distribution. Except for Colombia, which has not stopped growing, they have only recently recovered growth, a growth focused on the internal market. Manufactured exports have been few and unstable. Per capita incomes are still low, with the exception of Uruguay which, however, has recently experienced a decline. Debt-related balance of payments problems, particularly acute in

Venezuela, have affected their investment and import capacity. On the average, interest payments absorb between one-fourth and one-third of exports.

ii Their industrial structures are generally immature and complementary to major primary activities (agriculture, agroindustry, mining, oil exploration), with a limited import substitution in basic consumer goods[13]. Colombia and Venezuela have in addition sought to develop a capital goods sector in connection with oil exploration and refining. The results so far have been mixed.

iii) They all depend on foreign technology to develop their industrial base. Their limited technological capability, or their focus on primary sector related areas, limits considerably their capacity to unbundle technology. A limited market, particularly in the case of Uruguay, creates further problems for technology access. In Venezuela, attempts to accelerate growth have not been matched by the development of local capabilities.

iv) Educational levels are higher than the Latin American average, but still low by international standards in comparison with countries of similar economic size. About one-third of the population is still of rural origin, but urbanisation has been intense, particularly in Uruguay, and in Venezuela more recently. In Uruguay and Colombia past political developments affected negatively the development of an S&T infrastructure, which remains focused in government and academic institutions. In Venezuela the oil boom, in contrast, allowed for the rapid build-up of a scientific infrastructure, albeit excessively focused in oil-related activities and agricultural state institutions.

v) In general, these countries have a weak R&D infrastructure which is concentrated mostly in traditional sectors (agriculture, health, oil). Collaboration between universities and industry remains limited in spite of recent efforts to create stronger links (e.g. in Venezuela). The large countries (Venezuela and Colombia) have made considerable efforts in training S&T personnel, including sending large numbers of students for foreign training. In Uruguay, by contrast, political repression under the military regime led to a considerable brain drain which has only just begun to be reversed.

## The quasi-continental economies (China and India)[14]

i) Potentially, both countries have enormous internal markets, larger in numerical terms than any other country. Still, income levels remain very low in both, though more equally distributed in China than in India. Even with low per capita incomes, their markets are large enough so that both countries have pursued development strategies which are heavily focused on the domestic market. Demand patterns are quite homogeneous, though perhaps more so in China where until recently at least there was a small elite and middle class. In the last several years, both countries have encouraged exports, China more heavily and successfully than India.

ii) Industrial structures differ quite widely between the two. In China, about two-thirds of industrial output originates from state owned enterprises which, until recently, had very little autonomy. In the last few years they have gained greater financial and some production autonomy. The collective enterprise sector, which comprises a much larger number of firms, has had much greater autonomy and has accounted for a growing share of industrial output. Recently it has been reined in an effort to "cool off" the economy. In India, there is also a sizeable state enterprise sector, but outside that sector central planning has a limited effect on production decisions. In both countries, the most sophisticated product and manufacturing technologies are generally concentrated in the military sector, whereas civilian industries have tended to lag behind technologically. This applies to capital goods production as well. Finally, both countries have had stringent local content requirements which have created backward linkages to components production, but such production remains fragmented and inefficient.

iii) Foreign participation has been strictly controlled historically, with foreign investment only allowed in China for little more than a decade and foreign equity participation limited to minority status in most Indian enterprises. Both countries have sought to limit dependence on foreign technology by pursuing policies of substitution of local for foreign technology (in the Indian case) or of reverse engineering foreign technologies to be able to produce local equivalents (in the Chinese case). In both instances, the countries have come to recognise the need to liberalise technology imports to have access to the many new technological developments where they have "fallen behind"[15].

iv) The state's role has differed markedly between the two countries. In the 1950s the Chinese government established a highly centralised system of science and technology planning, which isolated the S&T system from the economy. That system was viewed as largely defence-related. China has had limited experience in technology policy formulation, as evidenced by the lack of co-ordination between technology import policies and local technology development. This suggests that access and absorption are treated as unrelated issues. Macroeconomic reforms appear to have had limited effect thus far on the incentives of large- and medium-scale state enterprises in China to upgrade technologically. The export promotion policies are focused on the coastal cities and provinces[16].

In India, state pronouncements on the need for diffusion of new technologies throughout the economy appear to be quite farsighted. Indeed, they look far beyond what may be feasible, given political and institutional constraints, in the foreseeable future. State policy reforms affecting high technology industries have been decreed since the early 1980s and have had a noticeable effect on investment and entry levels in fields like electronics, but policy inconsistencies and uncertainties still limit the scope for the development of competitive production of high technology products[17].

v) The indigenous S&T infrastructure remains weak in these countries, despite huge enclaves of advanced research and development related to space and nuclear projects. Linkages between the universities and research institutes and, especially, between the latter and production enterprises have been very limited. Low average educational levels and high illiteracy rates remain serious problems in both countries. Employment opportunities for scientists and engineers are limited. In India, this results in high rates of emigration. In China, more than a third of scientific personnel are estimated to be idle for lack of suitable work.

# BASIC COMMONALITIES AMONG THE NIEs

**Latecomer characteristics**

The newly industrialising economies share certain characteristics with industrial latecomers in earlier historical periods. At the same time, there are important new elements in the contemporary context which pose substantially different problems and offer new prospects to the NIEs. Among the central features of the new environment are the new technologies and their implications for global competitiveness.

Traditionally, the advantages of latecomers have been presumed to lie in their ability to utilise relatively advanced technologies previously developed in the early industrialising countries. This has allowed them to economise on R&D investment and equipment experimentation. In the early phases of industrialisation, indigenous innovative capabilities are weak in any case, so heavy reliance is placed upon imported technologies. Local efforts focus principally on adaptive engineering to modify the imported equipment to suit better local material and component availabilities, local skill levels, and relative factor costs. Copying, reverse engineering, and adaptive imitation are the major means of absorbing foreign techologies. Through a process of incremental learning, with time firms acquire capabilities to perform more innovation. At first the capital goods sector is not well developed and whatever capital goods production occurs is normally done in-house by the equipment users. Only at a later stage does capital goods production become a specialised activity and a major source of technological innovations, especially process innovations.

### Short history of rapid industrial development

Despite the diversity of development experiences of the NIEs, certain basic commonalities of latecomer industrialisation are shared by all of them. First, rapid industrial sector growth is a phenomenon of very recent origin, rarely dating back more than forty years. In many cases, the last twenty years are the relevant time horizon. Thus, the foundations of the industrial economies of the NIEs remain weak in several respects. While all the NIEs have engineering sectors comprising more than 20 per cent of manufacturing value added, the absolute size of this sector is still quite small in most NIEs. Since this sector is a principal user of capital goods, its limited size has also retarded the growth of capital goods production. As a result, practically all NIEs have yet to develop internationally competitive capital goods industries. This is reflected in the overwhelming dominance of OECD countries in world capital goods exports: 90 per cent of these originated in OECD countries which, however, accounted for little more than half of worldwide capital goods production[18]. While some countries like Taiwan can compete in terms of price for vintage equipment, even they face difficulties to remain competitive as prices of more advanced equipment fall and these have substantially better performance (in terms of durability, accuracy, etc.).

### Weak foundations of industrial structure

Related manifestations of the still underdeveloped industrial structures of the NIEs are the weakness of parts and components suppliers, of support services, like equipment repair and maintenance, and of subcontracting networks. The first is reflected, for example, in the high import content of both import substitutes and exports in the NIEs. That is especially pronounced for products — whether producer or consumer goods — with a high content of sophisticated components (e.g. electronic control units for CNC machine tools, very large scale integrated circuits for computers, etc.)[19]. The level of development of support services is a reflection of the level of complexity of the industrial processes performed. The more complex the processes and sophisticated the production equipment, other things being equal, the more demand is generated for specialised suppliers to support those processes and service that equipment. As with critical components, so with sophisticated capital equipment, the NIEs must still rely heavily on imports from OECD countries, whose firms do not always provide adequate support to user firms in NIEs which account for a small share of their global markets.

*Limited subcontracting networks*

With expanding markets for industrial goods and rising production scales of industrial enterprises, possibilities for creating backward linkages to domestic component suppliers increase. The growth of domestic component sourcing is not, however, synonymous with the growth of the local subcontracting network. For firms can increase domestic sourcing either by building up links to outside suppliers or by integrating vertically to supply their component requirements internally. There is no *a priori* basis for evaluating the superiority of one method over the other. Which is preferred will depend in part on the nature of the component and the degree of specificity of the investments required to supply it. For example, if highly specialised equipment and/or training is required to produce a component which is custom-made for a single firm's equipment, the advantages to vertical integration would be considerable[20].

The issue for NIEs is one of the broad competitive environment and the extent to which it allows for the flourishing of subcontracting networks wherever they are an efficient method of forging supplier-user links. Subcontracting networks are generally a more suitable organisational structure than highly vertically integrated firms for component sourcing, for example, when standardised components subject to large scale economies are needed by a number of user firms, none of whom accounts for a sizeable share of the total demand.

Subcontracting networks are also an efficient structure when learning economies are significant but technology- rather than firm-specific. Thus, to the extent that a subcontractor can accumulate experience by serving several customers' requirements, a new user of that subcontractor's services benefits from the learning economies without having to repeat the learning process. It is this latter sense in which subcontractor networks become a crucial source of flexibility in responding to rapid technological change. Subcontracting arrangements may involve the supply not only of complementary assets but also of supplementary capacity to the principals. Here, the primary advantage of such networks is to allow for additional degrees of freedom in responding to shifting market demands, for example, in rapidly expanding capacity in response to unanticipated surges in demand. Without such flexibility, firms risk potentially large declines in market share.

*Overwhelming reliance on generic technologies and product standards of OECD origin*

Reliance on foreign technologies is a matter of degree. In their early industrialisation most countries have relied quite extensively on imported technology. At present, technological self-sufficiency is beyond the reach of even the most highly industrialised economies. As technological innovation becomes an ever more central feature of the competitive environment, the OECD countries are, if anything, becoming more interdependent technologically.

The technological interaction between the NIEs on the one side and the OECD countries on the other tends to be even more lopsided. This is especially true with respect to the generic technologies which lie at the core of the new techno-economic paradigm. What technological capabilities the NIEs possess in these areas are generally second-order in the sense that they do not involve the capacity for sustained generation of new technologies that would extend the frontier but rather movements from a position well within the frontier to a point somewhere closer to it. The generic technologies are acquired from OECD countries and form the basis for selective product adaptation and development. Yet, even here there are strictly defined limits to such activities, at least where the NIEs seek to maintain a presence in world markets, since product standards are largely dictated by OECD market requirements. There are no examples of NIE developed products which have set standards for the OECD countries.

This fundamental technological asymmetry becomes increasingly problematical as barriers to technology diffusion become higher. Those barriers are increasing as OECD firms seek ways of increasing their returns from their R&D, and OECD governments seek in various ways to restrict outward technology flows, especially with regard to core technologies. A few countries within the OECD have enjoyed a dominant position in terms of innovative capacity for two centuries or more. Japan is among the few successful latecomers to technological innovation. While it is possible that a country may industrialise without achieving the level of technological sophistication of Japan, the industrial foundations of its economy will be weaker in proportion to the lesser development of its technological capabilities.

### A relatively weak human resource base

Probably more than in any earlier historical period, human resource "endowments" are a critical requirement for latecomer industrialisation in an era where "knowledge-intensive" industries are the most dynamic ones. All the NIEs are acutely aware of the need to strengthen their human resource bases. Even those with the most educated and skilled personnel fall far short of the OECD countries by almost any indicator. In terms of percentage of the population aged 25 and over which had completed secondary education in 1980, South Korea's 19 per cent (one of the highest among the NIEs) compares unfavourably with Japan's 40 per cent. In terms of post-secondary education, South Korea's 9 per cent and Argentina's 6 per cent are well below Japan's 14 per cent and very far below the United States' 32 per cent[21]. In 1983, Japan had 401 000 tertiary students in engineering to South Korea's 277 000, Mexico's 257 000, and Brazil's 165 000. Finally, and perhaps most importantly, in 1983 South Korea had 800 R&D scientists and engineers per million population and Argentina roughly 375, while Japan had over 4 000 and the United States over 3 000. Perhaps even more serious than the low density of skilled engineers and scientists in the NIEs is the shortage of experienced personnel who can effectively manage R&D projects. This lack of R&D management skills means that even the limited resources that are devoted to R&D in the NIEs are often used inefficiently, so R&D productivity is low.

## Increasing restrictions on market and technology access

At the same time that it is becoming ever more critical for developing countries to acquire access to new technologies, it is becoming increasingly difficult for them to do so. This is due in part to the rapid pace of evolution of those technologies, in part to the strategies of firms and the policies of governments within the OECD to cope with the challenges posed by intensifying competitive pressures.

The international trade environment is becoming much more protectionist and OECD market access is increasingly precarious for many NIEs. This growing protectionism reflects primarily the heightening political conflicts resulting from serious trade imbalances between OECD countries: in particular, between Japan on the one hand and a number of other OECD countries — most especially the United States — on the other.

Nevertheless, it is the NIEs that are increasingly the object of restrictive trade practices of OECD countries. In recent years, the number of "dumping" cases filed by OECD countries against one another has been declining while the frequency of cases filed against NIE exporters has risen dramatically[22]. From the perspective of the NIEs' efforts to maintain or even increase world market shares of more technology-intensive products, the potentially most damaging form of protectionism is the effort by certain OECD governments — led by the United States — to enforce more strictly intellectual property rights.

There is considerable dispute as to how effective legal protection of intellectual property has been in the past and is likely to be in the future[23], apart from a limited number of products (e.g. new chemicals and simple mechanical inventions). Still, a growing number of NIE firms are faced with lawsuits for patent or copyright violation. In the past, reverse engineering could be combined with selective modification of certain design features to minimise the risk of patent or copyright infringements. Reverse engineering may be becoming a less viable option for NIEs as technological complexity increases and OECD firms introduce customised features into their product designs to lower the probability of copying or at least to make it easier to detect. At the government level, by threatening to deny market access to producers in countries which have not given adequate protection to intellectual property, the US government has raised considerably the stakes for latecomer strategies. Such measures will hardly facilitate the debate, long overdue, on what constitutes an appropriate intellectual property regime.

The issue of intellectual property rights is a potentially divisive one within the NIEs. For those first-tier Asian NIEs where conditions exist for promoting sustained domestic innovation and product development, stricter enforcement of intellectual property rights may seem appropriate. On the other hand, those developing countries — and this means the vast majority — where innovative activity remains the exception rather than the rule probably see little to be gained by instituting measures which would tend to slow the rate of diffusion of new technologies. For example, there is no doubt that the utilisation rate of microcomputers in developing countries would be much lower than it is if (virtually costless) copying of standard software packages were tightly circumscribed. It is possible as well that lack of protection has retarded to a degree the emergence of an independent software industry in such countries. There are clearly trade-offs, but over time the terms of the trade-offs shift as countries' technological capabilities improve.

These "artificial" market barriers together with increasing restrictions on access to foreign technology, are forcing NIE firms and governments to make costly investments in R&D as an alternative means of assuring access to technologies that become more difficult to obtain from OECD countries. To the extent that OECD countries succeed in tightening their control, NIEs will have to pay a more sizeable rent for the technologies they are still able to procure. The technology exporters will thus have sufficient resources to upgrade their technologies in order to stay ahead of potential NIE competitors.

Entry costs into product markets are also becoming steeper. Product standards may themselves constitute an entry barrier, though they need not always do so. The role of standards is an ambivalent one in shaping conditions for NIE entry into OECD markets. Here one has to distinguish among technical norms, emerging technical standards and competitive equipment standards.

Today every major OECD country has a complex set of norms in a variety of sectors, which were used in the past to protect their markets from foreign competition. These are technically dictated norms which must be met to sell in individual OECD markets. Meeting such norms can be costly and time consuming, often requiring expensive equipment investments and detailed knowledge of the systems underlying the application of the norms.

A more recent phenomenon in some high technology areas like software is the emergence of virtual technical standards such as MS-DOS and UNIX[24]. The rapid diffusion of MS-DOS as an industry-wide standard for personal computers allowed for the penetration of NIE computer equipment manufacturers into a few major OECD markets. The emergence of a 32-bit software standard around UNIX holds a similar promise. As the 32-bit market gains in importance for all major OECD computer manufacturers, the setting of a UNIX standard becomes a strategic competitive issue. This raises the barriers to entry to NIE countries, in so far as the formation of regional (Europe's X/OPEN) or other competitive groups to diffuse a particular version of UNIX, makes it costlier to NIE firms to follow the developments in the area and often shuts them out of the standard setting groups, with an irremediable loss in terms of experience.

It is possible that the fall in prices of microprocessors will allow competing standards to coexist side by side within the same equipment or focused on individual applications sectors. Finally, a potentially positive development for NIE firms is the effort made by the US government to define an open UNIX standard which would then become the requirement for the government procurement market. There is no doubt, however, that NIE countries will for the time being have to conform with standards developed in OECD countries.


## DIVERSITY OF GROWTH PATTERNS AND INDUSTRIALISATION STRATEGIES

The contemporary economic structures and industrial performances of the NIEs are a reflection not only of differences in population size and natural resource endowments but also of different development strategies and policies. In this section we briefly examine the diversity of those development paths, especially inasmuch as they help to explain the differential access of NIEs to new technologies and their differential abilities to absorb those technologies. The experiences of the NIEs vary in five important respects:

    *i)*  Key market characteristics;

    *ii)*  Production structures;

    *iii)*  The nature and extent of reliance on foreign technologies;

    *iv)*  The role of the state in fostering industrial and technological development; and

    *v)*  The characteristics of the indigenous scientific and technological infrastructure.

**Key markets**

*Domestic versus external market orientation*

From the early 1960s, the first-tier Asian NIEs — with limited natural resources, low per capita incomes, and small domestic markets — based their growth primarily on manufactured exports. The second-tier Asian NIEs continued to rely primarily on their commodity exports to generate needed foreign exchange, while the manufacturing sector produced import substitutes for the narrow domestic market. Domestic market constraints to further import substitution led the second-tier Asian NIEs to promote export manufacturing from the early 1970s onward. In general, however, the export promotion policies created enclaves more or less isolated from the firms and industries producing principally for the domestic market.

In the first-tier Latin American countries, which possessed not only large natural resource endowments but also large domestic markets, pressures to export manufactures were less pronounced. Import substitution was supported by subsidised credit, high rates of effective protection, and overvalued exchange rates to hold down costs of imported components and materials. Import substitution advanced farther than in the second-tier Asian NIEs, but still many manufacturing industries remained heavily import-dependent for materials, components, and sub-assemblies. Severe balance-of-payments pressures since the early 1980s have intensified efforts at both import substitution and export-promotion, efforts which have been facilitated to a degree by currency depreciations in a number of countries.

The quasi-continental economies share certain characteristics of the first-tier Latin American NIEs but they have had even greater cause to focus their development strategies on the domestic market. Potentially at least, the economies of India and China, for example, are large enough to support highly integrated industrial structures. Still, effective demand remains low due to low per capita incomes. Real incomes have increased in China as a result of economic reforms launched since the late-1970s, but at the cost of widening income disparities. In India, liberalising reforms have generally been more cautious. Both countries have come to place greater emphasis of late on promoting exports, not as a substitute to domestic market development but rather as a means of obtaining foreign exchange needed to import advanced technologies as part of their modernisation efforts.

Since the early 1980s, an ironic reversal in relative emphasis on internal versus external markets has occurred between the first-tier Asian and Latin American NIEs. The high growth rates of the former have caused a considerable expansion in the domestic market potential, especially of the larger countries — South Korea and Taiwan. Meanwhile, the debt-induced stagnation of the Latin American NIEs, by shrinking their domestic markets, has forced many firms to become outward looking.

*Market homogenisation versus segmentation*

Market orientation has certain implications, though not always straightforward, for technological learning. First, the structure of demand in the export market and the domestic market is likely to differ, especially if the major export markets are the OECD countries. The higher income levels of those countries create demands for more differentiated products with somewhat higher quality standards than in the NIEs. That is why, to enter export markets from a domestic market base, NIE firms frequently must upgrade production, testing and quality control. This applies as well to suppliers of components to export-oriented firms.

At the same time, rapidly changing market structures in the OECD countries are forcing those NIEs which have traditionally focused on mass markets for standardized products to revise their strategies. For many products — from cars to computers — different brands are increasingly similar in terms of basic performance features and functions[25]. Thus, firms must seek new ways to differentiate their products so as to command a base of dedicated customers and thus a stable market share. In computers, for example, software availability plays a crucial role in differentiating sellers who offer similar hardware configurations. Board-level enhancements of the system performance are another differentiating factor. It has been noted elsewhere[26] that design differentiation of final products is increasingly determined at the component level. This is the result of the advance in miniaturisation of devices on the one hand and the improvements in flexibility of design tools on the other. Thus, an ability to use those tools to design ASICs would be important for entering differentiated product markets in the future, assuming that such capabilities are complemented by low cost fabrication of the ICs as well as by the development and manufacture of the products in which they are incorporated. As markets for standard hardware items near saturation in certain high technology products, a shift of focus to higher-value-added market segments may become critical to sustained growth. The high growth markets for standard mass produced items will be found increasingly in the NIEs themselves.

*Market orientation and technology access*

Most NIEs are dependent — though in widely varying degrees — on foreign technologies. Thus, gaining access to them through either trade or foreign direct investment is a critical concern. The relative merits of the two methods differ for different industries and different technologies as well as different countries[27]. If production is entirely or largely for export, the likelihood is high that foreign investors would choose to internalise completely the transfer of technology and other specific assets to a NIE via a wholly owned subsidiary. In that event, domestic enterpreneurs wishing to acquire access to the critical technologies, would need either to import them embodied in capital equipment or to license them from foreign suppliers, or both. Domestic absorptive capacity must be well developed for such a strategy to be effective — South Korea is a country where such an approach has been followed. Of course, there may be some "leakage" of technological assets from foreign subsidiaries into the domestic economy but that process is a slow one at best. In the case of domestic market oriented production, where the potential market is large, the prospects for accessing foreign technologies through FDI are somewhat better, since partial disclosure at least (for example, through mandated joint venture arrangements) may be traded for market access.

*Government procurement markets*

In a number of high technology areas, government procurement markets have been an important stimulus to industry and new technology development in both OECD countries and the NIEs. The classic OECD example is the US semiconductor industry, which was bolstered by defense- and space-related contracts. In the NIEs, government procurement has also played a decisive role in the development of the aerospace and nuclear industries of Brazil, China and India. It is now widely understood that such procurement can be a double-edged sword, especially where scarce R&D resources are competed away from commercial R&D and where civilian spinoffs from military technologies are minimal[28]. In the past, in the OECD countries, there have been some important spinoffs, but if anything the spinoffs in the future are more likely to run from commercial R&D to military applications. Thus, if NIE governments are to stimulate technology effort they will need to reorient procurement and related R&D support to civilian applications. The telecommunications system is an intermediate (i.e. "dual use" market where government procurement has played a pervasive role in the past and should continue to be an important stimulus to demand for high technology products and components. In terms of suppliers, the market for digital switching technology is one of the most oligopolistic of any high technology industry. It is extremely difficult for NIE firms to break into this field, even in their home markets (except of course as joint venture partners with one of the OECD-based oligopolists). System development costs can be extremely high.

Nevertheless, this has not deterred a number of NIEs. India, Brazil, and South Korea all have developed their own digital switching systems during the 1980s for the domestic market. Each of those three projects involved R&D costs a mere tenth of those of the latest switching systems developed by OECD firms. Engineering labour requirements were also roughly one-tenth.

The main source of cost saving is the fact that the systems developed in the NIEs were far less sophisticated than those of their OECD counterparts, reflecting the different market requirements. In the NIEs basic telephone services with high traffic density per line is the main characteristic. At this time, enhanced features like high volume data transmission and ISDN capability are not a priority, at least outside of a few major urban centres. Thus, the systems developed by these three NIEs are thought to be not only better suited to their respective domestic market conditions, but also potentially exportable to other developing countries with similar requirements for "no frills" technology at a low price[29].

Another area where the government procurement market is important is office automation. In many NIEs the government is the single largest computer user and generates sizeable demands for hardware as well as customised software. Traditionally, that demand has been mostly for large systems, where markets are only slightly less oligopolistic than in telecommunications equipment. The structure of demand is shifting toward smaller systems, including desktop PCs, which are technologically more accessible to domestic suppliers. The South Korean government has sought to stimulate the growth of the local minicomputer industry by undertaking a large-scale computerisation of public administration, while co-ordinating the efforts of domestic information firms (principally the *chaebol*) to develop the hardware and software configuration and produce the equipment for the system. On the other hand, the shift to desktops — with the large variety of low cost, off-the-shelf packages — may slow government demand growth for software and services.

Even if not in the core technologies, at least in many complementary technologies, government procurement demand may prove an important stimulus to local technological development, at least in the larger NIE markets. For example, as governments expand and upgrade their telecommunications networks (perhaps in some cases including ISDN capability)[30], a concatenation of related demands is generated — for telephone instruments, EPABXs, telefacsimile machines, interactive terminals, modems, etc. Of course, only in large markets would demands for most items be sufficiently large to justify local production, unless part of production can be exported. Another important set of demands is also generated — for a variety of components used in the equipment (e.g. integrated circuits, including large quantities of ASICs, laser diodes, couplers, multilayer printed circuit boards, connectors, cables, microphones, etc.). Given that sufficient volume of demand can be sustained, the telecommunications market could provide a strong boost — though probably not sufficient — to the upgrading of a country's component sector.

## The structure of production

### Industrial structure and firm size

The NIEs have vastly different industrial structures, average firm sizes, and size distributions of firms. These differences have implications both for innovative capacity and for the rate of diffusion of new innovations. Large diversified firms are better equipped to finance the enormous R&D and capital outlays required to compete in new technology markets (e.g. advanced electronics) at least in a world of imperfect capital markets. At the same time, a highly concentrated industrial structure may pre-empt many opportunities for learning and technology diffusion, which could occur if technological capabilities were more evenly distributed among a larger number of firms. These trade-offs are perhaps best illustrated by the contrasting industrial structures and firm sizes of South Korea on the one hand and Taiwan on the other. The former has a highly concentrated industrial structure dominated by the large conglomerates known as *chaebol*. The small- to medium-scale enterprises consist largely of suppliers to those conglomerates. In Taiwan, by contrast, small- and medium-scale enterprises are the most dynamic industrial sector and concentration levels are relatively low. There are only a few large diversified firms in technology-intensive industries.

The Taiwanese manufacturing sector has exhibited a high degree of flexibility in responding to shifts in demand in its major export markets. Faced with increasing barriers to the continued pursuit of a strategy of producing low-cost imitations of products designed mostly in OECD countries, Taiwanese firms have been able to shift to products involving some design enhancements and complementing rather than directly competing with products offered by OECD firms. On the other hand, Taiwanese firms have not been able to invest heavily in R&D activities which might enable them to compete for market share in areas on the technological frontier. Nor have they been able to make the capital investments required to produce high technology components like advanced integrated circuits (ICs).

South Korean firms, by virtue of their greater financial resources, have been better able to hurdle the escalating barriers to entry into products requiring large capital investments and where economies of scale are still significant. They have also substantially increased their investments in R&D. Still human resources for R&D remain a critical constraint. The *chaebol* face the risk of spreading scarce scientific and engineering resources too thinly and may be forced to concentrate their efforts on a limited range of new technologies, if they hope to keep apace of rapid technological developments[31].

As already noted, the high concentration of South Korean industry poses a potential barrier to diffusion of new technologies throughout the industrial structure. Of course there are incentives to limited technology transfer built into relationships between the *chaebol* and their subcontracting networks. The concern is that firms outside the network may have limited access to new technologies being developed and diffused within the more dynamic sector of industry. Moreover, even within the network there is bound to be technological asymmetry between the *chaebol* and the subcontractor firms which inhibits technology absorption by the latter. This problem should be diminished at least by the recent proliferation of R&D investments by small and medium enterprises in response to government financial incentives. Despite this, the large *chaebol* still dominate in terms of quantity of resources and quality of research.

In the quasi-continental economies, large- and medium-scale state enterprises play a more prominent role than in the first-tier Asian NIEs, although even in the latter state enterprises have sometimes been established in key industries with high investment and scale requirements (e.g. South Korea's steel industry). State enterprises are also important in the first-tier Latin American NIEs, notably Brazil and Mexico. In terms of competitiveness, Mexico's state-owned enterprises lag well behind those of Brazil. Both the quasi-continental economies and the first-tier Latin American NIEs have evolved industrial structures which are highly vertically integrated (although Argentina's has become an exception of late). The large number of entrants into certain sectors — for example, various electronics products in Brazil — makes backward integration by such firms into component production highly inefficient. Furthermore, in many cases those firms are producing a very diverse range of products whose characteristics are not sufficiently similar to allow for economies of scope. Interdependent supplier networks either hardly exist or, where they exist, are financially and technologically weak.

The quasi-continental economies, as well as some of the first-tier Latin American NIEs, have well-developed research capabilities in certain fields, but they have not been effective in translating technological innovations into commercially viable products[32]. In part this is due to a high degree of dualism between the military and civilian sectors. Moreover, the fragmentation of industrial capacities is accompanied in many instances by a fragmentation of R&D activity. Finally, while these economies possess sizeable capital goods industries, they have been slow to innovate and to incorporate new technologies in machinery design. Even where technology is relatively up-to-date, due to the recent origin of certain investments, the lack of competitive pressures on the capital goods and engineering industries of the quasi-continental economies may retard their effective adaptation to new technological developments.

The second-tier NIEs of Asia face a somewhat different set of constraints. Their industrial sectors are essentially dualistic, with one set of firms producing — frequently at high cost — for the domestic market and another set producing largely for export. Both sectors rely heavily on imported technologies, with the technology in the former generally being less advanced. Absorptive capabilities for relatively advanced process technologies exist, but innovative product development is lacking. With a few exceptions, domestic firms are too small and financially constrained to engage in significant R&D activity. Even vertical supplier networks are largely confined within the foreign-owned sector, though some backward linkages from foreign firms to domestic component and tooling suppliers are beginning to develop. In some countries the degree of dualism in the industrial structure is diminishing, as some (partly foreign-owned) firms which had traditionally produced almost exclusively for the domestic market are moving strongly into export markets.

*Inter-industry linkages*

All the NIEs face the problem of how to develop an integrated production structure without seriously compromising efficiency of certain key sectors. The disarticulation of the national production structure takes different forms in different countries. In the Asian NIEs it is manifested in the dualism of the components sector, with South Korea, for example, exporting large numbers of standard components at the same time that it is heavily import-dependent for key components. South Korean firms are investing heavily in the localisation of certain components, especially those where there may be supply interruption due to priority demand by foreign competitor firms. In the first-tier Latin American NIEs as well as the quasi-continental economies, the extent of linkages is perhaps somewhat greater but the efficiency is generally lower. Even in those countries, however, many high technology components (e.g. VLSI circuits) must be imported. The inefficiency of whatever linkages that do exist is suggested by the low degree of export competitiveness of their components sectors, as well as of the finished goods in which such components are incorporated[33].

While efficient linkages should be forged over time, it is not realistic to expect that even the large quasi-continental economies could develop fully integrated production structures. Some degree of specialisation in terms of both final product and component production is inevitable, especially in high technology areas where even OECD countries have been forced to focus development efforts and rely on imported technologies to fill gaps in their own product ranges. Still, the NIEs have considerable scope for strengthening linkages, especially from large export oriented firms to domestic small- and medium-scale engineering firms[34].

*Core industries*

Given scarce capital resources and the rapidly increasing capital intensity of certain high technology industries, many NIEs are faced with the dilemma of having to decide whether to channel resources into high risk new technology-intensive sectors or to concentrate on upgrading and expanding sectors like steel, chemicals, etc., which have traditionally been the core industries in the industrialisation process. This dilemma is epitomised by the "steel-versus-electronics" debate which took place in China in 1971-72[35]. In light of the fact that electronics are coming to play an increasingly important role as inputs into products where steel used to be the predominant input (e.g. automobiles, machine tools) there is certainly a strong case for acquiring competency in this field. As indicated earlier, such competency generally involves some local design, engineering, and even production capabilities for certain high technology products. Yet selectivity is necessary and complementarity desirable. Thus, for example, a NIE with strong steel and auto making capabilities might be well advised to focus its electronic development efforts on computer controls for metalworking machinery (on the process side) and automotive electronic components and subsystems (on the product side). This does not preclude entering other electronics or high technology sectors. Rather it highlights the fact that microelectronics may be a core technology of increasing importance, but this does not imply that for all (or even most) NIEs electronics manufacture must supplant other key sectors as the core industry.

**The nature and extent of reliance on foreign technologies**

Foreign technology has been a major contributor to the industrial capabilities of most if not all NIEs. The channels through which they have acquired new technologies from abroad differ across countries and over time within any given country. So do the countries' abilities to absorb and make effective use of those new technologies[36].

There are widely divergent, even diametrically opposed, views regarding the desirability of foreign direct investment as a means of technology acquisition. The transaction costs theory of FDI[37] suggests that the appropriation of the returns to firm-specific technological advantages is a major motivation to FDI. Evidence on the sectoral distribution of FDI shows a higher frequency of such investment in industries with characteristics generally associated with high technology levels (e.g. R&D expenditures as a percentage of sales). Even if, from the firm's perspective, FDI may under certain conditions be an efficient means of transferring a technological asset to another country, the question remains whether such technology diffuses widely or generates significant spillovers to other firms or industries in the economy where it is employed.

Within the Asian region, the first-tier NIEs have generally adopted fairly liberal policies regarding FDI, reflecting a perception by governments that there are some potential learning economies and spillovers. South Korea has probably had the most restrictive policy in this regard. From the mid-1960s onward, the government displayed a distinct preference for joint ventures involving minority foreign ownership over majority or wholly foreign owned ventures. Still, in wholly export-oriented ventures in more technology-intensive sectors (e.g. electronics), wholly foreign owned subsidiaries remained the rule at first. Nevertheless, the growth of a core of domestic enterprises with considerable managerial and technical expertise in the period of export-oriented growth lessened dependence on "packaged" foreign technology and created the conditions for effective unbundling. Thus, from the mid-1970s technology licensing begins to eclipse FDI as a source of foreign technology. Only a small percentage of such licensing agreements were tied to joint ventures, the vast majority involving wholly South Korean owned firms. Moreover, licensing has been most widespread in those sectors with high to moderate technology requirements (*viz.*, industrial machinery and electronics, followed by chemicals)[38].

Clearly, the ability to make effective use of licensed know-how depends greatly on the absorptive capacity of the licensee. While licenses may be an adequate means of acquiring codified know-how, tacit technical knowledge may be involved in the implementation of a licensed process. In that event, the licensee who lacks the learning ability to "fill out" the technology set may be at a loss to exploit the licensed know-how. A firm which possesses such absorptive capacity may eventually dispense with licensing once it has effectively internalised the fundamental "know-how" and "know-why". For the vast majority of NIE firms, this prospect will be confined to more mature technologies. It is doubtful whether that will be possible for leading edge technologies.

Even OECD firms in high technology industries have extensive cross-licensing agreements with other firms possessing complementary technological assets in an effort to pool R&D resources. Moreover, OECD firms are relying increasingly on cross-investments, forming joint equity ventures to pool capital resources in face of escalating entry costs into certain high technology fields. Those capital requirements are also a consideration in what seems to be a more accommodating attitude toward FDI in high technology fields by certain NIE governments which have historically downplayed FDI's importance. Certain NIE firms are resorting to strategic partnerships with OECD firms as a way of lessening R&D costs and gaining access to strategic technologies as well as markets. Given technological asymmetries between most NIE firms and their OECD counterparts, it is not yet certain how much potential exists for NIE firms to attract strategic partners.

There are clear limits to the extent of technology diffusion which can occur in the NIEs through either FDI or licensing. Neither allows much autonomy to NIE firms in the area of product design and development. By unbundling the technology, however, licensing allows greater scope for local enterprises to learn the mechanics of product design through reverse engineering. Significant design modification and especially innovative new designs require qualitatively different skills and intimate familiarity with user preferences in the major markets. Lacking those, NIE firms will remain locked into OEM supplier relationships with OECD firms.

The new technologies have ambiguous consequences for NIE firms seeking to move beyond accustomed design and marketing dependencies on OECD firms to establish themselves as independent, brand name suppliers in foreign markets. On the one hand, new automated design tools and methodologies make product design more affordable and accessible to NIE firms. On the other hand, those same tools give heightened flexibility to OECD-based design firms or in-house design departments to respond quickly to changing demands and allow higher degrees of product differentiation. Theoretically, such advantages are also available to NIE firms but the accumulated learning that OECD-based designers have acquired over years of close user-supplier interaction is not. That learning gets incorporated in design databases which are either firm-specific or which, if sold with design automation hardware by systems integration firms, substantially raise entry costs to NIE firms. Moreover, even if design barriers could be effectively surmounted, marketing and distribution barriers still remain to discourage entry by all but the most intrepid and financially strong NIE firms.

The design barriers are also being raised by calculated measures adopted by OECD firms and governments to "protect intellectual property", as well as by the inherent complexity of certain of the new technologies. The explicit measures affect principally the feasibility of pursuing a strategy of reverse engineering, while the inherent features of the technology complicate both that and more especially a strategy involving innovative design. With regard to the intellectual property regime, there are conflicting processes at work. On the one hand, firms are seeking to improve their returns from innovation by seeking to prevent early imitation of new product design. At the very least, they are seeking to discourage unauthorised (unlicensed) imitation.

On the other, proprietary designs may inhibit the emergence of standards. If firms are excessively protective of proprietary know-how, they may risk losing out in the standards battle. The 32-bit computer is a useful illustration of this trade-off. IBM pursued an open architecture strategy in earlier generations to encourage third party software development for its system and thereby established its machines as industry standards. With the 32-bit generation however, it is following a more "closed" architecture strategy, partly in an effort to pre-empt the "clone" makers, partly in an effort to differentiate its machines from other UNIX-based systems and set the 32-bit standard. In the meantime, however, the process of standardization is being drawn out and the rate of diffusion of 32-bit machines has slowed down. In order to increase the attractiveness of its machines, IBM has agreed to license its PS/2 technology to clone makers for a royalty fee of 3 per cent of sales. Given the small margins in the clone market, IBM expects that this strategy will limit its competitors' ability to cut into its market share[39]. Perhaps the most that NIE firms can hope is that multiple standards will emerge so they are not locked into a direct confrontation with IBM. At the same time, if competition among the major OECD computer vendors is intense, then all parties may be forced to adopt liberal licensing policies as part of their competitive strategies.

The second-tier Asian NIEs are faced with somewhat different issues regarding foreign technology access. Until now they have been heavily dependent upon bundled technology, either in joint ventures — as in import substituting and low technology export industries — or in wholly foreign owned subsidiaries — as in more technology-intensive export manufacturing. Relatively few domestic firms are employing extensive technology licensing, though brand name and trademark licensing is quite common. Absorptive capabilities would appear to be the main constraint to following this route to technology acquisition.

Yet a growing number of second-tier Asian NIE firms are reaching a level of technical competence, especially in low cost manufacturing techniques, where they could become important OEM suppliers of certain products of moderate technical sophistication. This route to technology upgrading may be partially blocked, however, if the first-tier Asian NIEs face difficulties "graduating" from OEM supplier to brand name supplier status. Of course, the first-tier Asian NIEs are likely to face competitive pressures to reduce costs as well. What this may mean is that, while the first-tier Asian NIE firms become OEM suppliers of latest generation products where margins are still relatively high, they slough off more mature OEM products to affiliates or licensees located in the second-tier Asian NIEs. Some evidence already points to such a process, with a number of investments recently by certain South Korean *chaebol* in Southeast Asian countries to manufacture low end telecommunications and consumer electronics products. As the first-tier Asian NIEs become increasingly important foreign investors in the second-tier Asian NIEs, this raises a new issue for further study, *viz.*, whether such investments will provide those economies with better, worse, or roughly comparable opportunities for technology upgrading than, say, the major OECD investor firms.

The first-tier Latin American NIEs, even after the resolution of the debt crisis, will face tremendous problems in the acquisition of technology through foreign direct investment because of the depressed state of their internal markets. On a more specific level, the economic crisis that hit these countries largely disarticulated their public S&T infrastructure, as highly qualified researchers and engineers migrated to the private sector and to defence-related industries. While the leading export firms have absorbed most of them, small and medium firms have had serious problems in retaining personnel. More importantly, the degradation of research teams at universities will affect the calibre of training, and ultimately their capacity to absorb foreign technology. The debt crisis also led to a new import substitution phase particularly in some high technology sectors. Imports of foreign technology have been dramatically reduced in Brazil, which leads one to predict that the industry will increasingly lose touch with the technological frontier. A country like Mexico may be in a somewhat better position given the recent influx of investment geared towards exports to the US market. Good management of this investment from the perspective of technological learning could contribute significantly to an increase in Mexico's technological absorptive capacity.

As for the second-tier Latin American NIEs, reliance on foreign technology has grown somewhat in those countries which pursued an export drive, for example, Colombia, as well as Venezuela, where an import boom accompanied the accelerated process of industrialisation facilitated by the oil boom. In a process similar to Mexico, it led to a severe debt crisis and to a weakening of an already fragile industrial structure. The rapidity of the industrialisation drive did not allow for the extensive development of technological absorption capacity. In Chile, in contrast, a more drastic liberalisation policy led to a boom in imports and to a devastating process of deindustrialisation similar to what happened in Argentina, although in a more limited scale, given the smaller size of Chilean industry. Here, a development similar to Mexico's is taking place, that is, a greater internationalisation of the economy, with a surge in FDI. The main source seems to be the opening of both countries to the Pacific sphere of economic influence[40].

The quasi-continental economies have been least reliant of all on foreign technologies, tending until recently to pursue policies of maximum self-reliance. China has historically relied heavily on turnkey projects and the hiring of foreign consultants to acquire needed technologies. In recent years, the government has sought to attract more FDI, especially in high technology areas, but foreign firms are hesitant to move in too rapidly due to the uncertainty of business prospects[41]. India has adopted a somewhat less restrictive policy toward FDI in high technology areas but within an overall environment that still makes many firms hesitant as well[42].

**The role of the state in fostering industrial and technological development**

Almost without exception, the governments of the NIEs have taken part in the process of fostering new technology development. The degree and form of state involvement has varied widely across countries, however. In some cases, the state (e.g. in Hong Kong) has limited its involvement to creating a broad policy environment and providing the necessary infrastructure (including educational institutions) to facilitate private sector initiatives. At the other extreme, the state has been a major investor in certain R&D projects and even productive enterprises (e.g. in China). An intermediate regime would be where the state's role is principally one of co-ordinating the decisions of private investors, encouraging them by certain incentives and administrative measures to focus their investments in certain priority industries or activities (South Korea and Taiwan). Evidence to date on the experiences of NIEs with different policy regimes and degrees of state intervention, would tend to favour an approach somewhere between the two extremes. On the one hand, extensive state involvement in the production system would tend to introduce rigidities incompatible with the requirements of the new competitive environment, unless of course state enterprises are granted substantial autonomy in strategic decision-making. At the same time, large-scale public R&D runs the risk of becoming insulated from the needs of industrial enterprises and of thus producing results which — however technically sophisticated — have limited commercial potential[43]. On the other hand, the minimalist state ignores certain of the potential external economies to which the new technologies give rise. For example, in Taiwan, state encouragement of the formation of a firm to fabricate application specific integrated circuits (ASICs) has had the effect of encouraging a large number of start-up firms in design services, since users know they can obtain their customised chip designs with short turnaround times. Had the state not played an active role, it is doubtful at best whether a private firm would have risked investing on its own in an ASIC silicon foundry.

There continues to be heated disagreement on the subject of government "targeting" of certain high technology products or processes for special treatment. While there are notable examples of success of such a strategy, the risks can be quite high and the costs of failure steep. Moreover, the risks are apt to be greater the newer and more rapidly changing the technology. Still, if the strategy succeeds, the payoff — financially as well as technologically — may be high. For the risk averse, an alternative might be to structure incentives to encourage certain activities which tend to be associated with high technology sectors rather than choosing the sectors themselves. Tax incentives for R&D, design, and human resource development would be examples.

The proper place of the state in the NIEs, beyond its accustomed provision of education and physical infrastructure, cannot be viewed in isolation from the changing role of the state in OECD countries. As OECD governments continue to escalate their intervention in the trade and technology systems to heighten the appropriability of the gains to innovation by domestic firms and limit access to new technologies by foreign firms, NIE states may well have to become more interventionist in order to neutralise the negative consequences of OECD measures for their own firms' market and technology access.

### The characteristics of the indigenous scientific and technological (S&T) infrastructure

However important a domestic scientific and technological (S&T) infrastucture may have been during the early phases of industrialisation of the NIEs, there is no doubt that indigenous S&T capabilities will become increasingly essential to sustaining the industrialisation process in the future. All the NIEs have come to recognise that fact, but not all are equally capable of making the necessary adjustments and improvements in their S&T infrastructure in a relevant time frame. Their differential capabilities to adapt to the new environment depend in part at least on how their S&T institutions have evolved to where they are presently. To understand those differential experiences, it is useful to distinguish several key elements of the S&T infrastructure:

*i)* Institutions engaged in basic scientific research, including government laboratories and universities;

*ii)* Industrial research and development laboratories;

*iii)* Engineering and capital goods firms;

*iv)* Mechanisms for financing innovative activities;

*v)* The "appropriability regime"[44]; and

*vi)* Institutions for education and training of skilled personnel, including both general educational institutions and specialised training institutes.

In order to appreciate fully the strengths and weaknesses of a given country's S&T infrastructure, moreover, it is not enough to consider each of these elements in isolation but also the dynamic interactions among them. In particular, the interface between basic research and industrial R&D would seem to be a crucial one. Also, it is necessary to consider how the indigenous S&T infrastructure is articulated with the international scientific and technological community. Is there dynamic interaction between the two? While the following discussion cannot provide an exhaustive treatment of this complex set of relationships, it attempts to suggest at least how the diversity of S&T infrastructure in the NIEs shapes their opportunities and constraints in the new technological environment.

Both India and China have a long-standing tradition of basic and applied research which, at least in certain military-related fields, is very near the frontier. Yet, despite their scientific expertise, they have been slow to acquire proficiency in commerical application of new technologies. In short, there would seem to be sizeable barriers to diffusion of scientific knowledge into the industrial economy. Such diffusion is by no means an automatic process, but involves a number of intermediate links (or "bridging institutions") which may be only imperfectly formed in those economies. Arguably, one weak link in both China and India has been their inefficient engineering and capital goods sectors. Normally, firms in this sector should face strong incentives to design and manufacture new and more efficient machines which then become the basis for cost-saving innovations in user industries. In both countries such incentives have been lacking. Capital goods producers have become locked into a specific, increasingly outmoded technology system — based largely on electromechanical processes — by virtue of the cumulative learning and large sunk investments associated with that technology. The technological trajectory on which they initially set out, no doubt in response to relative factor "endowments" and costs, has turned out to be a technological rut. Only belatedly are the capital goods sectors of those countries shifting to a new trajectory, which involves new technologies (like microprocessor controls and complementary inputs) and which permits a much greater degree of flexibility in the design and development of capital equipment for user industries.

Meanwhile, the first-tier Asian NIEs, which began their industrialisation process with less developed capital goods sectors than China or India, have perhaps benefited by virtue of being latecomers to this sector. The South Korean case, while not necessarily representative, is nevertheless informative. In the initial stages, the large domestic capital goods producers relied extensively on foreign licenses and, then, through systematic learning began reverse engineering certain of the equipment (Amsden and Kim, 1986). In the case of small firms using simpler technology, the movement was from reverse engineering to foreign licensing in order to upgrade products and processes. A noteworthy feature of the South Korean industry is that the largest toolmakers are usually part of the *chaebol*, and thus may benefit from economies of scope in that their electronics divisions could provide technical support in the integration of microprocessor and computer controls into the design of new machinery or the modification of conventional machinery. Taiwan has advanced further than other NIEs in its machinery making capabilities, especially for more sophisticated machine tools. With government encouragement, Taiwanese firms have been designing their own CNC units and a government research institute has developed full-scale flexible manufacturing systems (FMS). Still, most machine tool exports are of the conventional type and CNC machines have a high import content, principally the control unit imported from Japan[45].

It would be misleading to suggest that the first-tier NIEs have resolved all their capital goods supply problems. On the contrary, they face very high barriers to entry into the production of the more sophisticated equipment required to sustain process upgrading in fields like advanced semiconductor fabrication. Given that the production of certain types of processing equipment is becoming increasingly controlled by a few oligopolistic suppliers in one or two OECD countries, the costs of external dependency for such equipment are likely to rise and NIE firms may be vulnerable to pressures from competitors in OECD countries on their common equipment suppliers.

Another shortcoming of the S&T infrastructure in the quasi-continental economies (as well as in Brazil) has been the high degree of concentration of R&D activities in government laboratories and state enterprises, and a relatively narrow focus of such R&D on defence-related applications. This may partially explain the advanced state of aeronautics and space-related research, as well as of nuclear-related research in China, India and Brazil. Spillovers to the civilian sector have been limited[46]. In the Asian first-tier NIEs, by contrast, a much higher percentage of R&D focuses on commercial applications. Taiwan's R&D sector, for example, is populated by a number of quasi-public research institutes with close links to the private sector, and scientists are even encouraged to establish their own firms to commercialise the results of their R&D. In South Korea a reorganisation of the R&D infrastructure is occurring: the government is encouraging private firms to set up research institutes to facilitate industrial restructuring and technological development. At the same time, government research institutes are emphasising more improvements in production technology to support the needs of private sector firms.

The educational level of the population also varies widely across countries. The Asian NIEs in general have very highly educated populations and educational access is fairly evenly distributed, at least at primary and secondary levels. Moreover, educational institutions there have been quite flexible in adapting to the demands generated by the restructuring of the economy and the changing skill composition of the workforce. For example, the percentage of tertiary students in engineering in South Korea is at least double the figure for the Latin American NIEs and India[47]. In countries like India and Brazil, on the other hand, educational opportunities are far more unevenly distributed and the average educational level is below that in the Asian first-tier NIEs. In Latin America, moreover, the fiscal constraints of a number of countries have caused the quality standards of educational institutions to deteriorate. Many of the NIEs, including (or perhaps especially) the most dynamic ones, face the problem that the business sector provides an attractive financial inducement to many in academia to forego an academic career, in which financial rewards in many countries are quite modest. In Brazil, firms in the growing computer industry have attracted many graduates from the best engineering faculties.

The "appropriability regime" refers to the environmental factors which shape an innovator's ability to capture the rewards generated by an innovation. One important aspect of that environment is the efficacy of legal means of protection, the presumption being that innovations will be reduced to the extent that innovators have limited prospects of earning a financial return for their efforts. The relevant dimensions of the appropriability regime include the legislation governing intellectual property rights (e.g. patent and copyright laws), the enforcement apparatus, and the nature of the technologies in which a country possesses some innovative capabilities. Some technologies lend themselves more readily to copying than others. Almost all the NIEs are moving toward more restrictive legal frameworks for intellectual property protection. Virtually all the NIEs, for example, with the notable exceptions of China, Thailand, and Argentina, have introduced provisions to give copyright protection to computer software. A significant number have also amended (or in the case of China introduced) patent laws to give greater protection to product innovations[48]. To a large degree such measures were instigated by foreign pressures — especially from the United States — and would probably not have been adopted voluntarily. Whether they will serve to stimulate local innovative activity — at least in software development — remains to be seen[49]. To the extent that such local innovative activity does not materialise, increased protection could simply make it easier for OECD firms to maintain a presence in NIE markets through exporting from their home bases rather than having to undertake FDI in those countries to protect market shares.

Financing is a critical element of the S&T infrastructure. Given the riskiness of much R&D, both from a technological and from commercial point of view, risk-averse private firms may well neglect this activity. Whether they can afford to or not depends upon the broader competitive environment and the extent to which it induces such risk-taking. Clearly, firms forced to compete in both their home and export markets may have to invest in R&D as part of their strategies for maintaining or increasing market share. The size of the required investments will vary greatly depending on industry and on the particular market segment a firm is targeting. In the future, greater investments in R&D will be a condition for maintaining competitiveness in the face of accelerating technological change and the need to adopt new technologies. Thus the question of R&D financing will become even more important.

As technological innovation has become more widespread and systematic in certain NIEs, specialised financing institutions have evolved to enable firms to undertake high-risk investments in R, D and E. In short, venture capital markets have developed in certain Asian NIEs and Brazil, but they function imperfectly. In South Korea, for example, a large share of loans and equity investments by venture-capital firms are channeled to the more established large-scale conglomerates which are relatively good risks and have substantial collateral. In Taiwan, venture capital is more widely accessible to small start-up firms, and informal credit networks are more developed than in South Korea. The venture-capital firms themselves are entrepreneurial upstarts in Taiwan, whereas in South Korea they tend to be firms started at the government's initiative.

# NOTES AND REFERENCES

1. Since the sixth factor is country-specific to a large degree, only the first five are used to classify different groups of NIEs.

2. The Philippines has suffered declining educational standards lately, in part due to severe fiscal strains imposed by the foreign debt.

3. In Argentina, where historically income distribution was more equal, it has worsened in recent years.

4. Castillo and Cortellese, 1988.

5. See Kim, 1988 and for Brazil, see *Conjuntura Economica*, 15th January 1988, pp. 7-8 and July 1989, pp. 119-23.

6. UNCTAD, *Trade and Development Report 1987*, Part Two *Technology, Growth and Trade*, pp. 86-91.

7. Fajnzylber, 1988.

8. UNESCO, 1986.

9. See reports on the Brazilian electronics sector, prepared for the OECD Development Centre project "Technological Change and the Electronics Sector — Perspectives and Policy Options for North-South Industrial Co-operation".

10. UNESCO, 1986. For a comparison of higher education see Fajnzylber 1988 and Dornbusch and Park 1987.

11. Amsden and Kim, 1986:110.

12. Because of their limited importance as suppliers and exporters of manufactured products, we are dealing with these countries in a very marginal way. For details on the electronics sector, see the country case studies on Venezuela and Uruguay for the OECD Development Centre project, "Technological Change and the Electronics Sector ... ". For further details see: Gonzales, 1988; Villalobos, 1986; Avella, 1988; Florez, 1988.

13. In Colombia, for example, the industrial GDP accounts for about 16 per cent of the GDP. E. Florez, 1988, p. 111.

14. For India, see Gupta, 1986; for China, see Lalkaka and Wu, 1984.

15. China would like more FDI in high technology areas but is having trouble attracting it. India, on the other hand, appears to be much more ambivalent. For India, see Muralidharan, 1988 and for China see Simon, 1989.

16. See the report on the Chinese electronics industry, prepared for the OECD Development Centre project "Technological Change and the Electronics Sector ... ".

17. See the Report on the Indian electronics industry prepared for the OECD Development Centre project on "Technological Change and the Electronics Sector — Perspectives and Policy Options for North-South Industrial Co-operation".

18. OECD, 1988:61.

19. In the case of South Korea's electronics industry, for example, 60 per cent of domestic component requirements must be imported. See report on the Korean electronics industry, prepared for the OECD Development Centre project on "Technological Change and the Electronics Sector ... ".

20. Williamson, 1985.

21. UNESCO, 1986.

22. Westlake, 1989.

23. For details, see report on the legal protection of software and circuit design prepared for the OECD Development Centre's project on "Technological Change and the Electronics Sector ... ".

24. See the reports on the computer and software industries, prepared for the OECD Development Centre's project on "Technological Change and the Electronics Sector ... ".

25. For example, most cars offer roughly comparable fuel economy, safety, speed, and comfort. Due to similar developments in the computer industry, the borderlines between different market segments (i.e. micro, mini and mainframe computers) have become increasingly blurred.

26. See UNCTC, 1986.

27. The question of FDI is addressed at greater length below.

28. Mowery and Rosenberg, 1989, pp. 8-16.

29. See B. Göransson, "Manufacturing telecommunication equipment in Brazil, India, and the Republic of Korea — Third World challenges to world telecommunication hegemony", paper presented at Conference on "Telecommunications, Economy, and Society", Budapest, 5th-7th October 1988.

30. ISDN (Integrated Services Digital Network) refers to the capability built into many advanced communications systems to transmit simultaneously and interactively a variety of digitised information streams corresponding to voice, images, text and data.

31. See report on the South Korean electronics industry, prepared for the OECD Development Centre's project on "Technological Change and the Electronics Sector ... ".

32. For the electronics sector, see the relevant country case studies prepared for the OECD Development Centre's project on "Technological Change and the Electronics Sector ... ".

33. Once more, the foreign dominated transport equipment sectors of Brazil and Mexico constitute an exception.

34. A similar argument has been made for the United States in a background study on linkages, prepared for the Office of Technology Assessment's study on "Technology, Innovation and U.S. Trade", 1989 (forthcoming).

35. Simon, 1989.

36. See UNCTAD, *Trade and Development Report 1987,* Part Two *Technology, Growth and Trade,* Chapter II, "Trends in the International Flow of Technology", Geneva, 1987, pp. 85-100.

37. Teece, 1977; Kay, 1984.

38. Sung-Hwan Jo, 1988.

39. Report on the computer industry prepared for the OECD Development Centre's project on "Technological Change and the Electronics Sector ... ".

40. In contrast, the trend in Brazil and Argentina seems to be more inward looking toward the Latin American continent. This may initially hinder FDI, but in the long run may be favourable to it, due to market expansion and the opening of new markets.

41. See study on Technological Change and Industrial Development in China, prepared by Richard Conroy for the OECD Development Centre, 1989 (forthcoming).

42. See Encarnation, 1988, in particular Chapter 5, "India in Comparative Perspective".

43. Chinese R&D institutions are being encouraged to address this problem through the formation of alliances with productive enterprises to facilitate the movement of innovations into the production system. See report on the Chinese electronics industry prepared for the OECD Development Centre's project on "Technological Change and the Electronics Sector ... "; see also Conroy, 1989.

44. Teece, 1987.

45. Brazilian firms can also produce CNC machine tools but they are not competitive at present in export markets.

46. Agricultural research has also absorbed substantial resources, given the political importance of food self-sufficiency.

47. Dahlman, 1982.

48. UNCTAD, 1988.
49. For a critical assessment, see the report "The Legal Protection of Software and of Circuit Design — Implications for Latecomer Strategies in NIEs", prepared for the OECD Development Centre's project on "Technological Change and the Electronics Sector ... ".

*Chapter IV*

# "FORCED" INDUSTRIAL RESTRUCTURING: CONSTRAINTS AND STRATEGIC OPTIONS

## CONSTRAINTS

In broad terms, all the NIEs face a common set of external constraints on their growth prospects. The international trading system is becoming more highly regulated, with a proliferation of non-tariff barriers against NIE exports to the OECD. While the implications are as yet unknown, the integration of the European market after 1992 could affect dramatically the prospects for access by NIE exporters. This is especially so in light of recent "local content" regulations which have been devised as a means of forcing non-European firms to set up full-scale production facilities within the EEC to be able to qualify as "European" producers. While large Japanese and US firms may possess the resources to make such investments, it is doubtful whether the majority of NIE exporter firms do. In the case of the United States market, NIE exporters also face an increasingly hostile trade environment, with a proliferation of measures aimed at stemming the market penetration of Japan and the NIEs. The very fact that, in trade and industrial policy debates, the two are often treated as comparable threats to US industry suggests that political passions may be winning out over reason and evidence in shaping US trade policy toward the NIEs. The one offsetting consideration is that Japan's market may become at least marginally more accessible to NIE exports than it has been in the past. Between 1983 and 1988, for example, Japan's manufactured imports from the first-tier Asian NIEs increased from 13 per cent to 19 per cent of total manufactured imports[1]. In absolute terms, however, Japan's imports from the Asian NIEs are only about one-third of US imports from those countries[2].

In terms of technology access, once more all the NIEs face an equally hostile environment. For a number of years, the United States has been lobbying actively in international fora for a more restrictive intellectual property regime. In bilateral trade negotiations with specific NIEs, it has exerted substantial pressure to have countries legislate and enforce protection of patents, and copyrights for software, audio and video recordings, integrated circuit designs, etc. The effectiveness of those pressures is apparent in the flurry of legislative initiatives related to intellectual property rights in NIEs over the last several years. Such measures may well slow the rate of diffusion of new technologies to the NIEs — especially to small- and medium-scale firms lacking resources to pay costly technology fees — in the future. How serious a problem that is depends on the ability of NIE firms to "invent around" patents or adapt creatively a range of products so as to avoid costly litigation.

It is to be expected that US firms in particular will continue to be aggressive in prosecuting alleged copyright or patent violators.

Perhaps even more threatening to the NIEs is the prospect that the scientific establishments of certain OECD countries may become more xenophobic, for example, restricting participation of foreign scientists in certain conferences and further limiting circulation of research results relating to "strategic" technologies. The joint R&D programmes ongoing in Europe (e.g., ESPRIT and EUREKA) remain off limits to outsiders, and the various R&D consortia in Japan and the United States have similar *de facto* rules of exclusion. Of course, as with "strategic partnerships", one factor which has blocked the NIEs' participation in such ventures has been their firms' limited expertise in state-of-the-art technologies like superconductivity, optoelectronics, vacuum microelectronics, etc. For the moment, the university systems of most OECD countries remain fairly accessible to students and scholars from the NIEs, one of the few remaining "windows of opportunity". Moreover, serious bottlenecks in critical skill areas in OECD countries create the need for OECD firms to have continued access to skilled personnel wherever they are to be found, including in the NIEs.

**Roadblocks to further success: the first-tier Asian NIEs**

Paradoxically the constraints facing the Asian NIEs are a product of their "success". Inasmuch as they have achieved the highest degree of market penetration of all the NIEs in OECD countries, they have also confronted the most severe protectionist pressures. Thus, for example, in a move of primarily symbolic significance, the United States government "graduated" the four first-tier Asian NIEs from the Generalised System of Preferences (GSP) beginning in January 1989. Similarly, after Japan, South Korea is the country facing the next largest number of bilateral restrictions on access to the US market. Both South Korea and Taiwan were strongly pressured to revalue their currencies against the US dollar to reduce their export competitiveness and reduce their trade surpluses with the United States. South Korea's currency revaluation is still in midstream while Taiwan's has been largely effected. Both countries face slower growth as a result.

At the same time, the even steeper appreciation of the yen against the US dollar has highlighted a key vulnerability of their economies, that is their continued dependence on imported components and parts from Japan. Furthermore, the rapid growth during the last decade in all the first-tier Asian NIEs has led to tightening labour market conditions, especially in Taiwan and Singapore, and increasing labour costs. Combined with currency appreciation, this has been forcing many firms to relocate their labour-intensive operations to lower wage countries. Thus far, most of that investment has flowed into ASEAN countries, especially Malaysia and Thailand.

Meanwhile, the first-tier Asian NIEs have had to try to upgrade their domestic production structures to reposition their industries to enter higher value-added product markets. For governments of the region, this has involved heavy investments in education and training of skilled personnel as well as more active promotion of R&D, while for firms it has meant both rising R&D investments and increased procurement of foreign technologies. Even then, the shortage of skilled labour remains a short-term constraint in countries like Singapore and Taiwan. Singapore's solution has been to liberalise immigration policies for categories of professionals in short supply. Taiwan has provided incentives for nationals working abroad to return to establish their own high technology businesses.

A more serious constraint in the long run may be access to licensed technology. A number of NIE firms make extensive use of licensing agreements to acquire know-how for new technologies. In general, however, the technologies available on license are not state-of-the-art but a generation or more old. The South Korean *chaebol*, due to fortunate timing of entry into the D-RAM market, for example, were able to license a state-of-the-art technology from US firms possessing superior designs but inferior production capabilities. As such firms become anachronisms, so does a strategy involving such "easy" licensing opportunities[3].

Most OECD governments are seeking to strengthen "appropriability regimes" precisely to limit the "leakage" of new technologies at an early stage of commercialisation. The ability of Asian NIE firms to continue to gain access to licensed state-of-the-art technologies is coming to depend heavily on their having key technologies or other complementary assets to offer in exchange. Considering that even smaller OECD firms are being bypassed as large OECD firms scout for strategic partners — unless they possess highly specialised expertise — it is doubtful whether many first-tier Asian NIE firms will be able to attract partners possessing the advanced technologies they seek.

Nevertheless, there are a few instances of "tactical", if not strategic, partnerships involving OECD and NIE firms. For example, certain of the South Korean *chaebol* have entered agreements with US semiconductor firms, in which the former act in effect as OEM suppliers (or silicon foundries in the industry parlance) to the latter. The US companies see the relationship as a way of combining their design know-how with low cost manufacturing capacity of the South Korean firms; the latter see it as a point of entry into more sophisticated chip markets. Both see it as a way to compete with the Japanese semiconductor giants[4]. This sort of partnership is different from those between different OECD firms however. Intra-OECD partnerships involve pairs or sets of firms that have roughly comparable R&D capabilities but different comparative strengths. A firm which has refined a particular process technology might license it in exchange for that developed by another firm. Alternatively, two firms might design complementary chips to fill out a particular family — for example, microprocessor and peripherals. No NIE firms are yet in the position to enter partnerships with OECD firms on an equal footing. An important question for research is whether, by entering as "junior partners" they might stand to gain more technologically than their "senior partners" and might thereby use such partnerships to narrow the technology gap[5].

**Confronted with tough pressures at an early stage: the second-tier Asian NIEs**

The second-tier Asian NIEs are in the unenviable position of facing some of the same sort of adjustments in their production structure and market orientation but without as much flexibility and resilience as the first-tier NIEs. The protectionist barriers in traditional industries like textiles and garments hurt them doubly since, in the first place, they depend more heavily on those industries (with the exception of Malaysia) than do the first-tier Asian NIEs and, in the second place, the MFA quota system tends to preserve market shares of first-tier NIEs which they would otherwise lose to their second-tier neighbours.

At the same time, labour costs are also beginning to rise. Thus, certain firms in second-tier NIEs like Thailand are pursuing a strategy of upgrading to target higher value-added segments of traditional markets. Their first-tier competitors, however, are pursuing a similar strategy but with the advantage of higher rates of diffusion of new production technologies and greater accumulated experience in international markets. Moreover, traditional industries like textiles/garments in the second-tier Asian NIEs have a strong involvement of Japanese and first-tier Asian NIE firms, which prefer to maintain the higher value-added activities in their home economies. So, these countries have difficulty moving up market at the same time that rising labour costs make it harder to remain competitive in the low end of the market with countries like China, Indonesia and Pakistan. If the first-tier NIEs should gradually phase down their traditional industries, this could provide an opening for certain second-tier NIEs. This is no reason, however, to expect that the first-tier NIEs will be any less reluctant to restructure such traditional industries than OECD countries, especially since they are still dependent on them for export earnings and more so for employment.

In the more technology-intensive industries, the second-tier countries face the problem of limited access to technology. A much higher percentage of the investment in these industries is foreign investment, and most operations are relatively labour-intensive (with the exception of semiconductor assembly). Many of the investments are part of vertically integrated international firms whose more skill- and knowledge-intensive activities are performed elsewhere. There has been some development of local supporting industries in these countries, but the core technologies are largely inaccessible to domestic firms[6]. Given the limited exposure to those technologies, the weak scientific and technical infrastructure and the small capital goods sector, absorptive capabilities for the new technologies also remain very low.

In the last few years, the second-tier Asian NIEs have been the recipients of large foreign investment flows from Japan and the first-tier Asian NIEs due to currency revaluations and escalating costs in the latter. A very sizeable percentage of such investments has been in lower value, standard products within the technology-intensive electronics industry. Consumer electronics, for example, has been a major area of activity. This area is very component-intensive.

Given the high cost of imported components from Japan or the first-tier Asian NIEs, it is likely that a substantial portion of component supply — excluding certain key components — will be established locally. In some cases this may mean that equipment manufacturers seek to replicate their subcontracting networks within the region; in others, where a local supplier base exists, the equipment manufacturers may transfer know-how to those local firms so they can meet quality standards and product specifications. The sheer volume of such investments is bound to have some effect on the local component and supporting industries within the region.

Whether opportunities exist for building up technological competence in certain of the core technologies remains to be seen. There is preliminary evidence to suggest that, for more mature products at least, foreign firms may begin to perform some product development in these countries, since design personnel in their home bases are needed for more advanced product design tasks. Still, without a strong base of local entrepreneurial firms able to absorb know-how from the foreign sector, prospects for diffusion into the domestic industrial structure remain dim.

The acceleration in the rate of technological innovation could work to the disadvantage of the second-tier NIEs relative to the first-tier NIEs. For, as learning curves become steeper and product cycles shorter, those countries with slower learning processes will have greater difficulty adopting new technologies. In a sense, one critical advantage the first-tier Asian NIEs enjoy over their second-tier neighbours is that they have gone further toward speeding up learning processes by strengthening their indigenous engineering as well as R&D capabilities. They possess more highly developed, institutionalised mechanisms for internalising foreign technologies within domestic production organisations. Those countries without such mechanisms (or with only weak ones) will have increasing difficulty in keeping pace with new product and process developments.

### First-tier Latin American NIEs and the foreign debt burden

In Argentina, Brazil and Mexico, without doubt, the overwhelming constraint on their industrialisation at present is the foreign debt burden. Although firms in these countries are able to absorb new foreign technologies, the reduction in their capacity to import has slowed the rate of diffusion of such technologies. Contraction of domestic demand has caused the stagnation of investment, precisely when rapid technological change is making new investment imperative. The financial austerity occasioned by the debt crisis has hit especially hard the small- and medium-scale enterprise sector, narrowing the scope for the emergence of an efficient and flexible subcontracting network. For example, a study of Mexico's small and medium industries suggests that those which have been able to survive the crisis have not been able to modernise[7].

The fiscal crisis, resulting from the debt crisis, has had serious repercussions for the state's capacity to finance investments in physical and social infrastructure. A major casualty of government spending cutbacks has been education. Given the vital importance of educated labour in shaping a country's prospects for competitiveness in high technology industries, reduced educational resources will have serious repercussions for the first-tier Latin American NIEs in the years to come. It remains to be seen whether, in the long run, the restructuring of the state sector which has been undertaken in an effort to reduce fiscal deficits will substantially improve the efficiency and performance of state-run enterprises.

With the reduction in domestic demand, firms have been seeking to boost exports. While the depreciation of currency values has made exports more competitive, the Latin American countries also face stiff trade barriers in the US market. Mexico, for geopolitical reasons, has been less adversely affected by such barriers than its neighbours to the south. Indeed, in recent years both US firms and other firms (especially Japanese) seeking a low cost production base from which to sell into the US market have established assembly plants in the Mexican border region. So far, such plants have only limited linkages to local suppliers. Over time, such linkages may expand and may at least partially replenish the strength of the small- and medium-scale industries. Nevertheless, the proximity of the United States suggests that key components will continue to be sourced from there. In a sense, the predicament of the Mexican *maquiladoras* resembles that of the "export processing", or "free trade", zones of second-tier Asian NIEs. The difference is that, given a more highly developed engineering and capital goods sector, Mexico's ability to absorb foreign technologies is considerably greater. On the other hand, Mexico's border industries are especially vulnerable to any increase in unemployment in the United States in the event the US government should pursue contractionary policies to reduce its twin deficits.

A potentially serious long-term problem of the first-tier Latin American NIEs is that, once the economic crisis is resolved, their enthusiasm for exporting may wane. Firms may become complacent once more given the potentially large internal markets, especially if governments encourage such complacency by reverting to import-substituting policies. Clearly, it would make little sense for the first-tier Latin American NIEs to promote exports at the expense of slowing the growth of internal demand, but by the same token discriminating against exports would be self-defeating in view of the urgent need to sustain an inflow of foreign exchange to finance imports, especially of certain key technologies needed to upgrade domestic production structures. In the final analysis, foreign debt is a fundamental but not the only problem. The real issue is how to generate genuine competitive advantages based on the application of new technologies and not on continuous devaluation and lowering wages[8].

### Industrial stagnation or retrogression: the second-tier Latin American NIEs

The second-tier Latin American NIEs face much greater obstacles than their Asian counterparts in adjusting their economic structure. First, although their production capabilities are roughly comparable, their market size and economic conditions make them unattractive to foreign direct investment. Secondly, their inward-looking orientation, despite the export spurts engendered by the debt crisis, has not given them the needed learning experience that can only be acquired in a large internal market or in a sustained export effort. Thirdly, as the state sought to offset quickly the stagnation in private investments with public sector investment, it provoked a surge of machinery imports. This led to a significant reduction in the share of local capital good producers in the formation of fixed capital in machinery and equipment. In Colombia, for example, it fell from 34 per cent in the late 1970s to 17 per cent in the 1980s, as a result of the increase of public investment[9]. A similar process seems to have occurred in Venezuela and Chile. In the latter, however, the sustained export drive accompanied by a total import liberalisation, led to a more drastic deindustrialisation.

Fourthly, the region lacks an investment and potential demand locomotive comparable to Japan for the Asian NIEs. Neither the United States with its growing commercial deficits, nor the first-tier Latin American NIEs burdened by the debt and their own growth problems, seem to be in a position to play this role. Fifthly, their low educational levels (with the exception of Chile), limited industrial experience and fragile S&T infrastructure, pose a challenge to the effective absorption of technology. Sixthly, given the small size of their markets, specialisation would be a logical course. The broadly diversified nature of their industrial structure constitutes a formidable challenge to their future industrial development.

Lastly, and most importantly, in spite of the lip service paid to the need for greater opening to the world economy, economic nationalism and a perhaps overly pessimistic assessment of world trade prospects have tended to move these countries in the opposite direction. They are pursuing growth strategies centred on the internal market and a deepening of the industrialisation process. The rationale given for this decision is that, since their products are not competitive in the global market, they have to recentre on the internal market and to develop the scientific, technological and organisational capabilities that will allow them to export in the future. There is a risk, however, that this strategy may have precisely the opposite consequences for technological learning than intended — retarding rather than accelerating it.

### The specific constraints facing the quasi-continental economies

In general, the economies of China and India are far less severely affected by an adverse international trade environment than are those of the other NIEs, simply because foreign trade remains a relatively minor factor in relation to overall economic activity (though in the case of China it is large in absolute terms). Moreover, their recent export drive has come up against trade barriers. China, for example, faces growing problems of access to OECD markets and trade disputes are becoming more common. At the same time, China possesses greater political leverage than most other NIEs in seeking a favourable resolution.

Both India and China have liberalised the importing of certain key technologies — for example, in India's case, semiconductor components and computer peripherals. But acquiring more foreign technology through foreign investment will not be easy. First, they have historically been reluctant to allow foreign direct investment, even in high technology areas where domestic capabilities are weak. While policy has shifted somewhat, foreign firms still appear cautious in investing, especially in advanced production facilities. Of course, the lure of the vast China market has helped to diminish the anxieties of quite a few OECD firms. Limited assurances of protection of intellectual property rights (at least prior to the early 1980s) have dissuaded technology-intensive investments. Foreign investors, especially those without extensive international experience, may also be intimidated by the bureaucratic procedures and regulations surrounding their activities. This concern is especially acute in the case of high technology firms, which desire maximum flexibility in order to be able to respond to rapidly changing market conditions and meet tight production schedules.

Beyond these similarities in their external constraints, the particular internal constraints faced by each country are probably far more significant.

*China*[10]

Internal pressures to adopt new technologies have been minimal until now. The abundance of labour has discouraged labour-saving innovations, while the strong growth in domestic demand over the last decade has given enterprises substantial room to expand sales even on the basis of relatively inefficient production methods. This heyday of demand-led growth has already begun to show up some vulnerabilities of the production structure. Inefficient use of inputs is creating bottlenecks in certain sectors, raising costs and constraining output growth. The low technology base is also making it difficult for export manufacturers to achieve competitiveness in any but low-value-added product markets.

Despite widespread inefficiencies, industrial restructuring is blocked by a number of internal barriers. Plants producing the same product have widely differing costs, but high cost producers are effectively subsidised and allowed to remain in production. On the other hand, instances of enterprises shifting product lines, merging with or being taken over by more efficient enterprises are more frequent than in the past. The domestic S&T system has also been ineffective in fostering technological improvements in the productive sector, and in a number of cases, imported technologies (e.g. computer equipment) have hardly been absorbed efficiently. Finally, the core state enterprises, which could use their substantial resources to upgrade technologically, are among the slowest to adopt technological innovations (perhaps due to political privileges), while the smaller collective enterprises are potentially more dynamic but lack the assets (skilled labour, financing, etc.) to develop and commercialise new technologies. Manufacturing industries in general have suffered from a severe shortage of qualified technical personnel, at the same time that many highly educated scientists and technologists are idle for lack of suitable employment. In short, there appears to be a serious mismatch of skills.

Until the early 1980s, a number of factors stifled the technological development of Indian industry. Perhaps to a greater degree than China, India pursued a strategy of technological "self-sufficiency", which involved the development of indigenous technology with minimal recourse to foreign technology. While technology imports were effectively curtailed, domestic R&D did not effectively substitute for it. Not only were high local content requirements imposed — as in China — on manufacturers of high technology products, but small-scale producers were favoured in the components sector, with the result that many components were produced at extremely uneconomic scales and with very basic technology. Furthermore, the production of a number of key high technology products was reserved for state enterprises, which meant effective monopolies, while high rates of import duties and other protective measures led to oligopolistic arrangements among private sector producers. High indirect taxation also raised domestic production costs, hampering the development of products with export potential.

New policies introduced in the early 1980s addressed certain of the aforementioned constraints. The relaxation of rules on entry and expansion stimulated domestic competition in several high technology sectors. Importation of certain components and materials was liberalised, as was the importation of standard software packages. Foreign collaboration has also expanded very substantially since 1984 in areas like computers and peripherals, and telecommunications equipment. Yet, there is a concern that these sectors are now becoming overcrowded with inefficient producers, the main reason being that they still enjoy high effective rates of protection. Moreover, exit is not as easy as entry has become.

Most foreign technology collaborations involve licensing[11], which may become a less and less effective means of acquiring access to advanced technologies in the future. A strong bias against foreign equity investment may not be rational with regard to high technology industries, where FDI may be one of the few means of acquiring access to the latest technologies. Arbitrary equity restrictions may not be an effective means of assuring access to the technologies controlled by foreign firms but may simply pre-empt certain potentially rich technology flows.

A more important route to technology may be Indian engineers working for foreign firms. Given their strong educational background and training, some may be quite effective in absorbing know-how from their on-the-job experience, which they can then use to "spin off" domestic firms. Moreover, access to India's large market is a strong bargaining chip in negotiations with prospective foreign investors on favourable terms of technology access and training of Indian nationals.

## STRATEGIC OPTIONS IN THE INTERNATIONAL CONTEXT

The diversity of constraints faced by the NIEs as they seek to adjust to the changing global competitive environment are to a significant degree a reflection of their different growth patterns and industrialisation strategies. Together with the particular competitive strengths and advantages possessed by different NIEs, those constraints define the sorts of strategic options from which individual NIEs may be able to choose as each seeks to advance farther along the road to industrialisation. What is of particular concern here are the conditions under which different NIEs may be able to reap the potential afforded by the new technologies to enhance their positions in world markets.

## The limits to international assembly subcontracting

### Assembly plants

A number of NIEs began their export-led industrialisation by capturing segments of the booming demand in the 1960s and 1970s for contract assembly services, especially for electronic components like semiconductors. The history of that experience is by now well documented[12]. The early assessments of assembly subcontracting were highly sceptical of the possibilities for utilising that route to upgrade technologically. This perception was based on the fact that assembly is the most labour-intensive and least skill-intensive portion of the production process, whether of a component, of a sub-system, or of a final product. While that may have been true in the 1960s through the mid-1970s, by the late 1970s and very dramatically in the 1980s, automation has become widespread in certain types of assembly — most especially in semiconductor device assembly.

Contrary to the prediction that such assembly would lead to a shift in comparative advantages away from the NIEs and the transfer of assembly back to the OECD countries, some NIE assembly subcontractors have invested heavily in automation and become highly competitive in assembling the latest generation of products (e.g. highly miniaturised integrated circuits). The increasing technological complexity of assembly operations has tended to consolidate the positions of those NIE subcontractors which have made the transition to the new automated technologies, since they have accumulated expertise over many years. Anam Industrial of South Korea, for example, was one of the earliest entrants into assembly subcontracting and now is a worldwide leader in automated IC assembly technology[13]. By contrast, many OECD countries no longer possess the expertise to operate efficient assembly businesses and would have to undergo a "relearning" process should there occur a "transfer back to the North"[14].

At the same time, there are much higher barriers to entry into assembly subcontracting than there were when the NIEs first entered. These are due in part to the much higher capital investments required in, for example, automated assembly equipment and, in the case of semiconductors, magnetic heads, etc., the strict clean room standards. In addition, the learning economies that pose a barrier to re-entry to OECD countries pose even more formidable barriers to entry to newcomers. Thus, except for simple consumer electronics products like electronic toys and board-level assemblies, it is increasingly problematical for developing country firms to capture a share of the subcontracting market. Some of those NIE firms, on the other hand, which have established reputations for quality and reliability, are able to expand vigorously in step with the growing demand for contract assembly services.

Whereas in the early days of assembly subcontracting, such activity created very few linkages to other sectors of industry, more recently linkages have been expanding. The transition to automated assembly has fostered those linkages by creating demands for a variety of specialised tooling, such as, dies, jigs and fixtures to be used with the automated machinery. Thus, in some countries (i.e. Malaysia) assembly operations have stimulated the development of the precision engineering sector.

In general, as assembly subcontracting has become more automated, it has required more skilled operators as well as a pool of skilled technicians to maintain, repair and troubleshoot the automated equipment. The increased skill-intensity, infrastructure-intensity (higher energy consumption, e.g.), and engineering-intensity of subcontract assembly strongly suggests that only a relatively few NIEs which possess an abundance of those "factors" are likely to be major participants in assembly subcontracting for more technology-intensive products in the future. Assembly of low end products may be an option for certain other developing countries, but those are the least dynamic market segments and involve few opportunities for technology upgrading. At the same time, however, such standard products normally involve large production volumes and can be an important source of export earnings and employment for some countries.

*Assembly of software and services*

A new form of international subcontracting has emerged in recent years involving the assembly of software and services rather than of hardware. At the low end of the spectrum are data encoding operations which require little skill and are still quite labour-intensive, involving operators inputting data or other information from hard copy onto computer tape or disk. This is often associated with computerisation of large databases — medical records, telephone directories, etc. Given that conversion is a one-time operation, the demand for such services cannot be expected to continue in the OECD countries indefinitively. Considering, however, the low level of computerisation in many developing countries and the large databases which would eventually require conversion — for example, in countries like India, China and Brazil — demand for this service should accelerate outside the OECD for some time.

At the low end of the spectrum there is also a demand for the periodic updating of databases for OECD service sector firms like financial service firms and airlines. This has opened up opportunities for remote data processing, something that has been done mostly in the Caribbean countries by US firms. The limiting factor to this development would be the diffusion of real time computers and large database storage requirements.

Another sort of software job which can be — and has been subcontracted — to NIE firms involves the conversion of application programmes written for one vendor's operating system to run on the operating system of another vendor. For example, when an organisation outgrows its existing information system and when buying a more powerful system, decides to switch vendors (perhaps because the original vendor does not supply a system in the range required), customised software needs to be converted to the new operating system. The skill requirements are somewhat greater than those needed for simple data entry but are not substantially more than basic programming skills. Computer language translation programmes, so called "compilers", are available to facilitate the task.

Still another step higher in terms of skill requirements would be jobs involving the translation of the basic conceptual design for a new software programme into detailed specifications ready for programming. This requires the services of software engineers and systems analysts and not just routine programming skills. It also requires closer communication between the higher level software personnel in the NIE firm and their counterparts — the system designers — in the OECD countries. Even within this broad category there are varying degrees of complexity of the software to be developed.

An example of one of the most sophisticated such software subcontracting arrangements would be that of Texas Instruments (United States) in Bangalore, India, where seventy Indian software engineers develop programming tools for use in integrated circuit design. Their output is transmitted via a dedicated interactive satellite link to computers at TI's European hub facility in the UK[15]. Even with its high volume point-to-point traffic, TI cannot use all the capacity leased and, to recoup costs, must find other firms willing to sublease. Thus far only one other firm (DEC) has leased capacity. Other firms' data transmission requirements have led them to prefer to use a new packet switched network, but links between inland cities and the packet switching gateways on the coast or in New Delhi are still unreliable.

There are a growing number of examples of offshore software development involving OECD firms contracting jobs to NIEs. Singapore has become a major software centre for several OECD firms (e.g. NEC and HP), as has Taiwan. Like subcontracting for hardware assembly, the main input supplied by the NIE firms is labour, in this case more highly skilled labour. Of course, an efficient telecommunications network, electricity grid, and other physical infrastructure are also essential. As in hardware assembly, also in software new automation technologies are reducing the demand for low skilled labour. New software productivity tools substantially reduce the routine, time consuming tasks like error checking and "debugging". Thus countries which have abundant programming labour but few higher level software personnel are less well placed to attract such software subcontracting activities in the future[16].

A problem faced by most NIEs, but less so by certain first-tier Asian NIEs and Brazil, is that their software personnel, however highly educated or trained, lack accumulated experience which is critical to productivity. Given the relatively small size of the software sector in most NIEs until recently, this constraint will take some time to overcome. If the government can stimulate domestic demand for software — as a major user of computer systems — it may help to build up a cadre of experienced programmers and software engineers. As with contract semiconductor assembly, however, the NIEs which already possess substantial accumulated expertise in software development will be preferred locations for contract software production, even if its experienced personnel is somewhat more expensive than in other countries.

Unlike the Asian NIEs, the Latin American NIEs have had very limited experience in assembly subcontracting with the exception of Mexico's *maquiladoras*. The successive waves of offshore investments in semiconductor assembly by multinational firms almost completely bypassed the region. The reasons for this have much to do with the historic focus in many countries on import substitution for the domestic market to the neglect of export market opportunities. This is the case with Brazil where the information technology sector, for example, is dominated by national firms producing almost exclusively for the domestic market.

As explained above, the barriers to entry into this industry are higher now than they were when the Asian NIEs entered. Yet, Latin American NIEs are being pressed by macroeconomic factors to explore export possibilities more seriously. Given their limited historic experience in international markets, assembly subcontracting may be the easiest point of entry, since marketing expertise is not a requirement. Some subcontracting activity has begun, for example, in Brazil as a response to the growing assembly needs of the emergent computer and other informatics firms. While much of it is focused on the domestic market at present, some firms have started performing contract assembly (mostly "board-stuffing") for foreign firms. Quality remains a problem but presumably not an insurmountable one. More seriously, profit opportunities in the domestic market continue to divert many firms' attention from export markets. More aggressive institutional support for such activities is beginning to emerge in Brazil but there are doubts about the durability of the government's commitment.

There have also been some software subcontracting ventures between Brazilian firms and OECD firms such as Nixdorf, for the development of hospital system software[17]. Similarly, a Brazilian firm which sold point of sale automation equipment to a large Portuguese supermarket chain (in competition with NCR, IBM and Nixdorf) is developing the software for the operation of the system. In these cases, the experience which counted was not only the labour cost, but also the experience acquired either with a particular niche language, MUMPS, or with a specific sector's requirements, for example, supermarket automation. In other words, "dual-skilled" personnel are critical for penetration of such markets — people with thorough knowledge of computer equipment and languages, as well as of specific user industries or application requirements.

**Selective imitation of standard low-end products: the classical OEM strategy**

While the Southeast Asian NIEs and Mexico have relied more heavily on assembly subcontracting in the past, the first-tier Asian NIEs — most especially South Korea and Taiwan — focused more on supplying finished products to original equipment manufacturers (OEMs). They then either marketed the products without further modification under their own brand names (e.g., colour televisions) or incorporated the products into their systems, again to be sold under the OEM's brand name (as, for example, with computer peripherals). Most OEM suppliers started out with simple consumer electronics products and gradually worked their way up to more sophisticated consumer products like VCRs. With the personal computer (PC) boom since the late 1970s, however, some existing OEM suppliers as well as many new ones moved vigorously into supplying low-end PCs, once more moving up the technology ladder, as more powerful systems became standard. In all cases, the success of the strategy, to a far greater extent than assembly subcontracting, depended on an effective low cost component sourcing network. For OEM suppliers were not provided with the bulk of materials and components on a consignment basis by the customer, as are assembly subcontractors. Moreover, the sorts of products involved (e.g. televisions and PCs) are far more component-intensive than the semiconductor devices (and more recently magnetic heads) which have made up the bulk of assembly subcontracting activity. From the start then, a country which does not possess a relatively strong component sector or at least ready access to a supply of low cost components is pre-empted from pursuing such a strategy.

The advantage of the OEM strategy is that the products involved are generally very high volume ones, with the result that even if margins are thin, total earnings from such activities may be substantial and may help finance selective technology development in preparation for eventual upgrading of the OEM relationship to include higher value-added products, or perhaps even "graduation" from the relationship. Moreover, once such a strategy builds up momentum, the demand generated for components and materials should itself permit localisation of much component production at economic scales. The ability to mobilise flexible supplier networks seems to have been a key element of the success of the OEM strategies of certain NIEs. The logistics of maintaining low inventories of components without running into frequent bottlenecks that disrupt production and delivery schedules are formidable when hundreds or thousands of components are utilised in a given product. Of course, as the number of components required, e.g. in a colour television, continues to be reduced with improved circuit design, those logistical problems may become less severe.

At the same time, as more sophisticated products become affordable to a growing number of consumers or users in OECD countries, the demands placed upon OEM suppliers in terms of quality and reliability of products, and the sophistication of the components they contain, are certain to increase. In other words, whether OEM suppliers like it or not, their technological capabilities have to be upgraded if they are to stay in the market. At the same time, the opportunities are shrinking for new OEM suppliers to enter on a large scale the production of the low technology products which the early OEM suppliers are abandoning. There is no longer a growing OECD market for them.

There has been some degree of technological learning involved in OEM relationships, but effective learning presupposes some technological capabilities on the part of the NIE firms involved. OEM suppliers are either given detailed product design specifications by the customer or they are expected to conform to some international standard (e.g. IBM PC compatibility). To be able to produce a product of complex design to specifications at competitive cost already requires certain engineering as well as managerial know-how. Improving upon that design is an ever more demanding task. Yet, in the PC market at least, there are a number of cases where NIE-based OEM suppliers or "clone" makers have produced machines with performance characteristics superior to those whose design they had originally set out to imitate — for example, an IBM PC compatible machine with a higher processing speed, enhanced functionality, or greater memory capacity. Still, the fact of being tied into an OEM contract clearly limits the degree to which the NIE firm can capture the rewards of improved product design. Against that, of course, must be weighed the enormous investments required to build an independent brand name market presence.

**Beyond international subcontracting: what are the options?**

There is an obvious need for NIEs to transcend the narrow confines of international subcontracting and to proceed to more sophisticated forms of world market-oriented latecomer industrialisation. In what follows we first discuss two options which still subscribe quite clearly to the logic of "Fordist" mass production and its inherent division of labour[18], that is, the brand-name, mass-market strategy and the supply of strategic components. We will then show why "catching-up" strategies, even in their most sophisticated version, are unlikely to work. It is on this basis that we will finally discuss two unconventional strategic options, that is, the supply of complementary technologies and the strategy of focusing on "vertical market niches".

*Options within the traditional "mass production" paradigm*

***The brand-name, mass-market strategy:*** Thus far, of all the NIEs, South Korea and Taiwan are the only ones where the brand name, mass market strategy is being pursued, in the former more vigorously and more widely than in the latter. Certain firms — e.g. Tatung and Acer in Taiwan; Goldstar, Hyundai, Daewoo, Samsung in South Korea — are seeking to break free from the "OEM trap", which would indefinitely postpone the development of their own design capabilities. At least in certain products (e.g., colour TVs and simpler VCRs), they have been able to establish a reputation for acceptable quality and reliability which should help to bolster consumer loyalty, thereby enabling them to increase their margins while protecting market shares. For products like simple consumer electronics, specialised support and repair services are not critical. As long as the *chaebol* or other brand name manufacturers are able to convince large scale retail outlets, in the United States, for instance, to give them shelf space, they do not need to make large investments in distribution. They will need to invest, however in the advertising and marketing needed to establish a strong brand name recognition.

In products where customer support and services are more important, as for example, in PCs and most professional electronics, the establishment of a strong distribution network requires substantial additional investment, considerably raising the barriers to entry. Moreover, in those markets, brand loyalty is far less pronounced. Thus a sustained promotional effort is required, backed by strong R&D and product development to keep up with new competing products. In the PC market at least, the possibilities for reaping rewards from brand name identity are severely constrained by the strong influence exerted by the market leader over product standards and the extreme difficulty of establishing a competing standard. Thus, the entry barriers are far more formidable in professional electronics than in consumer electronics. Once in the market, there is no guarantee one will stay in it very long, as the long list of "has-been" brand-name PC manufacturers attests.

*Supply of strategic components:* Most NIE firms, even if they have begun to manufacture moderate to high technology products, still depend upon foreign suppliers of critical components. They have learned from that experience the significant leverage which the component supplier can exert over its customer and the premium prices it can charge. Often that dependence involves a licensing agreement with the component supplier to build a product to the specifications of the licensor, which means there is no other such component on the market which can be substituted for that of the licensor. Such "lock-in" arrangements may be contractual and/or technical. In customised components then, a NIE firm becomes the sole, or primary, source if it has a unique system in which the component is an integral part of its design. Semi-custom logic circuits are an example of an area in which NIE firms may have the ability to become key component suppliers, at least to domestic equipment or subsystem manufacturers.

The Taiwanese strategy is a case in point. There, a number of local firms have acquired the tools and know-how to design application specific ICs (or ASICs), which can be used by Taiwanese equipment and subsystem suppliers to differentiate their products and thus capture more value in export markets. In this case, the ASIC component designers work closely with the users, and it is the complementary assets of the two which give their "joint product" greater market leverage. The process features of ASIC fabrication, which allow for "batch" production of specific designs, make such a strategy possible even when the volumes required of a single ASIC design are relatively low. Without competitive equipment and subsystem suppliers available locally, however, the ASIC designers would have difficulty surviving. To design ASICs for semiconductor firms or equipment or subsystem vendors located in OECD countries would require investments in design centres and related infrastructure close to major customers in those markets. Entry barriers are rather high in that event, and as yet no NIE firm — even in Taiwan — is in a position to scale those barriers.

Supply of certain standard components used in large volume in high technology products may be a source of considerable leverage in world markets. This was learned, for example, by the South Korean *chaebol* which entered into large-scale production of computer memories (D-RAMs) several years ago. When a number of factors converged in 1987-88 to create a severe shortage in that market, South Korean D-RAM manufacturers received an enormous windfall as prices increased several-fold. The other side of that strategy, of course, is that prices fall just as dramatically as they rise — and more commonly. Learning curves are very steep and late entrants — even if they have extensive experience in semiconductor fabrication — face great difficulties moving down their learning curves fast enough to recover their large capital investments before new product/process developments render their plant and equipment obsolete. Such a strategy is not as design-intensive as the ASIC strategy but does require advanced process engineering capabilities. It is also a far more

90

capital-intensive strategy than the former and one which depends very heavily on reaping scale economies. The absolute capital barriers to entry are greater in this field than in almost any other high technology industry: the investment required for state-of-the-art wafer fabrication rivals that for a steel mill.

While in the past more or less standard designs for memories meant that a firm could "leap-frog" to a new generation of memories if only it had superior process capabilities, now, even in memories, design capabilities are becoming a more important feature of competitiveness. New automated design tools are making product differentiation possible, and intensifying competition in standard memory markets is making it necessary. Thus, in static RAM markets for example, firms compete by offering chips with shorter and shorter access times (i.e., the time needed to locate a bit of information stored in one of the memory cells). In certain market segments at least, entry requirements in the future are likely to be more stringent than in the past. Still, it may well be that the more advanced NIE firms in a country like South Korea face fewer difficulties supplying mass chip markets — where reliability is critical but brand name counts for little — than supplying final equipment markets, where marketing and distribution barriers are more difficult to scale. Moreover, leveraging chipmaking capacity by incorporating chips into one's own systems is feasible only where a firm's design capabilities are well developed.

*Why catching-up strategies are unlikely to work*

Some developing countries fear being trapped in the vicious circle of a "low-wage, low-growth" development pattern if they remain confined to producing only mature products which have "exhausted their technologial dynamism". To spare them this fate, some analysts[19] have sought to define the conditions under which certain NIEs may be able to catch up with the OECD countries. By this they mean "acquiring the capacity for participating in the generation and improvement of technologies as opposed to the simple 'use' of them"[20]. Their argument rests on a product life cycle theory of innovations in which "each product cycle develops within a broader family which in turn evolves within an even broader [technology] system". The knowledge, skills, experience, and externalities required for the various products within a system are interrelated and synergistic. In this view, different systems offer different time horizons for learning and catching up, as well as varying scope for development and growth. The analysis of entry opportunities for the individual product parallels that for the system of which it is a part. In the former case, entry is alleged to be "easiest" in either the first (pre-paradigmatic design) phase when the investment costs and experience requirements are low but the threshold of scientific and technical knowledge is high, or in the last (maturity) phase when knowledge requirements are low since technology is largely embodied in machinery and skills are codified, but fixed investment requirements are much higher than in phase one. From a catching-up perspective, only early (phase one) entry matters. While externality barriers may be high in that phase, it is assumed those can be offset through selective government "rebates". As for scientific and technical barriers, the heroic assumption is made that most of the knowledge required to enter in the pre-paradigmatic phase is available in the public domain, in particular through the university system.

At the system level, it is asserted that the advantages of early entry into a given product cycle are merely magnified, since the given scientific and technical knowledge needed at the outset to enter the system has substantial multiplier and cumulative learning effects on which the early entrant can capitalise. It is alleged, moreover, that those with resources committed to a mature, competing system may be slow to abandon it in favour of the new system, thereby allowing time for learning on the part of the newcomer. "So early entry into *new* technology *systems* is the crucial ingredient for the process of catching up"[21].

The main vulnerability of such reasoning is that it rests very heavily on the assertion (undemonstrated) that the scientific and technical knowledge needed to enter the new technology system is in the public domain. Indeed, with the strong tendencies toward greater "privatisation" of even basic R&D, and limitations being imposed on international scientific exchanges in the interests of maintaining national competitive advantages, it is highly doubtful whether NIEs can have free access to the scientific and technical knowledge needed to enter a new technology system. Assuming — and this assumption seems more realistic in the present environment — that NIE firms must invest heavily in the purchase of technology as well as in their own R&D, then the claim that the entry barriers are relatively low in periods of transition between technology systems is highly questionable. Even in the case of technologies — for example, computer memories — which are no longer in an early phase of the technology life cycle, R&D costs as well as fixed investment costs are extremely high. Commercialisation of new technologies is estimated to cost several times as much as development itself, since scale-up and testing are very expensive operations[22]. Perez and Soete do admit that, once entry has occurred, "the problem becomes whether the endogenous generation of knowledge and skills will be sufficient to remain in business as the system evolves." They also acknowledge that "this implies not only constant technological effort but also a growing flow of investment"[23]. This is precisely what makes a catching-up strategy such a risky and difficult one for most NIEs, and one for which very few are presently well situated to succeed.

Analyses of the prospects NIEs have of closing the technology gap with the OECD countries or, alternatively, for sustaining growth in the face of a widening gap, vacillate between extreme pessimism and guarded optimism. Certainly the naive expectation that new technologies would unleash "revolutionary" possibilities for shifting the balance of economic power between North and South is still only by the most imperturbable visionaries. Those who would like to consider themselves "hard-nosed" realists — among whom the present authors would number themselves — view the prospects for the vast majority of developing countries to break out of the "vicious circle" as severely limited. Yet, even if "catching up" may be an overly ambitious goal for most NIEs, there remain other, perhaps less ambitious but moderately promising options, some of which we now explore. Unlike the strategies enumerated above, they involve attempts by the NIEs to strike out in new directions.

*Supply of complementary technologies*

Few NIE firms are either willing to able to confront large OECD-based oligopolies head-on in world markets for high technology products. Even the large South Korean conglomerates are marginal participants in many markets they have sought to enter. Moreover, rising costs in the faster growing NIEs are making a mass market strategy more difficult to sustain. Some NIEs have thus moved in a new direction in an effort to capitalise on dynamic growth markets without having to contend with the cut-throat competition that characterises core products in a given market. An illustration of this would be PCs, where the basic CPU is the core, surrounded by various peripherals from keyboards to printers, monitors, and disk drives. Most of those peripherals are themselves commodities subject to intense price competition. Yet there is a proliferating array of add-on cards that can be plugged into the CPU and which substantially add value. These include graphics cards, modem cards, "turbo" cards (which accelerate processing speed), memory cards, and interface cards. The major computer vendors have encouraged the "value adders" since they stimulate sales of their own machines, which in turn benefit the latter. In this sense they are complementary technologies. Taiwanese firms have quite effectively pursued such a "niche" strategy, as have some Hong Kong firms (for example, AST Research). Such a strategy requires a high degree of enterpreneurial initiative to keep up with the latest needs of users and to constantly upgrade or develop new products. There is always the risk that, if a particular enhancement becomes very widely accepted, PC makers may incorporate that feature in the standard design of the next generation of machines. Depending on how well the NIE firm is protected by patents or trade secrets, it may or may not be able to license or sell its know-how to one or more PC maker and continue to earn revenues from its technology.

The Taiwanese ASIC strategy discussed above could be considered complementary to this approach, since it supports the "value enhancers" by providing them with access to IC design know-how which can help them develop new products more effectively. Such design capacity can also support the unique design requirements of a host of other small- and medium-scale firms producing a variety of products from computer peripherals to telephone equipment and consumer electronics products. The critical unknown is how innovative such firms will turn out to be in differentiating their products in such a way as to anticipate emergent user needs. Strong market intelligence capabilities will undoubtedly be essential to the successful pursuit of such a strategy.

*The "vertical market niche" strategy*

This strategy differs from the preceding one in at least one important respect. It seeks to capitalise more explicitly on learning related to the application of new technologies to traditional industries or activities within a given NIE. For example, a country may be a leading producer of some processed primary commodity or basic manufactured good. If it is competing in world markets for that product, presumably it must keep up-to-date in terms of process technologies. Increasingly, those processes draw upon the new generic technologies like electronics — for example, with electronic process controls in chemical plants, dyeing of textiles/fibres, steelmaking, smelting, etc. (Malaysia's palm oil processing industry is a case in point, where a local microelectronics group developed new technology to be used in process control.) To the extent that the NIEs' traditional industries have become efficient and sophisticated users of the new technologies, it is possible that expertise has been acquired which may itself be commercially exploitable in vertical markets — that is, in the design and implementation of specialised control systems or subsystems for particular industrial processes. The country which acquires a lead in developing such systems may then be in a position to export them to other countries where such industries exist and are in need of renovation. The Indian government has sponsored computerisation programmes in such major sectors as hydrology, railroad management, and power generation and distribution. While developed for the domestic market, there may be export opportunities for such systems. Already the railways management system is being sold to a foreign railway. Of course, if expertise is developed in-house by a natural resource processing firm or basic manufacturing firm, there may be barriers to diffusion if the innovation offers the firm a sizeable competitive advantage. Diffusion would be facilitated if a separate sector of systems integrators was the source of such innovations, though even then there might be some attempt by a client firm to limit third-party access to new technologies whose development it has financed. Such a strategy is viable for independent systems integrators when the design and development of a new vertical niche product is possible without having to invest in highly specialised equipment or other assets. But to do that, the systems designers need advice from experts who are highly knowledgeable about the industrial process to which the new technology is to be applied. If the technology is complementary to the user firm's core technology, then that firm might be more willing to allow commercialisation of a new niche product since it would not threaten significantly its competitive advantage in that core activity. This leads back once more to the discussion above of the tolerance shown by the major personal computer vendors toward marketers of add-on niche products.

This strategy, then, is a variation of the aforementioned complementary technologies strategy, with the major difference that countries which have achieved competitiveness and high world market penetration in certain traditional industries, but have had limited success breaking into new technology markets, may be able to exploit their experience in the former to make possible selective entry into the latter. The chances of succeeding in international markets, however, are limited if there are no close user-producer links and if the new technology being developed involves substantial hardware costs (for example, a superminicomputer or mainframe processor), and the hardware is not produced locally, or is produced but at high cost. Where the software content or other local value added (at world prices) is high, then the prospects substantially improve.

## THE ALTERNATIVE OF REFOCUSING GROWTH ON DOMESTIC AND REGIONAL MARKETS

Even if a particular NIE possesses the necessary conditions to pursue successfully one or more of the strategies mentioned, it must contend with the problem of increasingly restricted access to dynamic OECD markets. Thus the need to consider alternative market strategies is greater than ever before. In particular, NIEs must explore more systematically the possibilities for refocusing growth on their domestic markets. This is true despite the fact that unequal destribution of income often constrains internal demand growth. There are claims that new technologies might be able to relieve certain of those constraints, but only the most ardent "technological determinist" would place much stock in such possibilities. Perhaps more important in the context of our study, the scope for South-South trade needs to be carefully addressed. Can it compensate for slower growth of North-South trade, especially when the question of continued access to new technologies is involved?

As the Latin American experience has shown, there are serious limitations to the accustomed pattern of production for the internal market when protection is high, internal competition low, and production capacity fragmented. For example, Brazil's consumer electronics industry, which produces 2 million colour television sets a year for the domestic market, consists of 10 firms with 81 per cent of total output originating from plants of less than minimum efficient scale[24]. Moreover, given that fragmentation and the fact that manufacturers operate in an industrial "free zone" where they are allowed quotas of imported components at low or zero duties, a potentially component-intensive industry has generated very few linkages to domestic component suppliers. There are similar instances in other Latin American NIEs, giving rise to the paradox that the "import substituting" strategies of these countries have been at least as heavily import dependent as the "export-led" growth strategies of the Asian NIEs.

This is not to imply that the domestic market cannot be a stimulus to efficient industrial development. It is seldom sufficient, however, even in the large quasi-continentel economies. Institutional safeguards of some sort must exist against the calcification of industrial structures, so that firms are continually driven to upgrade their product and process technologies. In some cases import competition has played that role, in others, pressure to compete in export markets. Where neither is present some equally potent incentives must be found to induce innovation and the assimilation of new technologies.

Regional markets may be an attractive alternative for NIE firms not yet able to weather the storms of international competition against the OECD technology leaders. Such regional orientation may also — though not necessarily — enable countries to avoid being integrated in a subordinate role into the international division of labour. The main difference between regional South-South trade and North-South trade is the greater similarities in demand patterns, production structures and technology levels between different regional NIEs than between the NIEs as a group and the OECD countries[25]. Thus specialisation is possible within industries and not just across industries. Argentina has a consumer electronics industry, as does Brazil, as does Mexico, as does almost every other Latin American country. More than that, each to a degree duplicates the industrial structure of the other, with the same large number of firms producing in each at the same uneconomic scales, all in the name of "consumer choice". If the same number of brands (say, nine) were to be produced, but with three brands each produced in Mexico, Argentina and Brazil and traded for those not locally produced but locally consumed, the advantages of diversity of choice would be maintained while economies of scale would not be sacrificed, and there need not be any serious negative effects on a single country's balance of payments. Similar arrangements are conceivable over a wide range of industries but, given existing policies in many NIEs, are not politically feasible. It is even conceivable that such production rationalisation, by allowing firms to produce efficiently for the regional market, could serve as a jumping off point for entry into the international market.

## ASSESSMENT

The discussion of strategic options provides a broad framework which seeks to capture the main features of the various strategies which have been or are being pursued by specific NIEs, as well as those which offer the prospect of allowing the NIEs to meet the competitive challenges they face as they seek to advance their industrial development in a period of rapid technological change.

Several salient points emerge from the preceding discussion. The first is that none of the strategic options outlined is unproblematical. Each poses formidable challenges to the NIEs which choose to pursue it. This is reflective of the general tendency toward increasing entry barriers into high technology markets. Clearly, a particular NIE need not restrict its options to only one of the aforementioned strategies. Different groups of firms within a NIE may adopt different strategies; even a single firm may pursue a mixed strategy to spread its risks. Similarly, NIE governments may promote through industrial and other policies, a combined strategy. Nor does the above set of strategies exhaust the possibilities. Innovative new strategies are bound to emerge as global competitive conditions change and as the capabilities of individual NIEs evolve.

The second point is the striking difference between the Asian first-tier NIEs and the Latin American first-tier NIEs in terms of the strategic options they face. For the first-tier Asian NIEs, the urgent task is to find ways of graduating from the stage of international subcontracting. Their high growth rates and attendant macroeconomic adjustments have made it virtually impossible for them to sustain such a strategy. They must move upmarket. They are under pressure to diffuse more widely advanced manufacturing technologies (AMTs) in an effort to keep production costs down in the face of escalating labour costs. At the same time, they must move beyond the imitation of OECD firms' products and undertake substantially more local product development. Different firms and states have adopted different strategies for moving beyond accustomed dependencies on imported technologies. The South Koreans have opted more for brand name mass marketing, the Taiwanese more for supplying complementary technologies. Singapore has been seeking to move strongly into software-intensive activities. All have made a strategic commitment to high technology markets and are in the process of adjusting their industrial structures accordingly; the contribution of traditional industries to GDP is already waning. All have rapidly growing internal markets, but since only South Korea and Taiwan have even moderately large populations, there are limited possibilities for refocusing growth toward domestic demand to compensate for restricted OECD market access. Still, these countries need to explore actively other non-traditional export markets, with Japan as well as other countries in the region being prime candidates.

The Latin American first-tier NIEs that focused too exclusively on internal markets in the past — often at the expense of production efficiency — are now confronted with the challenge of balancing that historic orientation with more dynamic export growth. Given that they are latecomers to such an approach, they have much learning to do. Limited international experience, combined with weak component and parts sectors in most countries, makes entry at the assembly subcontracting level most feasible. Software subcontracting is also a possibility, given skilled labour availability, but the regional market — where language is not a barrier — may be more promising than the international market in this area. In general, the regional market holds good prospects — given a suitable policy environment — for allowing firms to acquire valuable export experience before venturing into somewhat more distant and competitive markets. Mexico of course enjoys the advantage of accessibility to the US market. A major difference between the first-tier Latin American NIEs and their Asian counterparts is the relatively wider industrial base of the former. This provides them with an opportunity — shared by the quasi-continental economies — to use their familiarity with a broad range of industrial processes as a basis for selectively developing new technologies to upgrade those processes. In areas of strong competence possibilities may exist for marketing specialised know-how abroad either in the form of packaged systems or in the form of technical consultancy services. There may even be opportunities for regional technical co-operation in areas of mutual interest, along the lines of the Argentinian-Brazilian co-operation in aeronautics and informatics. However, the macro-economic imbalances and the lack of clarity about the industrialisation and technology strategy to be followed, make progress in this direction very slow and precarious. In any case, the strategy of refocusing growth on domestic and regional markets should be complementary and not a substitute to increasing the manufacturing and export capacity to markets in the OECD region.

Even the quasi-continental economies, vast as their internal market potential is, can no longer rest content with the accustomed strategies of maximum self-reliance. Nor can they remain indifferent to the need to penetrate export markets, to be able to keep abreast of new technological developments and upgrade their production capabilities. With somewhat more extensive — though not always more efficient — component and parts sectors than in the Latin American first-tier NIEs, these economies may be better positioned to develop rapidly OEM supplier relationships in addition to assembly subcontracting. Quality remains a serious constraint, however, beyond the low end of the OEM market. It will therefore take some time before such relationships move into higher value added products.

From the perspective of upgrading technologically, the vast markets of the quasi-continental economies are a decided advantage. Thus, their domestic markets can be expected to remain the centrepiece of their strategies, as is also the case in Brazil. Their large markets give them considerable leverage in gaining access to technologies from foreign suppliers, who may even be willing to bend their own rules in some cases to ensure a market presence. Certain factors constrain these countries from taking full advantage of the opportunities to acquire new technologies from foreign sources. China still has absorption problems, as well as restrictions related to military considerations. India also has some absorption problems, as well as problems with its trade and industrial policy. Technology suppliers still fear the inadequate protection of intellectual property in both countries. The same is true of Brazil which in any event has stressed heavily the generation of indigenous technologies in certain areas like computers and software. If Brazil opens its markets more to foreign firms when the reserve policy expires in 1992, it will certainly be in a better position to absorb the technologies than if local firms had not gone through this protracted learning process. Given the size and growth prospects of Brazil's market for high technology products like electronics, its bargaining position for gaining favourable terms of access to the foreign technologies should also be very strong.

The second-tier Asian NIEs have been strongly pursuing the strategies that the first-tier neighbours pursued at an earlier date. They too must consider other options as they face growing competitive pressures from a "third tier" of manufacturing exporters, such as China and India, as well as countries like Pakistan, Indonesia, and Bangladesh. The latter are not yet a major threat outside of traditional industries like textiles and garments. Still, their inroads there are causing the second-tier NIEs to focus their energies on upgrading quality in traditional industries to capture higher value added market segments, as well as to diversify into the dynamic new industries like electronics, especially in products where labour costs remain a source of competitive advantage (for example, consumer electronics). They are upgrading their assembly subcontracting operations as well, and expanding into software subcontracting in an effort to capitalise on relatively abundant supplies of educated labour. These economies are becoming increasingly integrated into regional supplier networks organised by Japanese firms which are internationalising production of certain less technology-intensive products. First-tier Asian NIE firms are following suit but on a more limited scale. All that remains is for domestic entrepreneurs in these countries to develop their own technological capabilities, which until now they have been slow to do. As a result, despite the large size of the electronics industry in these countries, for example, very few instances of OEM relationships exist. The challenge ahead is to create the conditions where such relationships can develop, bearing in mind the difficulties of meeting the increasingly demanding technical requirements in the upper end of the OEM market and the difficulties of competing with countries like China in the lower end.

In conclusion, all the NIEs are being challenged to reassess their industrialisation strategies and to chart new courses. Creative planning is required on the part of firms as well as states. Also, adapting to the rapid changes occurring in the competitive global environment requires a more flexible institutional and policy framework. Those NIEs with flexible planners and institutions, have navigated in the waters of international competition more easily.  Still, all the NIEs face growing challenges in the years ahead.  Even "forced" restructuring does not guarantee that all the NIEs can achieve their industrialisation goals in a world where disturbing tendencies toward growing protectionism in OECD countries threaten to close the NIEs out of major product and technology markets.

# NOTES AND REFERENCES

1. Park, 1989.
2. Bank of Japan, 1988.
3. In microprocessors, for example, Intel and Motorola traditionally licensed other firms as "second sources", but with their latest generation of 32-bit microprocessors they have refused to sell second-source licenses. (*The Economist*, 18th March 1989, p. 102).
4. For details, see Ernst, 1989 (forthcoming).
5. See Chapter VI "A Research Agenda".
6. Imai, 1988.
7. Looney, 1982:187.
8. We are grateful to Daniel Chudnovsky, Director of Centro de Economia Internacional (CEI), Buenos Aires, for drawing our attention to this important point. See also Fajnzylber 1988.
9. Nieto Pontes, Mauricio, 1988 "Renovacion del crecimiento, politica industrial y ortodoxia economica: Elementos para un analysis critico", *Desarrollo y Sociedad*, (September) 22, pp. 77-106.
10. This manuscript was finalised before the "massacre in Bejing" abruptly "froze" the modernisation of Chinese society. China will now find access much more difficult to advanced technologies.
11. For licensing activities in India's capital goods sector, see Chudnovsky, Nagao and Jacobsson, 1983, pp. 107ff.
12. Lim, 1978 and 1988; Ernst, 1983; UNCTC, 1986 and Gregory, 1986.
13. Ernst, D, interviews in the South Korean electronics industry, May and June 1988.
14. For example, when Intel set up an automated assembly plant in Albuquerque, New Mexico, it had to bring in engineers and technicians from its Penang, Malaysia, facility to assist in start-up operations. It has set up an assembly automation unit in Penang which services its worldwide assembly network. O'Connor, David, interviews with Intel Malaysia officials, 1985 and 1988.
15. Kaye, 1989.
16. See report on software engineering, prepared for the OECD Development Centre project "Technological Change and the Electronics Sector..."
17. See report on the Brazilian electronics industry, prepared for the OECD Development Centre project "Technological Change and the Electronics Sector...".
18. Piore and Sabel, 1984.
19. For instance Perez and Soete, 1988.
20. *Ibid.*, p. 459.
21. *Ibid.*, p. 477.
22. Bowonder and Miyake, 1988.
23. Perez and Soete, 1988, p. 476.
24. See report on the Brazilian consumer electronics industry, prepared for the OECD Development Centre's project on "Technological Change and the Electronics Sector — Perspectives and Policy Options for North-South Industrial Co-operation".
25. Amsden, 1986.

*Part Three*

# AN AGENDA FOR THE 1990s

*Chapter V*

# EMERGING POLICY ISSUES

## TOWARDS INCREASING INEQUALITY?

In this study, we have gone a long way towards analysing how basic transformations in the international economy, combined with the uneven diffusion of new technologies, affect the scope for latecomer industrialisation. We have shown that technological change affects developing countries mainly through its impact on global competition between the United States, Japan and Western Europe. Developing countries, including even the most successful first-tier Asian NIEs, find themselves to be marginal players in such games, unable to influence the rules of competition.

The post-war recovery of Japan and Western Europe led to a world where trade was dominated by three major trading blocks. This triangular relationship will be strengthened by the continuing success of Japan in international markets, the new alliance linking the United States and Canada, and the planned EC integration in 1992. New technologies, particularly those that are knowledge-intensive and that lead to highly integrated production systems, have worked principally to the benefit of this charmed circle of countries. Other nations have succeeded in achieving rapid economic growth only by entering the markets and production networks of one or more of thedominant groups. This applies in particular to first-tier and second-tier Asian NIEs. So far, such export-oriented industrial growth has, however, remained heavily dependent on imports of generic technologies and product standards from OECD countries, and the same applies to most of the machinery and the critical parts and components used.

By the late 1970s, some of these countries, in particular South Korea and Taiwan, had in place effective strategies to utilise foreign technology acquisition as an important instrument of latecomer industrial transformation. Based on strong monitoring capacities for international technology flows and sophisticated negotiation strategies, some of these countries were also starting to implement ambitious strategies to diversify their technology imports and to speed up the absorption of productivity-enhancing generic technologies. But just as the first benefits of such strategies were materialising, access to international technology became increasingly restricted. While international technology flows to China, India, South Korea, Taiwan and a small number of other Asian nations continued to increase, they began to stagnate and sometimes even to dry up for a growing number of other developing countries. As we have shown before, this applies in particular to imports of capital goods and to foreign direct investment flows. But even South Korea, the archetypical success story of export-led industrialisation, is finding it increasingly difficult today to gain access to those product and process technologies which it needs for an upgrading of its industrial structure and product portfolio[1]. In short, while new technologies contain a huge, and still largely untapped potential for unlocking new technology combinations and thus for increasing productivity, the blunt fact remains that most of the world appears to be locked out of significant options for productivity growth. Barring something to break the trend, the gap separating rich and poor nations is likely to increase.

In this sense, our findings would seem to lead to rather pessimistic conclusions. This is true in the sense that we cannot share the sometimes quite naïve hope that new technologies could act as a panacea to all the pressing problems of Third World underdevelopment. Yet, neither would we argue for an unqualified pessimism.

As a matter of fact, reality is much more complicated and uncertain than both the technology pessimists and optimists would want us to believe. There is nothing predetermined about how new technologies affect international trade and investment patterns and the distribution of competitive advantages. The same applies to the impact of new technologies on the development potential, the scope for industrial transformation and the world market integration of different groupings of developing countries. "In individual countries, the outcome will be largely the result of political, social, economic and historic factors that traditionally influence development. Technology will be a powerful tool mediating the effects of such fundamental structural factors"[2].

We have documented for advanced electronics (in particular computer-based information technologies) how new technologies both can drastically increase barriers to entry, and at the same time open up new possibilities for destabilizing established market structures[3]. The same applies to the spatial allocation of production and complementary support services where new information technologies can strengthen both decentralisation and reconsolidation trends. Our analysis has shown that technology indeed is of great importance in shaping industrial transformation and the spatial location of economic activities, both within and between countries. Yet, it is by no means the only factor involved. What really matters are the strategies and policies of the main actors participating in the generation and diffusion of new technologies, that is, firms and governments. Apart from business strategies of global competition, this relates in particular to patterns of economic and political conflict regulation, both in the national context and with regard to international economic transactions (the "international trade regime"[4]). In addition, the impact of new technologies is conditioned to a very large degree by the basic features of industrial, market and organisational structures and by the driving forces underlying the current internationalisation of industrial production and of related services.

In short, as long as the introduction of new technologies is primarily driven by neo-mercantilistic goals, concentration and inequality in the international economy are bound to increase. Such a policy approach does allow for often quite substantial short-term growth benefits. Normally, however, they are restricted to a small number of firms and privileged growth regions, and this is bound to erode even further the long-term stability of the world economy.

# THE EROSION OF GLOBAL ECONOMIC SECURITY: THE SEARCH FOR AN ALTERNATIVE POLICY AGENDA

## The growing concern with global economic security

Today issues related to global economic security receive much more attention than in any other period since World War II. A catalytic event like the "crash" of October 1987 has forced all kinds of actors, governments as much as private companies and trade unions, to acknowledge that increasing economic internationalisation has fundamentally destabilized our current world economic system. While interdependence among national economies has become pervasive, covering today not only trade and investment, but increasingly also knowledge generation and technology flows, and the markets for labour and capital, the scope for national economic policymaking has been drastically reduced. At the same time, established patterns of international economic conflict regulation are running into growing constraints.

These developments have become a major concern even for the most outspoken proponents of economic internationalisation, that is American, Japanese and European multinationals. In order to continue their strategies of worldwide sourcing and of global product development and marketing, these companies need a reliable framework for their international economic transactions. Governments and trade unions increasingly share such a concern, obviously however, for quite different reasons, related predominantly to security and welfare concerns. This applies as much to OECD countries, as to socialist countries, NIEs, and other Third World societies.

So, while the underlying motivations differ quite substantially, concern with global economic security is shared by an increasingly large group of actors. It is in this context that the current improvement of political relations between the United States and the Soviet Union can play an important role — it opens up new possibilities for reconsidering outdated ideologies and negotiation positions, and for engaging in new and unconventional forms of co-operation.

## National versus global economic security: the role of technology

It is important to understand that national concepts of economic security differ quite substantially from, and often are in direct contradiction with, any concept of global economic security.

Viewed from the perspective of a national economy, the main concern is to achieve at least some independence of action on the international stage, despite the increasingly pervasive economic internationalisation. In order to ensure a minimum of autonomy in national economic policymaking, government intervention, in the form of trade, industrial and technology policies, is spreading in all kinds of societies, irrespective of their political persuasion, and irrespective of whether governments admit to having such policies. Such policies are also spreading in some of the more developed societies of the Third World, particularly the NIEs.

Technology in this context is perceived to play a crucial role. A lack of international competitiveness in key industrial sectors producing generic technologies, such as microelectronics, and the slow diffusion of such technologies across the national economy is widely considered to lead to increasing economic and, consequently political dependence.

104

Two comments are in order here:

*i)* First, the concept of national economic security certainly violates mainstream economic thinking, but it is not necessarily wrong. The blindness of mainstream economists can be gathered from the fact that for them "market imperfections" are only temporary phenomena and "strategic industries" simply do not exist. Technology is at best viewed as a residual factor, which is equally accessible to all economic actors, and thus will not disturb the general equilibrium. Obviously, such theories can only be of limited help in the real world of global competition.

*ii)* Second, as ever more countries are pursuing national economic security with a vengeance, global economic security has been increasingly threatened.

Take, for instance, international trade. In a world with bitter trade wars and without a stable institutional framework for regulating international trade and finance, the scope for mutually beneficial export-led growth is obviously quite limited. Of course, individual countries can try to expand their exports, for some time at least, to the detriment of their trade partners. In the long term, however, such "beggar-my-neighbour" export promotion would be a disaster — it is bound to intensify the already quite explosive trade conflicts which, in turn, would further accelerate the erosion of the world economy.

The same applies to international technology flows, where an increasingly aggressive legal protection of industrial and intellectual property rights is leading to pervasive "patent and copyright wars" in pharmaceuticals and in advanced electronics (particularly software, computer memories and microprocessors). Add to this the still quite far-reaching system of export controls on so-called "dual-use technologies"[5], as codified in the current COCOM lists, and you get an impression of the degree to which the international flow of scientific knowledge and key technologies has become restricted today.

We would like to submit that current policies of export-led growth, based on "neo-mercantilistic" trade and industrial policies, are leading us into a dangerous impasse — blindly following the whims of global competition is certainly not sufficient any longer. At least, we should reconsider the manifold possibilities for revitalising international technology diffusion in a way which would improve the chances of global development. We thus need a drastic change in our dominant policy doctrine on how we should utilise technology in the international context.


THE POLICY AGENDA FOR NEWLY INDUSTRIALISING ECONOMIES

The world economy is at a critical juncture. Both the OECD countries and the NIEs are faced with difficult decisions about what direction to take as they seek to reorient their economies to the changing currents of international competition. Technological capabilities act as a rudder to help the NIEs navigate through turbulent economic waters. To strengthen those capabilities has thus become a strategic goal of highest priority.

How successful a particular NIE is in realising this goal will depend on its response to a number of emergent policy issues. These issues can be broadly grouped under five headings:

*i)* Access to technology and acquisition strategies;

*ii)* Technology diffusion and generation;

*iii)* Industrial transformation;

*iv)* Restructuring international trade and investment relations; and

*v)* The role of the state.

In some cases, the issues cut across a number of NIEs and may even require a co-ordinated or co-operative response. In others, the policy issues are specific to a particular NIE, but even where the policy initiative must come at the level of the individual economy, the likelihood is that other NIEs are faced with similar policy dilemmas. For example, all NIEs must address the needs of industrial transformation, though the particularities of a given NIE's industrial structure will strongly condition its policy response. Finally, how a specific NIE or group of NIEs respond to certain emergent policy issues can be expected to have ramifications for other NIEs, as well as other developing countries. For instance, how the first-tier Asian NIEs transform their industrial structures will certainly affect the position of the Asian second-tier NIEs at the least. These growing interdependencies among the NIEs themselves are an issue ripe for further study[6]. More generally, the discussion which follows of emergent policy issues sets a broad agenda for future research.

## Access to technology and acquisition strategies

Active worldwide technology sourcing strategies are required if the NIEs are to assure access to the key technologies they need for industrial transformation. *Laisser-faire* does not work. Firms must actively search for the relevant technologies, ferret out the best sources, and negotiate the best possible terms of acquisition. Governments must support them in those efforts, making available information which might reduce search costs, fostering contacts between domestic firms and foreign technology suppliers, and creating a policy environment in which technology flows freely.

### Diversifying technology sources

NIE firms need to diversify technology sources as much as possible so as to minimise the vulnerabilities that come with dependence on a single supplier. When that supplier is also a competitor, the risks are that much greater. At the same time, there are limits to such diversification, just as there are limits to diversification in product markets. Beyond a point, in both instances economies of scope[7] may give way to "diseconomies of scope". In other words, where assets are highly specialised, there are some advantages to be gained in terms of effective technology absorption, when a more durable relationship with a given supplier is maintained. For many NIE firms, however, the luxury of choice may not exist. They may have to "take what they can get" as OECD high technology firms become less generous with licensing or otherwise sharing their new technologies. Without active search though, NIE firms will not even know what is there for the taking. Given that search is costly, especially for small- and medium-scale firms, and that there are substantial external economies in the supply of information on technology sources, it is an activity where government support can be of great help. Of course, the more firm-specific the informational requirements are, the more difficult it becomes for government information dissemination to substitute for firm-level search procedures. Government need not be the sole or even the principal provider of such technology information services. In some countries, private trade, or industry, associations have been quite effective agents of acquisition and dissemination of information about new technologies to their members.

*Trading off different methods of technology acquisition*

Once technology sources have been identified, the appropriate method and terms of technology acquisition need to be determined. Wherever domestic absorptive capabilities and the technology itself permit, unbundling the technology package is preferable to obtaining it bundled with extraneous elements which nonetheless command a price, often a premium one[8]. In the broadest terms, this may mean choosing to license a technology rather than enter a joint venture with its foreign supplier. More narrowly, a firm may want to license only a component of a technology, using its in-house expertise to provide the complementary technological inputs. There are trade-offs to be considered when choosing the appropriate method of technology acquisition. The terms of the trade-off will differ across firms, sectors, and countries. For example, unbundling and licensing a particular technology may reduce costs of acquisition, but it may raise absorption (learning) costs if the licensee does not have sufficient internal expertise. Moreover, relying on licensing alone may limit access to state-of-the-art technologies, which OECD firms are increasingly reluctant to license. In some cases, competition among OECD firms to become the standard setters may force earlier licensing by those firms of new technologies than would otherwise have occurred. Japanese firms in HDTV are one example. In other cases, joint ventures may be the only way to acquire state-of-the-art technology, but then the foreign partner may seek to limit the NIE partner's access to key technology assets. Once more, the state of the NIE firm's own internal technical resources will shape its ability to benefit from such a partnership. One situation which may arise is where the foreign partner transfers all the know-how related to the efficient operation of the production process but withholds critical information about product design and engineering. Such strict segmentation of information flows is not always possible however, so a NIE firm with good adaptive engineering capabilities may be able to learn how to design and produce a modified version of the product covered by the joint venture. This is especially true in metalworking industries, where the interface is closest between design and production engineering[9].

In short, acquisition strategies must be closely related to internal design, engineering and production capabilities. As the latter evolve, so must the former. There is a logical evolution in a NIE's technology acquisition strategy as its technology absorption capacity matures. In early stages, options are more limited, with FDI probably accounting for a major source of technology and licensing being a less important one. Innovative forms of technology acquisition — for example, strategic partnering — are not yet within the realm of possibility. For more technologically mature NIEs, the range of options widens. Licensing becomes a more fruitful technology source and cross-licensing may even be a possibility where the NIE firm possesses highly specialised know-how. At this point, NIE firms are no longer in the position of passive recipients of whatever technologies foreign firms may have to offer. Rather, they actively search out the technologies they need and, if necessary, take equity positions in foreign firms as a means of gaining access to key technologies. The principal role of NIE governments is to accelerate the transition from a more passive to a more active technology acquisition strategy. This essentially means helping domestic firms strengthen their absorptive capabilities.

*Leveraging complementary assets*

Strategic partnerships between NIE firms and OECD firms are becoming more commonplace. A number of South Korean *chaebol* have technology tie-ups with OECD firms in high technology areas (e.g. Samsung with Intel and Hyundai with Texas Instruments in semiconductors)[10]. Such arrangements may be one way of countering the general tendency toward more restrictive conditions of access to new technologies. For by its very nature, a "strategic" partnership establishes a relationship between firms in which the technological progress of each is critical to the competitive success of the other. Thus technology exchange could be more extensive than in the traditional OEM arrangements NIE firms have had with their OECD customers. The key to being able to enter such relationships appears to be possession by the NIE firm of a key technology or some other complementary asset required by the OECD partner. The complementary asset may be an efficient manufacturing capacity and speed-of-delivery; it may be large cash reserves; it may be a strong marketing and distribution network within the national economy. The government of the larger NIEs at least — especially the quasi-continental economies — may be able to leverage the bargaining position of individual firms by trading market access for favourable technology arrangements with the foreign supplier. More research is needed on how promising such strategic partnerships may be as an avenue of technology acquisition, at least for more advanced NIE firms[11].

*Countering efforts to restrict access to new technologies*

Intellectual property rights protection has become an issue of heated debate in international trade and development forums. The OECD countries — led by the United States — are seeking to introduce intellectual property protection into multilateral trade negotiations within the GATT framework. This would raise the stature of this issue to a level comparable to that of trade liberalisation, the need for which probably commands far wider support among developing countries than the need for protecting intellectual property. Thus far, Brazil and India have been the most influential opponents to the introduction of the intellectual property issue into the Uruguay Round of multilateral trade negotiations. They maintain that the World Intellectual Property Organisation (WIPO) in Geneva properly has jurisdiction over such matters and that its mandate should be strengthened. Whether such an approach will prevail remains to be seen, but the enormous political influence of the United States makes such an outcome doubtful at best. Therefore, each NIE may have to devise its own pre-emptive strategy that will provide adequate intellectual property protection for domestic innovation, though any such system of protection involves the trade-off of escalating the costs of acquisition of foreign technologies. The terms of the trade-off differ for each NIE depending on its level of technological development and domestic innovative capacity. More research needs to be devoted to the effects of alternative frameworks for intellectual property protection on indigenous technological development and on the acquisition of foreign technologies by NIEs[12].

**Technology diffusion and generation**

*Creating effective demand through government procurement*

Policies to promote diffusion of new technologies among domestic users are an essential requirement for development of the internal market. Once more, active state involvement may be a necessary (but not sufficient) condition for fostering such diffusion. The government is an important source of effective demand for certain key technologies like communications equipment. Government procurement markets can be sufficiently large in some cases to give rise to an efficient local manufacturing capacity. If that is the case, then it would provide the conditions for establishing the close user-producer links so essential to the diffusion of new technologies. Those links would in turn make possible the effective adaptation of those technologies to local requirements. The development of digital switching systems tailored to local market conditions in South Korea, Brazil, and India are examples of this process. Local telecommunications equipment manufacture may in turn provide strong impetus to the development of a more sophisticated electronic components sector. Still, scale requirements — especially in the component sector — are likely to make it necessary to export some of the equipment to other developing countries with similar user requirements and market conditions. Given the highly politicised nature of telecommunications markets, exporter NIE governments may have to assume an active role in such export promotion.

Government procurement may also be an important stimulus to the development of the software industry. The issue of copyright or other protection for software must also be addressed in this connection. The development of a large user base is an important element in the creation of demand for local software development. With regard to large systems, that base formation is frequently facilitated by government and financial sector modernisation efforts. For smaller systems, especially PCs, the availability of low cost (which often means uncopyrighted) software packages is an important element in computer diffusion. Thus premature software protection might slow such diffusion substantially[13]. The other side of the trade-off is that inadequate software protection may well retard the development of a dynamic local software industry. The question of timing — that is, when software protection would be most appropriate — requires further study[14].

### Providing information and generating skills for effective use of new technologies

There are a number of barriers to the diffusion of new technologies in NIEs which must be addressed. One is a lack of detailed information — especially acute among small- and medium-scale firms — regarding the costs and benefits of new technologies. Another is a lack of the necessary skills to utilise the technologies effectively. These include the engineering and managerial skills required to integrate new capital equipment and related software into manufacturing activities. There is a substantial amount of learning involved in mastering new automation technologies. New skills are critical for repair and maintainence of sophisticated equipment. Given the shortage of such skills in many NIEs, firms which introduce costly automated equipment which they cannot adequately maintain are courting disaster. Recognising this diffusion bottleneck, some NIE governments have established — in some cases with the co-operation of automated systems vendors — institutes for training engineers and technicians in the appropriate use, maintenance, and repair of new equipment.

### Supporting financial and technical needs of small- and medium-scale firms

The amount of financing required to acquire new technologies may also be a formidable barrier to small- and medium-scale firms. Capital costs may be excessively high for such firms, even supposing they are able to raise the necessary capital at all. This does not apply to such low cost, all purpose technologies as personal computers, but rather to more specialised technologies — such as, customised production equipment or software. Again, small- and medium-scale firms are also likely to have fewer technical and managerial resources to absorb and utilise effectively the new technology. Thus special government financing schemes, computer leasing services, and "technology extension services" may be needed to accelerate the rate of diffusion among small and medium firms. Since such firms make up the backbone of the supplier networks so crucial to the flexibility of the production structure, NIEs should urgently foster their technology upgrading.

*Creating a more conducive macroeconomic environment*

The diffusion of new technologies in the NIEs is a macroeconomic issue as much as a microeconomic one. For many of the new technologies are embodied in capital goods whose demand is affected by the same factors that affect investment decisions in general. That is why, for example, the stagnation of debt-burdened Latin American economies has adversely affected the diffusion of new technologies. Firms there were not investing at all, let alone in new technologies. Thus a resolution of the debt crisis and a rekindling of growth in Latin America is a prerequisite for accelerating the rate of diffusion of new technologies.

Factor market conditions also affect diffusion rates and patterns: high interest rates may deter investors while tight labour markets — as in several first-tier Asian NIEs — should stimulate the introduction of new labour-saving technologies, as is occurring in Taiwan and Singapore. If raw materials are considered another productive factor, then tight conditions in this set of markets also affect the prospects for diffusion of new "materials-saving" technologies.

China faces this constraint most acutely due to the highly inefficient raw material use in many enterprises. Much of China's foreign exchange reserves are used up to purchase new materials, restricting the amount available to import critical technology and capital goods. New information technologies have allowed companies elsewhere to achieve substantial material savings in many production processes. Thus a special effort is required to identify those industries which could reap substantial material input savings with the application for new production methods. Organisational and managerial adjustments have to accompany the introduction of the new technologies if their potential is to be fully exploited. Whether existing rigidities in enterprise structure (especially within the state sector and large conglomerates) would permit the sorts of adjustments required is an unknown variable and should be a topic for future research.

*Upgrading product design and development capabilities*

Of particular concern to the first-tier Asian NIEs is how to upgrade their product design and development capabilities. Beyond OEM lies still largely uncharted terrain. To find their way without the reliable guide of an OEM brand, the first-tier Asian NIEs must rely to a far greater extent than previously on their own monitoring of market trends, user requirements, and technology developments. They must be able not merely to respond quickly to, but even to anticipate emerging demands. Given limited design and R&D resources at present, the first-tier Asian NIEs are being challenged to expand those resources rapidly while, even more importantly, making more effective use of the resources they already have. Thus the pooling of those resources through collaborative R&D is becoming imperative. The government has played a catalytic role in such R&D initiatives in the past and will continue to do so. Nevertheless, there are limits to the role the state can and should play in these economies: too heavy state involvement in R&D may lessen pressures on firms to undertake more vigorous R&D themselves. The state is perhaps most effective in the capacity of prime mover — demonstrating the feasibility of local assimilation of a new technology — after which design, product development and process engineering related to the commercialisation of the new technology are best left to the firms themselves.

### Deciding how fast to automate production

The second-tier Asian NIEs are still in a position where innovative product development is the exception and not the rule. To them the more immediate concern is how far and how fast they ought to adopt new process technologies. Their industries are clearly under pressure from lower labour cost locations, yet their labour costs are still low and cost considerations alone would not justify the introduction of state-of-the-art automated processes. Still one of the few prospects they have for remaining competitive is to upgrade product quality, improve customer support (for example, reliable delivery schedules, quick response to customer requests), and target higher value added market segments. All of this requires improved production, inventory, and quality control methods as well as stronger management skills. New technologies undoubtedly play a role in upgrading manufacturing capabilities. Yet, given relative factor costs, as well as the limited information and absorptive capacity of domestic firms in these countries, diffusion of those technologies might be excessively slow. Thus government support will be needed to accelerate the rate of diffusion.

Government-sponsored R&D should focus at this stage on refining production methods and upgrading product quality. Strengthening the technical capabilities of government standards bodies, and providing certain testing and quality assurance services to small- and medium-scale firms in particular may be necessary. The precision engineering sector, including mould and die making, is critical for the timely response of local firms to customer requirements. Given limited resources, government efforts would probably have the greatest long-term pay-off if they were concentrated on strengthening this sector.

## Industrial transformation

### Policies for "sunset" industries

All the NIEs must cope with the complexities of industrial restructuring in one form or another. Competitive positions are rapidly shifting and this, in many instances, involves the decay of whole industrial sectors and regions. Such "creative distruction" often carries with it tremendous economic and social costs. Hence the prominence given to policies for sunset industries in the current industrial policy debates. In this area, however, the effectiveness of state policy varies widely. In many NIEs the state has major investments in "troubled" industries and thus the state is far from a disinterested party[15]. Moreover, it must weigh the more immediate — and more visible — costs of restructuring, that is job dislocation, against the longer-term strategic objective of repositioning the industry to compete more effectively in global markets, for example. The South Korean government, for one, is currently grappling with how to minimise the social costs of restructuring financially troubled businesses (in this case Daewoo's shipbuilding operations) without effectively guaranteeing to bail them out when they go bankrupt. The currency adjustments and cost increases of recent years in South Korea, Taiwan and Singapore have posed with added force the issue of how to treat their sunset industries, which are struggling to remain competitive[16]. In Singapore, for example, the state has managed to phase out the textile and the motor vehicle assembly industries. Even without state intervention, the adjustments would occur but the process could well be more protracted, given the cumulative experience and sunk investments in a particular sector.

The second-tier Asian NIEs also confront major problems relating to industrial restructuring. One concern is the proper pacing of industrial transformation. The tendency in certain instances may be to try to move too quickly into high technology industries for which the foundations — in terms of scientific and technical expertise for example — frequently do not exist. This may result in the neglect of sectors which still could be highly competitive with some technological upgrading. For example, in Malaysia the textile industry has for some time been considered a sunset industry, a case perhaps of "premature obsolescence". In general, the problem is one of balancing the investment between upgrading the more mature industries and entering into new ones. Discouraging labour-intensive industries would be inadvisable because the second-tier Asian NIEs still have high unemployment and underemployment. As more labour-intensive industries shift out of Japan and the first-tier Asian NIEs, the second-tier has an opportunity to capture a large share of the FDI originating from those economies. The concern to move into higher value added activities is understandable, but at this stage it may be more advisable to augment value by capitalising on accumulated experience in traditionally more labour-intensive industries than by shifting wholesale into more capital and technology-intensive industries. Selective entry into a few such sectors, where local scientific, engineering and technical expertise permits, would be warranted.

The key element to any restructuring of "sunset industries" in the first-tier Latin American NIEs is to make them internationally competitive and flexible through the use of advanced technology, preferably internally generated. Mexico's recent restructuring of its state steel sector achieved increases in productivity and higher degrees of flexibility through technological upgrading based on sectoral government R&D[17]. While in certain sectors well focused direct state intervention may be needed, in others in which state procurement or investment levels are not so high (textiles, shoes, other consumer goods) state involvement should be more on the institutional level of creating the conditions for restructuring towards greater international competitiveness. The state efforts should be aimed at providing seed financial support and, more importantly, facilitating the emergence of regional or sectoral based institutions for technology development, joint marketing, international market intelligence, etc.

*Managing the trade-off between specialisation and diversification*

Two sets of trade-offs must be addressed in varying degrees by all the NIEs:
  *i)* The trade-off between diversification and specialisation, and
  *ii)* The trade-off between vertical integration and flexible networks of independent subcontractors.

The first trade-off refers to the organisational problems which may arise from an excessively diffuse product mix. The management and organisational requirements of high technology industries are very different from those of traditional industries, and vary widely among high technology industries as well[18]. The experience of diversified conglomerates which have moved from a base in the latter to an active involvement in the former has been mixed. Where the base bears a close enough resemblance to the new field to make possible certain economies of scope — for example, consumer electrical and electronic appliance manufacturers moving into industrial and professional electronics — the success rate has generally been higher than otherwise. At the same time, a base in trading can provide some advantages for moving into export manufacturing because links with foreign suppliers and customers, distribution channels, etc., are that much easier to establish. Finally, on the positive side, a diversified product mix appears to have been a source of competitive strength to large Japanese and, more recently, South Korean conglomerates, as they have been able to subsidise to an extent the costs of penetrating new high technology markets from the profits on more mature products.

On the negative side, there are examples where diversification appears to have been excessive. The Brazilian informatics sector is a case in point where, as earlier mentioned, firms have shifted frequently from one product line to another in search of the highest short-term returns, but at the expense of learning and scale economies in specific products. Even a powerful conglomerate like Samsung must rationalise its diffuse activities in order to focus more singlemindedly on strengthening its capabilities in the high technology sectors it has chosen to enter. A problem that has plagued the South Korean *chaebol* in general is how to transform management from its traditional family style, with a high degree of centralisation of decisionmaking, to a more professional and less centralised management system able to respond more flexibly to changing technology requirements and market conditions. Whereas South Korean firms have recognised the need, and have begun to move from a broad base to a more focused product range and technology effort, Brazilian firms have been moving in the direction of a more diffuse and fragmented production structure. Thus the rationalisation of this production structure in high technology sectors is an emergent policy concern.

*Managing the trade-off between vertical integration and flexible supplier networks*

Related to this dilemma is the second trade-off, between vertical integration and flexible supplier networks. As with the previous one, the terms of the trade-off differ across NIEs. The economising properties of vertical integration in certain contexts have been noted above[19]. To the extent, however, that backward integration into parts and components production comes at the expense of economies of scale, such integration may raise rather than lower costs of downstream industries. In the Brazilian case, pressures to localise component supply for purposes of saving scarce foreign exchange and achieving local content targets, have resulted in such inefficient integration. Government initiative to promote component standardisation could be a means of allowing certain components to be localised at efficient scales. Even where scale economies are not significant, excessive vertical integration may be a liability. For it may result in certain "lock-in" effects for the "captive" component suppliers, in the sense that they are not able to reap the potential economies of scope which arise from producing related components for different customers. To the extent that they must forfeit such economies, components locally produced are more costly than they would otherwise be. Thus government policy aimed at promoting the development, wherever possible, of an independent component sector is highly desirable. This may involve fiscal or financial incentives targetted explicitly at small- and medium-scale enterprises, which make up the bulk of such suppliers. These firms have the potential of becoming dynamic technological innovators, given the proper environment and encouragement. Large firms should also be encouraged to strengthen their technological links to small- and medium-scale firms to make them into efficient and reliable subcontractors.

To appreciate more fully the complexity of the trade-offs between vertical integration and "dis-integration", it is useful to distinguish between "core" and "peripheral" components[20]. This distinction is critical in high technology industries. The question confronted by firms not only in the NIEs but also in OECD countries is what components should a firm make itself to maintain competitive advantage in downstream markets. For example, an important policy concern in OECD countries is whether a computer firm which also produces certain critical semiconductor components has a strategic advantage over one which must source all of them from merchant suppliers. The same question can be posed at the level of national industries — that is, whether a particular country's computer industry can afford to import all its requirements of certain key components (D-RAMs or microprocessors, for example) from foreign producers, especially when those foreign producers are vertically integrated firms also making computers. The South Korean *chaebol* face this issue especially acutely, as they must depend heavily on Japanese suppliers of core components for a number of high technology products, while at the same time those same Japanese suppliers or their principal Japanese customers are the *chaebol's* major competitors in those product markets. Under what conditions would competitive indigenisation of core component production be possible? Why has it not proceeded farther already in NIEs like South Korea or Brazil? What are the principal constraints? These are issues for further research[21].

## Restructuring of trade and investment relations

### Avoiding "premature liberalisation"

The NIEs as a group face mounting pressures from OECD countries to liberalise their markets, at the same time that most OECD markets are becoming more restrictive. An emergent policy concern of utmost importance to the NIEs is how to respond to such pressures. The United States, for example, is pressuring South Korea and Taiwan to liberalise imports of high technology products, which are among the remaining areas in which US exports are still competitive but which those NIEs are also seeking to promote. Somewhat reluctantly, the South Korean government recently liberalised imports of personal computers, but lower-priced Taiwanese models, not US firms appear to have been the main beneficiaries[22]. In the case of consumer electronics, liberalisation led to an influx of Japanese products manufactured mostly in offshore facilities in the second-tier Asian NIEs. This is not the first instance where, ironically, the US government has spoken out most in favour of liberalisation and US firms have benefited least. The South Korean government is rightly concerned that "premature liberalisation" of strategic industries could undermine its efforts to strengthen the competitiveness of national firms in those industries[23]. First- and second-tier Latin American NIEs have also had negative experiences with hasty and unplanned liberalisation, the de-industrialisation of Argentina and Chile being the most extreme cases.

### Export market diversification

Export market diversification is as crucial a concern to the NIEs as is diversification of technology sources. In particular, those NIEs which have relied upon selling into the largest market — the United States — find themselves highly vulnerable to rising protectionism there. Diversifying is not, however, a simple matter. First, to compensate for a given reduction in US market share would require either a comparable increase in market shares across several other countries or a very large increase in one or two other key markets. The former gives rise to the problem that selling into many new markets in smaller volumes would involve additional expenses on the marketing and distribution end — since every market would require a separate and somewhat customised network[24] — and would also involve, in many cases, expensive product design modification to suit different technical norms and user requirements/tastes in different markets. Moreover, economies of large scale production could also be sacrificed if product market segmentation requires significant adaptation of production processes to different output requirements. To an extent, flexible production technologies may mitigate such difficulties by increasing economies of scope. If diversification takes the route of refocusing demand growth on one or two key export markets, there is the risk that market penetration levels sufficient to compensate for loss of US market share would be so high as to be politically unacceptable and would lead in turn to market restrictions in those new growth markets. Clearly the reaction of the importing country government will depend greatly on the overall macroeconomic performance and on how pervasive import penetration is.

Another potential problem with market diversification is that very few markets other than the United States have the same sophistication of demand, especially for high technology products. That sophistication, while it has made it difficult for NIE firms to break into the US market, has also meant that those which succeeded would be in touch with the latest user requirements[25]. They could thus respond to new technological developments before they had diffused to less sophisticated markets, although the rate of diffusion across OECD countries is generally rapid. The Japanese and European markets are the only ones which could adequately substitute for the US market as a "technology driver" for NIE exporters. Moves toward liberalisation notwithstanding, it may be some time before the Japanese market opens widely enough to become a major technology proving ground for NIE firms. In the case of the European market, much depends on how restrictive market access becomes after EC integration in 1992.

### The "reciprocal market access" game

The NIEs need not passively accept aggressive gestures by certain OECD countries restricting market access to their exports. As a number of NIEs realise, "two can play the game", especially if the second player has a population of a few hundred million people or more. This explains why, for example, China, India and Brazil are better positioned to assure access of their exports to the US market than, say, Thailand or Taiwan.

For those NIEs lacking such an advantage but intent upon remaining serious players, for example, in the US market, other strategies are necessary. One possibility is to establish sufficiently strong technical and/or manufacturing links with one or more firms in the market of choice so that the latter become guarantors of the NIE firm's market position as a matter of self-interest. Another alternative is to become a foreign investor in the target market to ensure access. This has been necessary for several South Korean and Taiwanese firms in the United States[26] and it will be necessary before long — and on a more massive scale — in the European Community. Rising capital exports, however, could generate political resistance in the NIEs, especially if unemployment is growing at the same time. Foreign direct investment to ensure market access is not easy for many small- and medium-scale firms in NIEs. One issue which needs to be examined is whether large trading companies could pool the assets of such small- and medium-scale firms and lower their entry costs into foreign markets. The problem here is that "trading" activities in the European market may not be enough to ensure a market presence if strict local content requirements are enforced after 1992. More extensive cross-investment or cross-production agreements could be a means of ensuring European market access, even with stringent local sourcing requirements[27].

If present trends toward rampant protectionism in the OECD countries continue unabated, the NIEs will be forced to search more intensively for alternative trade arrangements to offset the negative effect on their growth prospects. One possibility alluded to earlier is to refocus growth on internal and regional markets. For all but the large quasi-continental economies internal markets will not be sufficient to fuel growth. Thus regional integration and co-operation could become imperative for sustained industrial development. Clearly, trade is only one dimension of a broader set of co-operative relationships which would have to be forged, including cross-investment, increased mutual technology flows, perhaps labour mobility, etc. Such arrangements could enable NIEs in a given region to pool knowledge, capital, skills, and markets. Of course there are formidable political and institutional barriers which would need to be overcome if such integration were to materialise.

The history of regional co-operation among developing countries has been disappointing. As policymakers seek to create new links, a necessary first step is to assess those experiences critically and learn from past mistakes. Some of the reasons for past failures include: the disproportionate share of the benefits accruing to the larger and/or wealthier countries; the large share of the benefits captured by transnational corporations as opposed to firms of regional origin; inadequate financial mechanisms to support integration; and reluctance of individual countries to downgrade historic trading links to OECD countries. The last at least no longer poses a problem, since the OECD countries themselves are weakening such links by protectionism. One necessary requirement for durable regional relationships to emerge is that links to grow roots in the productive sector go beyond bureaucratic arrangements between governments. In short, cross-investments and cross-country technical co-operation between firms should help cement the regional bonds, with the result that they will have a greater likelihood of surviving political changes which might result in a downgrading of co-operative arrangements by certain regional governments.

Of course, making regional co-operation viable would require internal policy reforms in many developing countries. For example, trade liberalisation within the region would be necessary, as would the liberalisation of financial flows, foreign investment regulations, etc. Naturally, some safeguards have to be devised to avoid a recurrence of earlier negative experiences where multinationals benefited inordinately. Assuming this can be done, certain otherwise unpalatable policy reforms could become more feasible, such as the rationalisation of inefficient industries and the liberalisation of heavily protected markets.

Refocusing demand growth on regional markets may have the drawback of reducing the degree of exposure of NIE firms to the most sophisticated users. Keeping up-to-date technologically could become more difficult. This liability may be more serious on the side of product development, but less so for process technology. For the latter, there might even be some unanticipated benefits. For firms whose horizon (as in parts of Latin America) had been confined to the domestic market, regional markets may offer opportunities for economies of scale previously unattainable. For firms whose sights had customarily been set on the US market (mostly in the Asian NIEs and Mexico), producing for smaller, more differentiated markets may force the pace of introduction of new flexible manufacturing systems. Furthermore, NIE exports to other developing countries have been found to be more skill-intensive in general than their exports to OECD countries[28]. Since learning economies are greatest in skill-intensive sectors, regional trade could have more positive effects on technological learning than trade with OECD countries.

Patterns of foreign direct investment have been shifting significantly in recent years[29]. Outward FDI by US firms has slowed considerably while that by Japanese firms has accelerated. FDI by first-tier Asian NIEs has also become quite significant, at least in certain OECD countries and other countries in Asia. Certain NIEs — especially the second-tier Asian NIEs and the Latin American NIEs — still rely heavily on FDI as a source of technology[30].

*Second-tier Asian NIEs:* Two emergent policy issues are relevant to the second-tier Asian NIEs in particular as they evaluate investment policies in the light of changing realities. First, what does the change in the weighting of different sources of FDI imply for technology acquisition? The past experience of Southeast Asian countries with foreign investment suggests that Japanese firms have been quite effective in protecting proprietary know-how, at least with respect to core technologies — more so in general than US or European firms. As Japan becomes the dominant investor in the region, policymakers are concerned that their economies may reap even fewer technological spinoffs than before. At the same time, there may be new factors which are inducing Japanese firms to transfer more technology than they were accustomed to transfer in the past[31]. For one, the strong revaluation of the yen has greatly increased costs of components made in Japan, with the result that Japanese firms making equipment in the second-tier Asian NIEs have strong incentives to source components locally. Given their stringent quality standards, this requires either that Japanese component suppliers locate in the region or that local suppliers be given the know-how to enable them to meet exacting standards. Secondly, a large number of small- and medium-sized Japanese firms are moving to the region and these may have greater need to rely on external technical resources. Moreover, they may be less adept at maintaining tight control over their technologies.

The other unknown is whether FDI by first-tier Asian NIEs will provide a valuable alternative technology source to second-tier Asian NIEs. There is little doubt that the technology possessed by those firms is less advanced than that of their Japanese counterparts, at least on the product side. There are two senses, however, in which it might be more suitable for the second-tier countries. First, there is the familiar factor proportions argument, which suggests that their production technologies — developed in a context of relative labour abundance — may better match the relative factor proportions in the second-tier NIEs. Secondly, and more importantly, the first-tier NIE technologies may be better adapted to the domestic market conditions in the second-tier NIEs. The advantage here would be, to be able to accumulate experience in producing for the domestic market, where user-producer links are more easily established. The disadvantage would be the less sophisticated demands of domestic users relative to those in the OECD markets. Of course, if exports are destined principally for other developing countries this problem may not arise. The new patterns of FDI raise one important theme for further research, *viz.*, what possibilities do they create for greater regional integration and technical co-operation, especially within Asia[32].

A final emerging policy issue for second-tier Asian NIEs relates to investment incentives. Traditionally, generous fiscal incentives were designed to compensate for certain "structural competitive" weaknesses of a particular country. Foreign investors were quick to encourage competition among NIEs in granting incentives in order to minimise their overseas tax burdens. There is now growing recognition that a number of NIEs possess structural competitive strengths which they can use to attract FDI. For example, over the years they have developed skilled and experienced labour forces which are an important asset to a foreign investor. Thus policymakers recognise that it may no longer be necessary to offer "overly generous" incentives that needlessly forfeit valuable potential government revenue, which could be invested in further strengthening the economy's structural competitiveness.

*Latin American NIEs:* In Latin American NIEs, where foreign direct investment already plays a large role in traditional and new technology industries, policymakers should be concerned about developing suppliers for these firms which could reap potential technological learning effects. In the case of Brazil, one area for research is to what extent foreign firms have developed local supplier networks, and how their performance in this respect compares with equivalent Brazilian firms. Closely related, has technological learning diffused from firms within to those outside these supplier networks[33]?

Second-tier Latin American NIE firms and policymakers could attempt to develop specialised complementarities with small- and medium-sized foreign firms which might not be intimidated by their size in transferring technology, but which may find the possibilities of market access to larger markets in the region attractive.

*China:* While China has developed a reasonably comprehensive policy and legal framework to encourage FDI in the past ten years, and has been rather successful in attracting foreign investors, the environment could still be improved significantly[34]. The incentives to do so are considerable, given the current austerity measures, the deteriorating prospects for increased export growth rates, and the slow rate of technological change. FDI, especially in the form of joint or contractual ventures, is seen as a major mechanism for the rapid development and technological upgrading of key industries, particularly those producing technically sophisticated products. Success in this area is dependent on a number of factors. These include a recognition of the increasingly global nature of certain sectors, an acceptance that the benefits of FDI will take time to materialise and a willingness to liberalise FDI rules further. Given the often different objectives between China and foreign investors, the above conditions may be met only with some difficulty in the near future.

*India:* India faces concerns that are similar in some respects to those of China, *viz.,* how to achieve an appropriate degree of liberalisation of FDI policies to gain access to those key new technologies which are available principally in packaged form. India may be in a stronger position than many smaller NIEs to gain access to foreign technologies on favourable terms, yet it must come to grips with the reality of an international environment in which high technology firms are increasingly sensitive about not allowing their proprietary technologies to fall into the hands of potential competitors. While the government may choose not to alter its policy regarding local equity participation, it may have to weigh carefully the costs and benefits of making exceptions to the policy in cases where a key technology might otherwise become inaccessible[35].

## The role of the state

### Why the state's involvement is required

Mark Twain's quip that reports of his death were greatly exaggerated could apply equally well, *mutatis mutandis,* to the activist state in developing countries. Despite the decades of railing by development economists of a *laisser-faire* bent against the incompetence and inanity of the Third World state bureaucracies, "developmentalist states" in East Asia have turned in a creditable performance in steering their economies on a course of rapid industrial development. Even in other NIEs — for example, in Latin America — where state intervention is frequently chided as having been counterproductive, the record is at best mixed[36]. Still, it is probably correct to say that state intervention has been far less effective in the Latin American NIEs in strengthening industrial competitiveness than it has been in the first-tier Asian NIEs. Certainly there is something that can be learned from a comparative assessment of the Asian and Latin American experiences with state intervention. But the mere replication of the East Asian NIE model in Latin America would be not only inappropriate but impossible given the vastly different historical experiences, as well as contemporary political, social, economic and cultural realities. Already Malaysia has had to pay the consequences of an excessive eagerness to imitate the "Japanese model" of state support for strategic industries. Its thrust into heavy industries like steel, cement, and autos has been plagued by serious technical and financial problems[37].

There is no doubt that the state will continue to play a central role in most of the NIEs with the increasing importance of new technologies in shaping the prospects for industrialisation. The degree and form of state intervention is bound to differ widely, but there are several key policy areas which cannot be safely neglected by governments intent on creating the conditions for exploiting new technological opportunities. These include policies to: strengthen indigenous technology development and absorption capabilities; develop the human resource base needed for industrial development; provide an environment in which flexible adjustment of production structures in the face of changing demand conditions is possible; and facilitate access to information about, and the acquisition of, new technologies by domestic firms. A number of these issues have been discussed above and require no further elaboration here. The first two points, however, raise new issues requiring comment.

*Strengthening indigenous technology development and absorption capabilities*

This area is one where the state in many NIEs has been remiss in performing its responsibilities. There is an urgent need, for example, for bridging the wide gap separating government sector R&D from commercial applications. Except for a few first-tier NIEs, private sector firms are heavily reliant on state-sponsored R&D. Thus far, there has been very little of commercial use which has emerged from government laboratories. That must change if new technologies are to have an effect on industrial competitiveness. Of course, at the same time much more must be done to stimulate R&D activities within the industrial sector. Until individual enterprises grow large enough, however, to reap economies of scale in R&D, the government may have to serve as an R&D catalyst, identifying with the help of interested firms urgent R&D requirements, then mobilising both private and public sector resources in a collaborative R&D effort. For many NIEs R&D resources are still quite scarce, especially in terms of highly qualified scientists and technologists, so pooling of resources may be desirable, assuming they are employed effectively and managed properly. Excessive centralisation of R&D — either in government laboratories or in large firms — must be avoided. Decentralisation of R&D effort among smaller firms and research units, combined with some higher level co-ordination, would be most appropriate.

*Developing the human resource base needed for industrial development*

This is probably the most important function of the state related to long-run technological capabilities. Those countries which do not invest heavily in upgrading educational levels of the population as well as skill levels of workers will almost certain suffer a relative economic decline in the future. Great care needs to be given to human resource planning so that developing countries can anticipate potential skill bottlenecks and adjust educational and training programmes accordingly. While initially the priority may be numbers — increasing as rapidly as possible the numbers of people with higher level education and training in critical areas of science and engineering — before long greater attention must be paid to improving the quality of the "product" of the educational and training institutions. Some countries have placed high priority on upgrading quality. Singapore, for example, recruits worldwide for its faculty at the National University. It also has obtained UK accreditation for its training courses in computer programming and other technical subjects. Other countries may have longer university traditions, but they often face the problems alluded to with respect to government R&D institutions, namely, of being insulated to a degree from the needs of industrial enterprises. Thus forging closer links between industries and universities will also have beneficial effects. In the first place, it makes more effective use of the expertise within the universities to strengthen industrial technological capabilities. In addition, it reduces the risk that growth of industrial R&D will siphon off valuable intellectual resources from the universities.

**Countering "forced" de-coupling from the world economy: policy implications for the "other" developing countries**

The discussion thus far has focused almost exclusively on the policy concerns of the NIEs as they seek to sustain their industrialisation efforts. Yet an emergent policy issue of utmost urgency is how those developing countries which have barely begun to industrialise can avert the prospect of "forced" de-coupling from the world economy. Beyond the second-tier NIEs and perhaps certain third-tier countries, like Indonesia and Pakistan, there are scores of developing countries whose future growth prospects are clouded. Many of those countries lack the basic prerequisites to make effective use of the new technologies, even though those technologies hold great potential for strengthening their social and economic infrastructures. For most, foreign direct investment is not likely to be a major source of access to new technologies, since there are few attractions which would induce major investments outside the resource-extraction sector. Moreover, licensing is not a viable alternative since absorptive capabilities, both on the technical side and on the managerial side, remain extremely weak. Many such countries continue to rely heavily on official development assistance (ODA) as a major source of capital formation, but how effective ODA has been in developing human resources and strengthing skills that might be useful for applying new technologies is an area requiring further research[38]. Clearly, certain of the new agricultural technologies (bio-engineering) may be valuable in helping those countries alleviate the severe constraint on their industrial development posed by food scarcities. Still, technological "quick fixes" have not worked in the past and are not likely to work in the future. There are fundamental institutional and structural changes required in many of those countries for which new technologies are not likely to provide an adequate substitute. Only on the basis of such changes could it be possible to improve substantially the environment for generating effective demand for those technologies.

From the perspective of this study, the most relevant policy concern is how to create an international economic environment that, at the least, avoids the marginalisation of those countries or, more optimistically, progressively integrates them into a dynamic process of "trade-driven" growth. Rapid industrialisation may not be on the current agenda for most of these countries, but sustainable growth must be. Without a conducive external environment however — including high and stable prices for their primary commodities, greater capital inflows to help develop their physical infrastructure and their human resources, and greater technical co-operation with OECD countries but perhaps more importantly with the NIEs — it will be extremely difficult for those countries to undertake the necessary internal structural and policy reforms which will strengthen their prospects for joining the ranks of the newly industrialising economies.

## PERSPECTIVES FOR INTERNATIONAL TECHNOLOGY DIFFUSION

Are there any realistic options for re-establishing international transfer of technology as an instrument for promoting global economic security? And more specifically, is there sufficient scope for establishing viable forms of international technological co-operation which would include rather than exclude developing countries, and which would reap the mutual benefits of complementarity? Much depends on the future development of the international technology system. Will it become more closed and restrictive or will be barriers to entry for latecomers be reduced?

In what follows, we will discuss two alternative scenarios for the future development of the international technology system. We will conclude by presenting some issues for debate on perspectives for international technological co-operation.

The *pessimistic* scenario is one in which current trends towards a more restrictive system continue or even accelerate, and barriers to entry for latecomers become more severe. Its results will be devastating for global economic security. Yet, in the absence of major changes in our prevailing policy doctrine, it is quite plausible that it will become reality. Some would even argue that the die has already been cast, and that we are well on our way to an increasingly restrictive and balkanised international technology system. The *optimistic* scenario is one where the international technology system becomes more open and accessible to latecomers. While there are some factors at work which make the more optimistic scenario at least remotely possible, substantial modification of the OECD government policies and corporate strategies would be an essential prerequisite for such a scenario to materialise. From a long-term perspective, such changes would bring sizeable benefits both to OECD countries and to the NIEs. Nevertheless, policymakers and firms in the former may behave on the basis of shortsighted assessments of their interests, even at the expense of jeopardising those longer term gains.

In discussing each of the scenarios, we focus on the implications of the degree of openness of the technology system for three areas of economic interaction between OECD countries and the NIEs. These are:

*i)* The prospects for NIE manufactured exports;

*ii)* The prospects for the NIEs' import capacity; and

*iii)* The implications for cross-investment links and international technology diffusion.

Recent trends in OECD-NIE trade and investment flows have already been described above[39]. The discussion of future scenarios takes those as a point of departure.

## Scenario I: intensifying technological protectionism

### Key features

This scenario rests on two assumptions:

First, in industry after industry, we will witness a shift from US hegemony to a heterogenous and consequently highly unstable global oligopoly, with American, Japanese and European companies fighting to position themselves in the lead. Their relative strengths differ, of course, depending on the sector and the technology we are talking about.

The decline in US supremacy, both in manufacturing engineering and in product design, has been aptly documented in a series of reports recently commissioned by the US administration. One of them, a report prepared for the Pentagon and the National Science Foundation, and released in June 1988, had this to say: "... the United States no longer holds a world monopoly [in technology] as it once did. Moreover, it no longer even holds a position of broad dominance among key players poised at the frontier; indeed, technical leadership is now globally dispersed"[40].

This global oligopoly, however, is hardly a viable one. It has a built-in bias towards self-destruction, because none of the actors involved is in a position to shape the rules of competition. Furthermore, as world demand in a great majority of economic sectors is growing only slowly, if not declining, such intra-oligopolistic rivalries are bound to be zero-sum games. In such a situation, "mutual recognition" and gradual consolidation strategies are likely to give way to desperate *fuite-en-avant* strategies, leading to much more destructive forms of competition.

Second, we assume that at least some other actors, from the so-called ROW (rest of the world), in particular a few NIEs in Asia and Latin America, are finally able to enter this global oligopoly, at least in a few select industrial sectors and technology fields. In terms of industrial sectors, this would go well beyond clothing and toys and would include ship-building, steel, cars and components, consumer electronics (including VCRs), computer peripherals and (with some question marks) PCs, and semiconductor commodities (in particular D-RAMs) — to mention but a few in a long list of possible candidates.

In terms of technology, excellence in manufacturing engineering, as practiced for instance in South Korea and Taiwan, is certainly an area open to dedicated latecomer entry strategies. But even in such sophisticated areas as software engineering and circuit design, it cannot be excluded that some of these NIEs will accumulate sufficient technological capabilities, say within the next five years.

One could in fact argue that the relative success of latecomers to industrialisation is a reflection of the aforementioned intra-OECD rivalry and the concomitant destabilisation of existing global oligopolies. In a number of cases, growing intra-OECD rivalry may have improved considerably the scope for latecomer strategies. In principle, intensified competition among American, Japanese and European companies can drive down the cost of technology and of some of the capital equipment and final products which embody such technology. A case in point is the drastic long-term price decline for semiconductor commodities, in particular D-RAMs and simple micro-controllers and -processors which, depending on market structures and competitive pressures, can lead to equally drastic price falls in a number of electronic consumer devices and computer-based machinery. In the latter case, a vast potential for productivity gains would be opened up, at least for those countries that have sufficient resources (both in terms of finance and technological capabilities) to buy and absorb such technologies. To a certain degree, growing intra-OECD rivalry has also increased the diversification of the sources of international technology flows, thereby expanding considerably the options open to technology importers. In addition, latecomers can compare, and learn from, the experience of the leading oligopolists, particularly their failures, in reducing costs and adapting products and of the distribution system to buyer needs. Through judicious strategies of "creative imitation", latecomers can avoid being trapped into huge R&D cost burdens.[41] Finally, at least in areas where incremental technological change prevails, latecomers have the great advantage of being able to set clear targets for development and engineering activities.

Yet, we would argue that this is by no means the full story to be told. As a matter of fact, global oligopolies are not only intrinsically unstable and tend towards self-destruction, but they are also challenged from outside. In such a situation of extreme volatility and unpredictable risks, it is not at all clear to what degree latecomers can reap the potential benefits of increasing intra-OECD rivalries. It might be argued in fact that under conditions of "destructive" oligopolistic competition, all major actors involved in the global oligopoly will try to raise the barriers to entry by almost any means.

We have already described the impressive arsenal of policy instruments which governments in nearly all major OECD countries, and in some NIEs, have assembled so far, to implement an increasingly aggressive "high-tech neo-mercantilism". At the same time, corporate management in the United States, as much as in Japan and Western Europe, is experimenting with new strategies for sustaining technological leadership which would allow for strengthening of the "appropriability regime"[42] of new technologies and, at the same time, raising the threshold levels for their implementation. The following strategies should be mentioned in this context:

*i)* Internalising sources of technological change, that is, aggresive strategies of worldwide sourcing for technological building blocks, and increasingly also for applied and even fundamental research[43].

*ii)* Establishing absolute cost or differentiation advantages in technology development activities:

— Economies of scale and learning economies involved in R&D give large and experienced firms an absolute cost advantage;

— Due to the high fixed cost burden of R&D, the firm with the largest market share can realise the lowest unit costs of R&D;

— Particularly for the main building blocks of advanced electronics (that is, 32-bit microprocessors), investment thresholds for product development are dramatically increasing, which, for all practical purposes, precludes the entry of latecomers;

— Large and vertically integrated companies have a superior capacity to exploit technological interrelationships (cost-sharing of R&D through cross-subsidisation; transfer of skills from one activity to another; etc.); and, finally,

— Incremental product and process refinements are often much more scale-sensitive than basic innovations.

*iii)* Broadening the firm's skill basis, in particular through worldwide sourcing for human capital, whether through "brain drain" or through the relocation of at least some elements of the research/development/engineering chain to areas where skilled labour is available cheaply.

*iv)* Restricting the rate of technology diffusion, by means of aggressive strategies on intellectual property rights[44], and through a policy of "pervasive secrecy", treating all contacts with outsiders, even buyers, as a threat to proprietary know-how.

*v)* Increasing the threshold barriers to the implementation of new technologies. It has been argued for instance that threatened market and technology leaders may consider huge, very costly and highly centralised systems of factory automation as a convenient weapon to prevent new competitors from gaining a market share or even entering the market. Unable to shoulder such huge capital burdens and risks, less powerful companies are expected to rapidly lose market shares, to end up in small market niches, or to be driven out of the market altogether. While in its extreme form, like in GMs' "Saturn project"[45], such a strategy may hurt rather than strengthen the market leader, it can nevertheless drastically increase the barriers to entry for latecomers, particularly when it is applied in a more realistic manner[46].

Such strategies do not always meet with unalloyed success. Indeed, as suggested earlier, they often have contradictory results. Nevertheless, assuming that OECD firms and governments are capable of learning-by-doing, it can be expected that the international technology system will become less accessible to all but a privileged few NIE firms with sufficient muscle to stay in the bout. In fact, much of this has already become reality. This applies in particular to technology flows from the OECD region to developing countries, with the exception of a few NIEs in East and Southeast Asia and China. Since the early 1980s, the main indicators of the volume of international technology flows — foreign direct investment, capital goods imports, payments for licences and know-how, and official technical assistance — show an unprecedented shrinkage of technology flows to developing countries[47].

We thus would submit that one of the main issues to be addressed in future research at the OECD Development Centre should be the current drying up of technology diffusion to the overwhelming majority of developing countries, and the scope for countervailing policies which could further both the interests of OECD Member countries and of developing countries. In this context, a frank and open assessment of how different intellectual and industrial property regimes affect international technology diffusion and trade patterns would be of utmost importance[48].

*Implications for trade and investment links between the OECD region and NIEs*

If the international technology system become more restrictive, what will be the implications for trade and investment links between the OECD region and NIEs, and how will this affect international technology diffusion?

**Prospects for NIE manufactured exports:** The first and most obvious consequence would be an erosion of the competitiveness of NIE manufactured exports in OECD markets. Without continued access to new product and process technologies, NIE firms would not be able to keep abreast of rapid shifts to new generations of products, nor would they be able to upgrade their production capabilities to compete with the AMT being diffused in the OECD countries. To the extent that the growth of certain NIEs is driven by manufactured exports, their economies would slow down substantially and perhaps even stagnate. Nor would the more advanced NIEs be able to recover their competitive advantage in traditional labour intensive manufactures like shoes, garments, toys, etc., since there are already a number of

124

other less developed countries which have become highly competitive in these areas. Thus their export prospects would be far dimmer than in the past.

Anticipating such a scenario — which to an extent is already being played out — the NIEs have been trying to take countermeasures. Most importantly, they are more actively searching out all opportunities to gain access to the technologies they need. They have been forced to experiment with new forms of technology co-operation. A "window of opportunity" opened, for example, to South Korean *chaebol* a few years ago when they were able to trade low cost manufacturing capacity and quick plant start-up capabilities in semiconductors for design expertise of US semiconductor firms searching for ways to staunch the flow of Japanese chips into the US market. As the South Korean firms have become more sophisticated technologically, however, their erstwhile US partners are beginning to view them as a competitive threat, and are more reluctant to transfer their advanced technologies[49].

The NIEs are also working hard at diversifying their export markets, to lessen their dependence on the US market where a rising tide of non-tariff restrictions is making market access more difficult. In this scenario, such restrictions become more extensive in the future. In addition, the European Community after 1992 is likely to become much more highly protected from manufactured imports from the NIEs, with the exception of a few countries in the European periphery with close links to one or another European economy (something like Mexico's relationship to the United States). Large European technology-based oligopolists will continue to forge closer co-operative links in R&D, but to the exclusion of non-EC firms. Thus the European market does not offer much promise of compensating, even in small measure, for the reduction in US market penetration.

Third, we assume that the Japanese market will continue to open up under pressure of intensifying trade conflicts with the United States and the EC. In this scenario, however, the process is painfully slow and highly selective. In short, the Japanese government, faced with the prospect of growing domestic opposition to drastic liberalisation, might seek to manage it in such a way that trade concessions are made bilaterally with Japan's major trading partners — the United States and the EC — in exchange for continued market access. At the same time, the NIEs — which for Japan are a less strategic market at present — would bear the brunt of efforts by Japan to restrict liberalisation to levels that are politically acceptable to powerful interest groups[50]. Thus NIE exports would have only limited access to the Japanese market, and then only for less sophisticated products.

With no OECD market able to compensate adequately, then, for declining export growth to the United States, the NIEs would have to look toward developing country markets, but increased OECD protectionism is certain to slow the growth of the developing world and thus impair import capacities.

*Prospects for NIE import capacity:* The debt-induced crises of many Latin American NIEs since the beginning of the 1980s have dramatically demonstrated the impact of impaired NIE import capacity on US export performance. If the import capacity of other NIEs is similarly impaired by a steep decline in their export growth, there would be severe repercussions for the export performance especially of the capital and intermediate goods industries of OECD countries. For example, almost two-thirds of Japan's textile machinery exports are to other Asian countries, with South Korea, Taiwan, and China being the three largest markets[51]. A major decline in their textile industries would adversely affect not only Japanese but also Swiss, German, Italian and other textile machinery producers. Similarly, certain NIEs have become major markets for electronics industry-related production equipment, the bulk of which is still made by OECD firms. A serious retrenchment in South

Korea's semiconductor industry would have a strong negative impact on US and Japanese semiconductor equipment manufacturers. Likewise, the stagnation of the South Korean or Mexican or other NIE automobile industries would hurt Swedish, German, Japanese, United States, and other sophisticated machine tool manufacturers.

Beyond the reduction of the financial capacity of NIE firms to sustain imports of capital goods from OECD firms, their technological capacity would also be jeopardised in this scenario. Effective demand for sophisticated capital goods will only materialise if the NIEs have continued access to the technologies for producing goods they could sell profitably. In other words, if they cannot acquire the product technology for sophisticated products, whose production requires sophisticated capital equipment, they are not going to invest in that equipment. An example would be advanced computer memory ICs: if South Korean firms are deprived of access to the design and process know-how to make chips with the finest geometries, they will create no demand for the latest generation semiconductor processing equipment on the market.

*Implications for cross-investment links and technology diffusion:* This scenario involves a worsening of the environment for collaboration of all kinds between OECD and NIE firms. An atmosphere of hostility and suspicion toward the NIEs prevails in the OECD region. OECD firms become more guarded in their contacts with NIE firms, which they perceive primarily as potential competitors[52]. To the extent that OECD firms continue to invest in the NIEs, they insist, wherever possible, on 100 per cent ownership as a way of safeguarding proprietary technology. Appointing expatriates to key technical posts also becomes a major concern. Licensing agreements are linked to rather "peripheral" or mature technologies. Under such conditions, collaboration with NIE firms is aimed principally at securing low cost manufacturing capacity or at gaining access to a potentially large NIE market. Technology flows are minimised by every available means. In addition, governments of OECD member countries would also escalate bilateral pressures on major NIE exporters to tighten their protection of intellectual property.

Because in such a scenario NIE technology development would be stunted by the restrictive practices of OECD firms and governments, NIE firms would not have much scope for developing complementary assets which could make them attractive partners for OECD companies. In this restrictive scenario, technology exports from NIE firms to OECD firms, by definition, would remain insignificant. NIE firms seeking to gain access to those technologies by investing in OECD countries, would face drastically tighter restrictions[53] on their ability to acquire equity stakes in high technology firms.

The repeated frustration of NIE firms' efforts to gain access to foreign technologies would make them more isolationist in their technology policies, with more countries finding the traditional path of "self-reliance" pursued by India and China the "lesser of two evils". As a result, the prospects for OECD firms to export capital goods and in general to have access to NIE markets would become increasingly dim.

### Scenario II: barriers to international technology diffusion decline

This alternative (more optimistic) scenario is much less likely to materialise than the previous one, although it would certainly have much more positive implications for global economic security. Major changes are required, both in government policies and in company strategies, and this applies to all actors involved in the international economy. As a matter of fact, in nearly all major OECD countries the proliferation of high-tech neo-mercantilism has gathered such momentum that it will be very difficult to reverse. Important and often quite far-reaching changes have taken place in the industrial and trade policy doctrine, as in the relevant institutional set-up. Examples include the considerable softening of anti-cartel policies, both in the United States and Western Europe[54], and institutional innovations such as Sematech, the HDTV consortium, ESPRIT and EUREKA which, on a so far unprecedented scale, allow firms and governments to merge their increasingly aggressive competitive strategies[55]. Nevertheless, there are at least some chances that a break will occur in the current trend towards increasing barriers to international technology diffusion, which in turn could open up new possibilities for industrial co-operation between OECD Member countries and NIEs.

Two main assumptions underly this scenario:

  i) Fundamental shifts in the international demand structure, particularly for manufactured exports, will open up new possibilities for redirecting not only international trade flows, but also international investment and technology flows. In particular, we assume that Japan's role in compensating for a decline of US demand for manufactured exports will materialise earlier and on a larger scale than foreseen in our first scenario.

  ii) It is possible to imagine that states and firms would come to realise in time that current trends towards an increasingly restrictive international technology system, if allowed to continue, would have damaging (even disastrous) consequences for all concerned. As a result, the policy debate would shift from an exclusive concern with the "NIEs competitive threat" to a more balanced view, where competition would not necessarily exclude co-operation with NIEs. Under such circumstances, it might not be impossible any longer to see the emergence of broader and increasingly complementary forms of technological co-operation between OECD member countries and NIEs.

Our second scenario must be distinguished sharply from the neo-liberal dream of a free market world economy. The *invisible hand* of market forces will certainly not produce the fundamental changes required for reducing barriers to international technology diffusion. Rather, for our scenario to materialise, we need the *visible hand* of substantially modified company strategies and government policies.

We also do not intend to promote unrealistic expectations: a restructuring of the world trading and technology system in a way which would substantially redistribute power away from the technology-based oligopolists is unlikely to materialise any time soon. The scenario suggested here is unlikely to reduce substantially the huge gap in wealth and economic power between the OECD region and even the most successful NIEs. Rather, it is an attempt to identify the limits of the possible, given the severe constraints imposed by global competition. What we would like to underline in particular is that in some instances the leading oligopolists themselves may be in the best position to anticipate and benefit from movements in new directions which would reduce the barriers to international technology diffusion. At the same time, it would be a serious mistake to ascribe omnipotence to the IBMs, NECs and Philips of this world and other "high tech" potentates. Not only do they leave quite considerable markets uncovered, but even those they do cover they do not always cover well. Moreover, even they need a network of suppliers and subcontractors to maintain their pre-eminence in the main growth markets of the future[56].

In what follows, we will present some hypotheses on how the international demand structure for manufactured exports could change and what this could imply for international technology diffusion.

So far, the United States has been, by far, the main market for manufactured exports, and this applies in particular to those originating from developing countries. Between 1981 and 1984, US imports of manufactured goods from developing countries more than doubled, from $34 billion to $70 billion, while Japanese imports rose by only $2 billion and European imports actually declined. And in 1985, 62 per cent of the developing countries' exports of manufactured products to OECD countries went to the United States[57]. "... During the first half of the 1980s, when demand declined and then stagnated in the other developed countries, the US became the buyer of last resort and was a major impetus to growth for the developing countries"[58], that is, basically for the first-tier Asian NIEs.

In the future, the importance of the US economy for manufactured exports is bound to decline. This is a simple reflection of three fundamental structural imbalances which have accumulated in the US economy since the late 1970s: a record debt (more than $400 billion by the end of 1987); a booming US trade deficit (more than $140 billion by the end of 1987); and, finally, a towering US federal budget deficit (more than $150 billion at the end of fiscal year 1987)[59]. As a result of such major imbalances, drastic changes are bound to occur in the integration of the US economy to world markets. Given the limitations to an expansion of US exports, whether manufactured or services[60], most of this adjustment has to come from a drastic reduction of US imports, whether recession-induced or via selective import substitution, as part of a deliberate industrial policy. In other words, the heavy concentration of world industrial exports on the US economy has become an anachronism which cannot be sustained for long.

Consider the following basic facts:

i) Currently, the US absorbs about 70 per cent of the manufacturing exports of the developing world, while Japan absorbs only about 8 per cent[61]. With an economy roughly two-thirds to three-quarters as large as the American economy, that is obviously a situation that must change. On the one hand, any US administration must lower the balance of payments deficit, and thus will try to reduce import penetration[62]. On the other hand, Japan is coming under increasing pressure from practically everybody else, to internationalise its economy, that is, to open it to imports and foreign investment[63].

ii) Japan's extremely biased integration into world trade flows of industrial products is unlikely to continue. Today, Japan's dominant position in world industrial exports goes hand in hand with its low profile as an importer of manufactured products. In the early 1980s, Japan's imports of manufactured goods were about the same as those of Switzerland, a country with about 5 per cent of Japan's population. Of all major OECD countries, Japan is the only country where large exports in key industrial sectors are not matched by large imports. In fact, whenever Japan had a strong export industry, imports in that industry were likely to be close to zero. Finally, between 1975 and 1983, while the average import-penetration ratio for manufactured goods rose from 7 per cent to 10.3 per cent in the United States, and from 24 per cent to 35 per cent in Germany, and also in France and Italy, in Japan it only rose from 4.9 to 5.3 per cent[64].

In the future, however, imports of manufactured goods are likely to increase substantially in Japan. One reason is the yen appreciation which has acted as a catalyst for Japanese firms to drastically expand their global sourcing strategies[65]. Historical experience tells us that global sourcing strategies are bound to lead to growing import penetration, because they increase intra-industry trade. This may also induce Japanese companies to reconsider their so far highly restrictive policies on technology transfer[66].

Of even greater importance, however, is that intensifying international trade conflicts will force the Japanese government, willy-nilly, to proceed with market liberalisation in a growing number of industrial sectors. And while the US administration makes the most noise, exporters from Asian first- and second-tier NIEs, and from some European countries, may well draw the greatest benefits from such market liberalisation. Between 1983 and 1988, for example, Japan's manufactured imports from the first-tier NIEs (South Korea, Taiwan, Hong Kong and Singapore) increased from 14 to 19 per cent of total manufactured imports[67].

In short, the Japanese economy will become more internationalised, and its importance as a market for world industrial exports will increase quite substantially. Among the first to realise this and to adopt successful market penetration strategies, have been South Korean and Taiwanese companies, particularly in the field of consumer devices[68].

However, it is difficult to see how Japan, even under the best of circumstances, could ever compensate Asian NIEs for their declining share of the US market which is "... simply too large to be replaced by any single country"[69]. This becomes clear when we compare the absolute figures involved. In 1985, the US market for NIEs' manufactured exports was nearly ten times larger than that of Japan, $52.3 billion versus $5.8 billion[70]. And in 1987, Japan's imports from the Asian NIEs were only about one-third of US imports from those countries[71]. In short, while Japan's market is likely to become more accessible to manufactured exports from NIEs, this will be a relatively slow process.

iii) Markets in NIEs are bound to become more important for world industrial exports. This applies in particular to exports of capital goods and of related services, where a huge demand potential exists not only in the quasi-continental economies of China, India and Brazil, but also in a number of first- and second-tier NIEs in Asia and Latin America. While in Asia, particularly in the first-tier NIEs, this potential is already being translated into concrete projects, in Latin America the current debt crisis is a major barrier.

In order to illustrate this point, let us focus on demand projections for first-tier Asian NIEs in one of the archetypical high-technology industries: semiconductors. Particularly for "hot growth" products like cMOS integrated circuits and microwave transistors, a massive shift of demand is under way from the US to Japan, and increasingly also to South Korea, Taiwan and Singapore. In 1985, the Japanese market share for these two crucial product groups was 46 and 37 per cent respectively, and thus had overtaken a combined US/Canadian share of 32 and 27 per cent. There are strong indications that this is a long-term, irreversible trend. In other words, the US market, which used to be the Mecca of worldwide semiconductor demand, is unlikely to retain much longer such a privileged position.

In 1986, in fact, overall demand for semiconductors in Japan was $10.5 billion, well above the demand level recorded for the United States ($8.5 billion). By way of comparison, Europe's demand during the same year was $5.3 billion, corresponding roughly to one-fifth of the world market for semiconductors. Of particular interest in this context are recent projections by the Semiconductor Industry Association (SIA) that till 1990 the market volume in South Korea, Taiwan and Singapore will more than double from about $2 billion to $5.4 billion, where it is assumed that this growth, at a constant level of the yen, will be fully to the detriment of Japan[72].

*iv)* A particularly interesting development takes place in the CMEA region, where new possibilities for technology co-operation with NIEs could materialise. Take for instance the Soviet Union. In order to proceed with its current "modernisation drive", this country will have to increase drastically its international trade and technology imports.

Given the still quite rigid position of the US administration on technology export controls, European, Japanese and some NIEs are likely to play an increasingly important role in this context. To quote again the June 1988 study, commissioned by the Pentagon: "Significant market opportunities in the Eastern bloc will thus develop, with the Europeans, the Japanese, and South Koreans expanding the scope of their linkages already in place. (Their) economic ties (with CMEA countries) will thus accelerate far ahead of the Americans, and as the military threat lessens for the Europeans, US efforts to restrict trade, in concert with COCOM partners, will face greater resistance"[73].

Together with Asian NIEs, China, and India, markets in CMEA countries, and in particular the Soviet Union, will thus significantly increase their importance as future high growth markets.

In this context, we would like to underline the following important fact: both for CMEA countries and for China, trade requirements revolve primarily around low and moderately R&D-intensive products[74]. Apart from the already predominant countries from the EC (in particular the FRG), this opens up new and quite substantial export possibilities for NIEs. Take the example of 8-bit PCs. As their export to the CMEA has been prohibited for COCOM member countries till the end of July 1988, this has created new export possibilities for countries such as South Korea, India, Cuba, China, and even Peru. No doubt similar exports can be realised in the future, even for more sophisticated generations of data processing equipment.

Finally, two major questions are hanging over this possible geographic decentralisation of demand for manufactured exports:

*i)* What will be the implications resulting from the establishment of a Common European Market in 1992? Will this increase the attractiveness of Europe as an export market and as a partner for technology co-operation, or rather, will it lead to a selective isolation of Europe from the world economy, and add further to the already quite strong tends towards regional economic power blocs with a minimum of mutual interconnection?

*ii)* Will it be possible to overcome the deep and fundamental crisis of the international financial system? After all, international technology co-operation is simply not feasible in the context of global financial turmoil and crisis.

Particularly for Latin American NIEs, the spiralling debt crisis, combined with the growing instability of international financial markets, has drastically reduced their capacity to import capital goods.

*From international transfer of technology to complementary technological co-operation*

Our second assumption takes as a starting point some of the more creative efforts at technical collaboration between OECD firms and NIE firms. It also encompasses more extensive and richer technical collaboration among NIE firms themselves. Of course, we are also referring to the ongoing development of technology exchanges between the large South Korean *chaebol* and large-scale enterprises in other NIEs and their counterparts in OECD countries[75]. The mutual benefits from such exchanges increase over time, as the NIE firms become more adept at product and process innovation and thus have something more to offer than efficient manufacturing capacity or cash reserves. The relationships become more durable and even evolve to the point where technology development is a joint product of two or more firms. These cross-technology links also serve as avenues for assuring mutual market access.

Such co-operation need not — and ideally should not — be limited to links between the leading oligopolists in the OECD and the NIEs. One important source of technology for NIE firms in the past has been the highly dynamic start-up firms of Silicon Valley and their equivalents elsewhere. By taking small equity shares in, or buying technology, from such firms, the NIE firms could remain close to state-of-the-art[76]. Such opportunities may be disappearing soon, as this sort of firm becomes a candidate for the "endangered species" register. In some cases large NIE firms have taken over such firms to internalise their know-how. Far more frequently, OECD oligopolists have been the predators. Many have come to recognise that in their eagerness to internalise knowledge, they may be "killing the goose that lays the golden egg". In our optimistic scenario, effective policy measures as well as changes in firms' strategies would ensure the renewed vigour of the archetypal "born-in-a-garage" firm. Policy changes would be needed not just in certain OECD countries themselves, but also in many NIEs to inject more dynamism into the entrepreneurial small and medium firm sector. One development which might help to strengthen such small- and medium-scale firms financially, both in the OECD and in the NIEs, would be the formation of networks of such firms in different countries that may then be able to interface with comparable networks elsewhere. For example, trade associations of machine tool builders in an OECD country and an NIE may establish communication channels which would facilitate technical collaboration between members of the two associations. Some such links already exist[77].

The possibilities for establishing others are limitless. In some cases the interface between two networks could be mediated by "model" firms in each country that have themselves established broad-ranging technical collaboration. For example, a South Korean *chaebol* and a German conglomerate enter into a technical co-operation agreement which involves the mutual interaction of the two firms' subcontractor networks in the design and development of common parts and components, subsystems, etc.

Similar sorts of collaboration could be envisioned between different NIE firms. The technical co-operation accord between Argentina and Brazil covering a range of industries and technologies, while still at an early stage of implementation, at least suggests the possibilities that may exist[78].

Regional integration is also advancing in Southeast Asia, with growing intra-regional, intrafirm trade organised by large Japanese conglomerates and their supplier networks. Again the evidence does not yet exist to be able to assess what the implications of this development will be for the economies of the region and, more especially, for their technological capabilities. If such regional integration is to be fruitful, it needs to be accompanied by a greater opening of the NIEs towards trade with their neighbours and, in the case of the Asian region, a much more dramatic opening of the Japanese market to the exports of its NIE neighbours.

*Prospects for manufactured trade flows:* Our optimistic scenario would allow much greater scope for continued expansion of NIE exports of a variety of manufactures. By allowing the more advanced NIEs to scale down their production of certain more labour-intensive products without major social dislocations, it would also make it easier for other developing countries to step into the breach left by the first-tier NIEs. As a consequence, significant shifts in the composition of international trade flows would be likely.

First, complementarity of technologies and production structures between the more advanced NIEs and the OECD countries should increase. In other words, both may have advanced machine tool sectors, but they would produce complementary elements of a product set. Certain models might, for reasons of accumulated experience (skill availabilities, relative costs, etc.), be more suitably produced in one location, other models in another. Traditional "factor endowment" explanations of such patterns of specialisation would be of extremely limited usefulness.

Secondly, if this complementarity of production structures were to evolve, then intra-industry trade flows between the NIEs and the OECD countries would grow in importance relative to inter-industry trade[79]. Trade would tend toward greater balance, as manufactured exports from OECD to the NIEs would grow simultaneously with exports in the other direction.

Thirdly, capital goods producers in the OECD countries would experience robust demand in the NIEs as the latter invest in upgrading production. Links between the capital goods suppliers of the NIEs and the OECD would enable each of them to serve the other's market better since user/producer links are especially crucial in this sector.

*Prospects for cross-investment and technology diffusion:* Both investment and technology would have to flow increasingly in two directions. The same "creative tension" between collaboration and competition which characterises relations among the OECD firms[80] would come to characterise relations between OECD firms and their NIE counterparts. One would expect to observe a growing number of instances of OECD firms setting up R&D and design facilities in certain NIEs and vice versa. Cross-licensing agreements between OECD firms and NIE firms would proliferate as firms pooled technologies, production capabilities, and markets.

Those NIE firms which are not yet in a position to become technology suppliers, would at least be able to gain access to technologies on more favourable terms than under the pessimistic scenario. A growing number of NIE firms would become technology licensors in competition with OECD firms, giving buyers a broader range of options on more attractive terms. Increasing foreign investment flows from the more advanced NIEs into other developing countries would also broaden the foreign capital base. Yet whether technology diffusion via FDI by NIE firms is more effective than that occurring via FDI by OECD firms, cannot be known without more empirical evidence.

Other developing countries may be integrated more extensively into regional investment flows as the NIEs broaden their subcontracting networks and make more labour intensive components and sub-assemblies in lower cost regional locations. The OECD firms with investment ties and technology exchanges with NIE firms would also make use of those supplier networks, while the NIE firms presumably would utilise them within or on the perimeter of the OECD markets, for example, in Spain or Portugal for the EC market, in Mexico or Canada for the US, in Southeast Asia for Japan.

## ESTABLISHING VIABLE FORMS OF INDUSTRIAL CO-OPERATION BETWEEN OECD COUNTRIES AND NIEs: CONCLUDING REMARKS

How can viable forms of international technological co-operation be established, which would not be restricted to countries from the OECD and the CMEA, but would increasingly include NIEs and other, less-developed Third World societies?

Obviously, established concepts of technological co-operation require some careful reconsideration. OECD countries still tend to subsume such arrangements under the heading of technical aid, where the non-OECD country remains a mere receiver. Yet, at least for NIEs, such concepts have become quite obsolete. The challenge today in fact is to ensure a transition toward a more complementary relationship, where both partners would bring in their respective strengths, and which would open up new possibilities for expanding mutual flows of trade, investment and technology.

The case of the electronics industry shows that this is not any longer wishful thinking. In fact, South Korean electronics firms today are involved in a network of co-operation agreements with some of their major American and Japanese competitors, which range from straightforward subcontracting arrangements, to "silicon foundry services", and even to joint technology development projects[81]. The underlying rationale is a straightforward one: South Korean manufacturing prowess and speed-of-delivery versus product design and market access. Similar arrangements would seem to be plausible in other industries as well.

North-South technological co-operation which does not allow for more complementary relationships would hardly be of interest to NIEs. Viewed from an OECD country perspective, insisting on traditional concepts of "technical aid" would in fact be quite harmful; it would preclude reaping the benefits of increasing intra-industry trade and investment flows, and it would force member countries into increasingly tough rounds of mutually harmful neo-mercantilism. It is in the long-term interest of OECD countries to generate sufficient demand for new technologies and related capital goods in as many developing countries as possible. Strengthening the technological capabilities of developing countries should not be viewed as running counter to the interests of OECD countries. It could be an important mechanism for arresting the recessionary demand conditions that are likely to confront most of the OECD region's high tech industries in the years to come. As a matter of fact, the growth of the major OECD economies increasingly depends on the growth of world demand for the output of their high tech industries and related services[82]. Promoting the international diffusion of new technologies should and can be done without endangering the competitive position of OECD economies. According to a recent study, commissioned by the Overseas Development Council[83] "...the acceleration of technological development in the Third World will not undermine the US competitive position, because science-based development is a cumulative process in which the innovative capacity of US institutions and corporations will continue to support a technological edge, provided industrial growth keeps pace with scientific discovery". This, in turn, depends on whether or not demand growth is sufficiently large for US industrial exports which, it is argued, would not be possible without growing Third World markets. "Thus, the more rapid the adoption and diffusion of new microelectronics technologies in the world economy, the stronger the relative competitive position of the US is likely to be." Hopefully, such far-sighted concepts will gain in importance in future debates about industrial adjustment requirements of OECD member countries.

# NOTES AND REFERENCES

1. D. Ernst, interviews in the South Korean electronics industry, May, June and September 1988.
2. Castells and Tyson, 1988, p. 56.
3. See Chapters I and IV.
4. Strange, 1985.
5. Technologies which have been developed for "civilian" purposes but which are claimed to have considerable potential for military applications.
6. See Chapter VI, "A Research Agenda".
7. Economies of scope exist when for two or more products the cost of producing them jointly is lower than the cost of producing each separately. See W.J. Baumol, J.C. Panzer and R.D. Willig (1982) for a more rigorous, formal definition. In general, economies of scope are associated with the existence of multi-product firms.
8. An example would be microprocessors and peripheral chips, where peripheral chips are often substantially over-priced.
9. Amsden (1983).
10. For a discussion of the limitations involved in the Hyundai-Texas Instruments linkup see A.M. Hayashi, "Hyundai's Headache", *Electronic Business,* cover story, 6th February 1989.
11. See Chapter VI, "A Research Agenda".
12. *Ibid.*
13. See report on the legal protection of software and of circuit design, prepared for the OECD Development Centre's project "Technological Change and the Electronics Sector...".
14. See Chapter VI, "A Research Agenda".
15. The steel industry in Mexico is one example. Heavy industries in many NIEs have large state participation.
16. For example, South Korea's knitwear and shoe industries have been put under severe competitive pressure by the won appreciation as well as rising labour costs.
17. Villarreal, René P., 1988, "La reconversion en la siderurgia paraestatal en Mexico", *Comercio Exterior,* 33(3), pp.191-209.
18. The venture of Hyundai, a firm with a tradition in mechanical heavy and civil engineering, into D-RAMs and other advanced semiconductors without any prior experience in electronics is a case in point. See A.M. Hayashi, *op. cit.,* 1989.
19. See the section on "Basic Commonalities" (Chapter III).
20. Core components are those whose timely access is critical to the design and development of competitive new products. For example, Japanese computer firms which have access to new D-RAMs well before any competitors because of the virtual Japanese monopoly of this business may be at an advantage in designing the latest memory chips into new generations of computers. Peripheral components, by contrast, would be those where proprietary or advanced designs are not as critical to the competitive position of users (e.g. simple standard ICs, passive components, etc.)
21. See Chapter VI, "A Research Agenda".

22. For a price comparison of South Korean and Taiwanese IBM PC-XT compatible machines see report on the Taiwanese electronics industry prepared for the OECD Development Centre's project "Technological Change and the Electronics Sector...".

23. See report on South Korean electronics Industry prepared for the OECD Development Centre's project on "Technological Change and the Electronics Sector".

24. On the other hand, forging alliances with foreign firms or networks of such firms in key markets is one option which small- and medium-scale firms could explore to minimise this constraint.

25. The 32-bit engineering workstation market is a case in point. Of course, depending on the particular market segment, some users may be more sophisticated than those in the US market (e.g. the UK and Japan for consumer electronics; Sweden, Germany and Italy for robots; France for avionics).

26. For example, the major South Korean consumer electronics manufacturers — Goldstar and Samsung — have had to establish colour television plants in the United States to ensure continued access to the market.

27. See Chapter VI, "A Research Agenda".

28. See Amsden (1986).

29. For details see UNCTC 1988.

30. Of course, in Latin America the debt crisis of recent years has seen a reverse flow, where foreign firms are repatriating more capital than they are investing.

31. See Imai 1988 and Wakasugi 1988; for a more sceptical assessment see Park 1989.

32. See Chapter VI, "A Research Agenda".

33. Prime cases for study would be IBM and perhaps the foreign telecommunications firms.

34. See UNCTD (1988), pp. 276-79, for a discussion of policies regarding FDI in China.

35. For a discussion of India's new policy on FDI in high technology fields, see *Electronic Business,* 23rd January 1989, pp. 68-99.

36. Hirschman, 1986.

37. In the case of the steel industry, a major Japanese firm supplied technology for a cold rolling mill which never became operational due to unmangeable technical problems (see A. Bowie 1988).

38. See Chapter VI, "A Research Agenda".

39. See Chapters I, III and IV.

40. Haklisch and Vonortas, June 1988, p. 224.

41. In the case of incremental technological change, basic design features are well established, well understood and unlikely to change. In addition, basic features of the production process (material requirements and specifications) are well understood, and it is possible to extrapolate their future development on the basis of current trends. Such predictability however does not apply to demand growth and patterns of market segmentation.

42. Teece, 1986, p. 5.

43. For evidence see *OECD Science and Technology Policy Outlook 1988,* in particular Chapter V. For the underlying theoretical debate, see Chesnais, 1988.

44. US software firms, co-operating with the United States' government, apply tremendous pressure on South Korea to enforce more strictly its new software copyright protection legislation. Similar pressure is also applied to Brazil. See report prepared on the legal protection of software and circuit design, prepared for the OECD Development Centre's project on "Technological Change and the Electronics Sector...".

45. For details, see Jones, 1988.

46. For an analysis of the issues confronting such a strategy in the semiconductor industry, see Ernst, 1987.

47. UNCTAD, 1987, Part Two, Chapter II, "Trends in the International Flow of Technology".

48. See Chapter VI, "A Research Agenda".

49. D. Ernst, interview at Hyundai Electronics, June 1988.

50. See for instance, recent dumping charges raised by MITI against South Korean knitwear exports to Japan.

51. S. Itaya, "The outlook for industrial growth in the Asian NIEs, Thailand and Japan", Chapter 1 of " A Case Study of Japan's Textiles and Electronics Industries", submitted to OECD Development Centre, February 1989.

52. See the current obsession with the so-called "boomerang" effect.

53. Indicative for this more restrictive approach to FDI is the United States government's blocking of Fujitsu's takeover bid for Fairchild Semiconductor.

54. On the United States, see Mowery and Rosenberg, 1989; for Europe, see "European High Technology", *Financial Times Survey*, 22nd March 1989.

55. On Sematech (Semiconductor Manufacturing Technology Research Consortium) and the HDTV (high definition television) consortium, see report on "Industrial and Trade Policies in Advanced Electronics — What Lessons can be Drawn from the US Experience?", prepared for the OECD Development Centre's project on "Technological Change and the Electronics Sector." ESPRIT and EUREKA are covered in a similar report for the OECD Development Centre on the European experience.

56. For details, see Ernst, 1989 (forthcoming).

57. Thurow and Tyson, 1987.

58. Castells and Tyson, 1988, p. 82.

59. For details see: Office of Technology Assessment, "Paying the Bill. Manufacturing and America's Trade Deficit", Congress of the United States, Washington, DC, June 1988.

60. "The US must increase exports or decrease imports not by ten or twenty or even fifty billion of dollars, but by hundreds of billion of dollars" (Borrus, 1988, p. 1). In the context of worldwide demand stagnation and increasingly closed markets, there is simply not enough demand available for such a massive expansion of US exports.

61. Henry Nau — Introduction to Nau (ed.), 1989.

62. See the concluding chapter in OTA June 1988, entitled "Climbing out: how to reduce the trade deficit?".

63. See Prestowitz, 1988, Higashi and Lauter, 1987, and Pugel and Hawkins (eds.), 1986.

64. Balassa, 1986, p. 11.

65. The Bank of Japan, 1988, and Imai, 1988.

66. Imai, 1988 and Wakasugi, 1988. For a more sceptical assessment see Park, 1989.

67. Park, 1989.

68. See case studies on the South Korean and Taiwanese electronics industries, prepared for the OECD Development Centre's project on "Technological Change and the Electronics Sector ...".

69. Park, 1989, p. 28.

70. OECD, 1988 a, p. 21. This report's definition of NIEs includes South Korea, Taiwan, Singapore, Hong Kong, Mexico and Brazil.

71. Bank of Japan, 1988, chart 12 "Import/Exports of Asian NIEs to US and Japan, p. 40.

72. D. Ernst, interviews in the US electronics industry, May 1988.

73. Haklisch and Vonortas, June 1988, p. 81.

74. Wienert and Slater, OECD, 1986, Chapter 5.

75. See country case studies on the South Korean and Taiwanese electronics industries, prepared for the OECD Development Centre's project "Technological Change and the Electronics Sector...".

76. See for instance the link-up between Daewoo Telecom and Zymos, one of the early US pioneers in the ASIC market which has recently run into cash-flow problems.

77. For an example see D. Ernst, "Technological Cooperation between German and South Korean Industrial Firms — Possibilities, Constraints and Future Perspectives. Report to the South Korean-German Commission", Seoul, November 1987.

78. Chudnovsky 1988.

79. Such an increase in intra-industry trade links between OECD countries and NIEs would in fact be in line with earlier trends emerging since the mid-1970s, which, however, are endangered today due to the proliferation of neo-mercantilism. See Chapter III.

80. D. Ernst 1987, Chapter 2, "Strategic Alliances and Global Competition — Driving Forces".

81. D. Ernst, interviews in the South Korean electronics industry, May, June and November 1988.

82. D. Ernst, 1989 (forthcoming).

83. Castells and Tyson, 1988. The following quotations are from page 91.

*Chapter VI*

# A RESEARCH AGENDA

It is no easy task to assess how new technologies, and in particular new information technologies, are likely to affect the relative advantages and disadvantages of latecomers in different sectors of industrial manufacturing. It is even more difficult to devise appropriate strategies. There are many uncertainties still associated with the worldwide diffusion of the new techno-economic paradigm, and its interaction with emerging patterns of global competition. We know even less about the chances of different groupings of developing countries to gain access to, to absorb, and to develop further some of these new technologies. Finally, we are still on very unsafe ground when it comes to projecting the implications of new technologies for international trade and investment patterns.

Further research could clarify some of these issues and suggest policy directions in both OECD member and non-member countries alike to deal with them in an anticipatory manner. We have identified in our study a number of important gaps in our understanding of how new technologies are likely to affect the industrialisation prospects of NIEs. Using the analytical framework of structural competitiveness, we have developed a set of fairly concrete research hypotheses relating to the nature of demand for new technologies, to the structure of production and the crucial concept of linkages, the sources of technology generation and the barriers to technology diffusion, the acquisition and absorption of foreign technologies, and, finally, the role of the state in fostering industrial and technological development. Within this framework we were able to describe in some detail the great diversity of growth patterns and industrialisation strategies, and the constraints and strategic options confronting different groupings of NIEs. Finally, on that basis, our study has developed a detailed policy agenda for NIEs, again differentiated according to our country classification, which would allow these countries to exploit the potential benefits of new technologies and thus to strengthen their development possibilities. We were able to show that, under certain conditions, a number of possibilities do exist for broadening the basis for industrial transformation and that production and marketing systems built around new generations of technology in this context can play a crucial role.

## SUGGESTIONS FOR FUTURE RESEARCH

Our choice of the following research topics has been guided by two criteria: their policy relevance and the specific advantages of the OECD Development Centre. As for the policy relevance, we will refer to our arguments developed in previous chapters, in particular,

Chapters IV and V, and will not repeat them here[1]. Suffice it to say here that out of our discussion of emerging policy issues, we have chosen those where we felt that lack of empirical research has been particularly harmful in constraining appropriate policy formulation.

As a research institute linked to the OECD, the Development Centre is well placed to analyse changing patterns of interaction between OECD Member and non-member, in particular developing, countries and their implications for international trade patterns and structural adjustment. Second, the Development Centre could provide up-to-date information on the global restructuring of key sectors of world industry which condition to a very large degree, the scope for latecomer industrialisation in developing countries.

Lastly, but of at least equal importance, the Development Centre could act as a forum where different national experiences could be compared in the field of industrial and trade policymaking, thus acting as a catalyst for learning from each other's successes and failures. Such comparative assessments could not be constrained to developing countries, but could include experiences in OECD Member countries.

In our view, three research topics deserve priority attention in the context of the Development Centre's future work on "New Technologies, Industry and Trade"[2]:

*i)* How do regionalisation and global competition interact, and what does this imply for international trade flows and technology diffusion? And how will these basic transformations of the international economy affect the growth prospects and world market integration of different groupings of developing countries and their trade and investment links with OECD Member countries?

*ii)* To what degree have new information technologies broadened/decreased the scope for internationalising industrial manufacturing and services, and how does this affect the spatial allocation of R&D? Will homogenisation, globalisation and worldwide integration of production, marketing and R&D give way to a complex (and often highly interdependent) coexistence of centralised and decentralised markets and production systems? And how will this affect the division of labour between OECD Member countries and different groupings of developing countries?

*iii)* And, finally, how will new generic technologies, such as computer-based information technologies, affect the scope for technology sourcing, acquisition and absorption in different groupings of developing countries? And what institutional and organisational innovations are required to capture the tremendous productivity potential inherent in such technologies without destroying the "social fabric" of such societies?

### Regionalisation and global competition: implications for international trade and technology diffusion

Under this research topic, we suggest the following case studies:

*A study on how Europe 1992* will affect the trade, investment and technology links of this continent with NIEs and other developing countries[3]. Specific issues to be addressed, include:

*i)* The impact of non-tariff trade barriers on mutual trade flows (both EEC imports from NIEs and their exports, particularly of capital goods and services, to NIEs).

*ii)* The impact of stringent local content requirements on cross investment links.

*iii)* Can NIEs (and other developing countries) overcome some of the aforementioned constraints and ensure access to the huge European market through extensive cross investment or cross production agreements?

*iv)* Can large NIE trading companies pool the assets of small- and medium- sized firms and lower their entry costs into the European market?

*v)* What other strategies are open to NIE companies? An evaluation of recent experiences, their prospects, problems and limitations.

*vi)* An assessment of government-level co-operation agreements between European countries and NIEs (examples: Italy/Argentina; Spain/Mexico).

*vii)* Is there scope for strategic/tactical partnering between NIE and European companies, and under what conditions are such arrangements likely to work?

*viii)* Finally, in what areas is there scope for somewhat more complementary forms of technological co-operation between OECD and NIE firms, and how could governments foster this process?

*A study of emerging issues* related to the integration of East Asian and Southeast Asian economies through intra-firm linkages, with a particular focus on the recent involvement of Japanese, Taiwanese, Hong Kong-based, Singaporean and South Korean companies[4].

Concrete issues to be addressed include:

*i)* A series of industry-specific case studies on how regional sourcing and marketing strategies pursued by Japanese companies affect first-tier and second-tier Asian NIEs and the interactions (rivalries/co-operation) between them.

*ii)* Similar studies for regional sourcing and marketing strategies pursued by companies from Hong Kong, Taiwan, Singapore, and South Korea. Will such investments provide a valuable alternative technology source to second-tier Asian NIEs, and will they open up new, somewhat more sophisticated markets for them?

*iii)* Same for cross investment links with Australia and New Zealand.

*iv)* What new possibilities for regional technological co-operation are emerging, and which areas could be particularly fruitful? Example: Is it possible to establish a regional network of ASIC[5] design centres, based on the role model of the Australian informatics policy?

*v)* What are the implications of the aforementioned regional integration trends for the region's trade and investment links with the US, i.e. will it be possible to reduce, step by step, the overwhelming dependence on the US market?

*vi)* Finally, what will be the implications for the region's trade and investment links with Europe, and what role could Europe play in the regional integration process of East and South East Asia?

*A similar study on the emerging regional economic zone* which combines the US, Canada, Mexico and the Caribbean, and its implications for US trade, investment and technology links with the rest of Latin America, in particular Brazil[6].

Concrete topics to be addressed include:

*i)* A comparative assessment of foreign direct investment strategies of American, Japanese and European companies in the Mexican industrial "border zone". Are there differences in terms of local sourcing, local value added, linkage effects and transfer of technology?

ii) What are the strategic options for Mexico's latecomer industrialisation strategies?

iii) Implications of the Mexican experience for latecomer strategies in Argentina and Brazil?

iv) Scope for renewing Latin American regional integration schemes, by means of centering them on specific areas of technological co-operation? What is the importance in this context of new forms of bilateral economic and technological co-operation, like the one concluded between Brazil and Argentina?

**New information technologies and the spatial allocation of industrial research and development**[7]

This research topic would be much more focused than the first one. It consists of three components:

*A theoretical study,* which confronts the rich empirical material included in a number of sector and country case studies[8] with the current theoretical debate, and attempts to broaden the analytical framework for future research. Two issues should be addressed in particular:

i) A re-evaluation of the "Relocation Back to the North" hypothesis;

ii) An assessment of how the internationalisation of production, finance and marketing interacts with the "politicisation" of international trade and investment, and how this changes the constraints for internationalisation strategies.

*A comparative study* (for a common set of industries) of emerging issues related to the internationalisation of industrial R&D, the conflicting forces uderlying them, and their implications for international technology gaps and competitiveness. The following questions will be addressed in particular:

i) Why is it that, so far, R&D has remained much less globalised than production and marketing?

ii) What are the driving forces behind an increasing spatial decentralisation of R&D activities, and how do they square with the still powerful forces favouring centralisation of R&D?

Among the forces behind decentralisation, the following needs to be addressed:

— "Leading users" are not necessarily any longer concentrated in just one dominant market (i.e. the US), or in a handful of them. Not only is there decentralisation of leading users among OECD countries, but they are also present now in some growth poles of NIEs.

— Sourcing for scientists, technologists and designers transcends by far the limits of the OECD region, and concentrates increasingly on human resource pools available in NIEs and other developing countries.

— Access to national R&D subsidies and to national/regional collaborative projects has become a prerequisite for competitive survival. This also applies increasingly to access to government procurement markets in NIEs.

Among the forces constraining geographic decentralisation of R&D, the following needs to be analysed:

142

- The worldwide homogenisation of key market segments reduces the need/scope for specific local product adaptation or for autonomous product development;
- The economies of sophisticated S&T infrastructure;
- The economies of scope of R&D; and
- The need to minimise economic, political and strategic risks.

*iii)* How will an increasing decentralisation of R&D affect the scope for latecomer strategies in different groupings of developing countries, and how could these countries make best use of these new possibilities?

*Industry-specific case studies* on evolving patterns of R&D internationalisation, comparing the strategies of American, Japanese and European companies. Which of these strategies is most conducive to international technology diffusion and for the access of developing countries to productivity-enhancing generic technologies?

## New technologies and latecomer technology acquisition and absorption strategies

Under this topic, we suggest to address the following five issues:

*i)* A study of "strategic partnering" arrangements betwee NIE firms and OECD firms or among NIE firms as a method of improving access to technology and markets, with particular reference to possible complementarities, the distribution of costs and benefits involved, their evolution over time, and their relation to competitive strategies[9].

*ii)* A few empirical case studies on how computer-based information technologies have affected the scope for "technology unpackaging" strategies by NIEs and other developing countries.

*iii)* A conceptual study, based on limited field research in Asian first- and second-tier NIEs, on the impact of new information technologies on producer-user interactions, and how this affects the requirements for setting up viable supplier networks. An important issue to be researched in this context is under what conditions competitive indigenisation of core components, as defined above[10], would become possible?

*iv)* An evaluation study on how effective ODA has been in developing human resources and strengthening skills required for active technology acquisition and absorption strategies[11].

*v)* And, by far of greatest immediate concern, two or three comparative studies (for a common set of industries and technology areas) of how different intellectual and industrial property regimes affect international technology diffusion and trade patterns[12].

# NOTES AND REFERENCES

1. See references given under specific research topics.
2. For the underlying argument, see Chapters I, V and VI.
3. For the underlying rationale, see Chapter IV, "Restructuring of Trade and Investment Relations", in particular the section entitled "The 'reciprocal market access' game". For this project, research co-operation is suggested with the seminario de Sociologia de Nuevas Tecnologices, Universidal Antonoma de Madrid (Prof. Manuel Castells).
4. For the relevance, see Chapter V. Research co-operation is suggested with the Institute of Business Research, Hitotsubashi University, Tokyo (Prof. Ken-Ichi Imai), the Korean Advance Institute for Science and Technology (KAIST), Seoul (Prof. Chong-Ouk Lee) and the Chung-Hua Institution for Economic Research (Dr. Gee San).
5. Application and specific integrated circuits.
6. Research co-operation is suggested with the Centro de Economic International (CEI), Buenos Aires (Dr. Daniel Chudnovsky).
7. The need to study current internationalisation patterns of R&D was stressed by various participants in particular, Prof. Chris Freeman during the expert group meeting "New Technologies, Global Competition and Latecomer Industrialisation — Implications for International Trade and Structural Adjustment" (Dourdan, 20th-27th February 1989). See Appendix.
8. Within the Development Centre, see some of the case studies and reports commissioned for its projects "Technological Change and the Electronics Sector" and "New Forms of Investment". None of these studies however has addressed the issue so far of R&D internationalisation, which is one of the most important aspects of current internationalisation patterns.
9. For the underlying argument, see Chapters V and VI. See also Ernst 1987a.
10. See Chapter IV, "Managing the trade-off between vertical integration and flexible supplier networks".
11. See Chapter V.
12. See Chapter V. See also the report on intellectual property rights, commissioned for the OECD Development Centre research project "Technological Change and the Electronics Sector".

# BIBLIOGRAPHY

AMES, E. and N. Rosenberg (1963), "Changing Technological Leadership and Industrial Growth", *Economic Journal*, March.

AMSDEN, A.H. (1983), "'De-skilling', skilled commodities, and the NICs' emerging competitive advantage", *American Economic Review*, 73.2.

AMSDEN, A.H. (1986), "The direction of trade -- past and present -- and the 'learning effects' of exports to different directions", *Journal of Development Economics*, 23, pp. 249-274.

AMSDEN, A.H. and L. KIM (1986), "A technological perspective on the general machinery industry in the Republic of Korea", in M. Fransman, ed., *Machines and Economic Development*, London, Macmillan, pp. 93-123.

AOKI, A. (1989), "Global Competition, Firm Organisation, and Total Factor Productivity -- A Comparative Micro Perspective", paper presented at OECD Seminar on "Science Technology and Economic Growth", Paris, 5th-8th June.

ARTHUR, W.B. (1988), "Competing technologies" in G. Dosi *et al.*, (eds.) 1988.

AVELLA, R.C. (1988), "Un diagnostico de la crisis de la acumulacion de la industria Colombiana", *Desarrollo y Sociedad*, September, 22, pp. 13-73.

BALASSA, B. (1986), "Japan's trade policies", paper presented at conference on free trade in the world economy, Institut für Weltwirtschaft, Kiel/FRG, 24-26th June.

BANK OF JAPAN (1988), *Greater Role of Asian Economies in the World and Growing Interdependence Among Asia, the United States, and Japan*, Special Paper No. 166, Research and Statistics Department, August.

BAUMOL, W.J., J.C. PANZER and R.D. WILLIG (1982), *Contestable Markets and the Theory of Industrial Structure*, New York, Harecourt Brace Janovich., BORRUS, M. (1988), *Competing for Control. America's Stake in Microelectronics*, Cambridge, Mass., Ballinger.

BOWIE, A. (1988), "Industrial aspirations in a divided society: Malaysian heavy industries 1980-88", paper presented at annual meeting of Association of Asian Studies, San Francisco, 25th-27th March.

BOWONDER, B. and T. MIYAKE (1988), "Measuring innovativeness of an industry: An analysis of the electronics industry in India, Japan, and Korea", *Science and Public Policy*, October, 15:5, pp. 279-303.

BRAUDEL, F. (1979), *Civilisation matérielle, économie et capitalisme, XVe-XVIII siècle. Le temps du monde*, Paris, Librairie Armand Collin.

CARR, E.H. (1967), "Some Random Reflections on Soviet Industrialisation", in Feinstein, C.H. (ed.), "Socialism, Capitalism and Economic Growth", Cambridge.

CASTELLS, M. and L. TYSON (1988), "High-technology choices ahead: Restructuring interdependence" in *U.S. Foreign Policy and the Third World: Agenda 1988-89*, Overseas Development Council, Washington, D.C.

CASTILLO, Mario and CORTELLESE, Claudio (1988), "Small- and Medium- Scale Industry in the Development of Latin America", *CEPAL Review*, April, 34, pp.127-151., CHESNAIS, F. (1986), "Science, technology and competitiveness", *STI Review*, Paris, OECD, No. 1, Autumn.

CHESNAIS, F. (1988), "Multinational enterprises and the international diffusion of technology" in G. Dosi *et al.*, (eds.), 1988.

CHILD, John (1987), "Information Technology, Organisation, and Response to Strategic Challenges", *California Management Review*, Vol XXX, No. 1, pp. 33-49.

CHUDNOVSKY, D. (1988), "Economic integration between Argentina and Brazil: Capital goods as a starting point", *Development and South-South Cooperation*, December, IV:7, pp. 105-112.

CHUDNOVSKY, D., M. NAGAO and S. JACOBSSON (1983), *Capital Goods Production in the Third World: An Economic Study of Technology Acquisition*, London, Pinter.

DAHLMAN. C.F. (1982), "Analytical framework for acquisition of technological capability research project", (World Bank, Development Research Department, Productivity Division, mimeo.).

DORNBUSCH, R. and Y.C. PARK (1987), "Korean Growth Policy", *Brooking Papers on Economic Activity*, 2, pp. 389-454.

DOSI, G. *et al.* (eds.) (1988), *Technical Change and Economic Theory*, London and New York, Pinter.

DOSI, G. and L. SOETE (1988), "Technical change and international trade" in G. Dosi *et al*, (eds.), 1988.

EDQUIST, C. and S. JACOBSSON (1988), *Flexible Automation: The Global Diffusion of New Technology in the Engineering Industry*, Oxford, Basil Blackwell.

ENCARNATION, Dennis J. (1988), "Dislodging multinationals: India's strategy in comparative perspective", manuscript.

ERNST, D. (1981), "International transfer of technology, technological dependence and underdevelopment -- Key issues", Chapter 1 in D. Ernst, (ed.), *The New International Division of Labour, Technology and Underdevelopment*, Frankfurt am Main and New York, Campus.

ERNST, Dieter (1983), *The Global Race in Microelectronics. Innovation and Corporate Strategies in a Period of Crisis*, Campus, Frankfurt am Main and New York.

ERNST, Dieter (1987), "Global competition, strategic alliances and the worldwide restructuring of the electronics industry -- A European Perspective", paper prepared for Stanford Center for European Studies Conference "New Technologies and New Intermediaries", Stanford University, 4th-6th June.

ERNST, D. (1987), "Programmable Automation (PA) in the Semiconductor Industry -- Reflections on Current Diffusion Patterns", invited paper, INSEAD research symposium "Issues in International Manufacturing", Fontainebleau, 7th-9th September.

ERNST, D. (1989 forthcoming), *Global Competition in Advanced Electronics -- Implications for Barriers to Entry and International Technology Diffusion*, Paris, OECD Development Centre.

FAJNZYLBER, Fernando (1988), "Technical change and economic development: Issues for a research agenda", paper presented at World Bank Seminar on "Technology and Long-Term Economic Growth Prospects", Washington, D.C., 16th-17th November.

FERGUSON, C. (1988), "From the people who brought you voodoo economics. Beyond entrepreneurialism to US competitiveness", *Harvard Business Review*, May-June.

FLOREZ, E.G. (1988), "Aprecicion sobre la situacion y las perspectivas de las industrias de bienes de capital", *ibid.*, pp. 109-116.

FRANSMAN, M. (1986), "International competitiveness, international diffusion of technology and the state: A case study from Taiwan and Japan", in Fransman, ed., *op. cit.*, pp. 153-214.

FREEMAN, C. and C. PEREZ (1988), "Structural crises of adjustment, business cycles and investment behaviour" in G. Dosi *et al.*, (eds.), 1988.

GERSCHENKRON, A. (1962), *Economic Backwardness in Historical Perspective. A Book of Essays*, Cambridge, Mass., The Belknap Press.

GILPIN, R.G. (1988), "Implications of the changing trade regime for US-Japanese relations", in Inoguchi *et al.*, (eds.), *The Political Economy of Japan. The Changing International Context*, Vol. 2, Stanford, Ca., Stanford University Press.

GONZALES, N. (1988), "Balance preliminar de la economia Latino Americana en 1987", *Comercio Exterior*, February, 38:2, pp. 108-32.

GORANSSON, B. (1988), "Manufacturing telecommunication equipment in Brazil, India and the Republic of Korea -- Third World Challenges to World Telecommunications Hegemony", paper presented at conference on "Telecommunications, Economy and Society", Budapest, 5th-7th October.

GREGORY, Gene (1986), "East Asian electronics: System and synergy", Chapter 30 in G. Gregory, *Japanese Electronics Technology: Enterprise and Innovation*, Tokyo, The Japan Times Ltd.

GUPTA, A. (1986), "India" in F.W. Rushing and C.G. Ganz, eds., *National Policies for Developing High Technology Industries: International Comparisons*, Boulder and London, Westview, pp. 89-110.

HABAKKUK, H.J. (1962), "American and British Technology in the Nineteenth Century", Cambridge, Cambridge University Press.

HAKLISCH, C. and N.S. VONORTAS (1988), *Export Controls and the International Technical System: The US Semiconductor Industry*, Center for Science and Technology Policy, New York, Rensselaer Polytechnic Institute, June.

HAYASHI, A.M. (1989), "Hyundai's Headaches", *Electronic Business*, 6th February, pp. 25-32.

HIGASHI, C. and G.P. LAUTER (1987), *The Internationalisation of the Japanese Economy*, Boston, Mass., Kluwer Academic Publishers.

HIRSCHMAN, A.O. 1958), The Strategy of Economic Development, New Haven.

HIRSCHMAN, A.O. (1986), "The Political Economy of Latin American Development: Seven Exercises in Retrospection", paper for the XIII International Congress of the Latin American Studies Association, Boston, 23rd-26th October.

IMAI, K. (1988), "Japanese corporate strategies towards international networking and product development", paper presented at the Japanese Corporate Organisation and International Adjustment Conference, Australian National University, Canberra, 19th-20th September.

IMAI, KEN-ICHI and BABA, Y. (1989), "Systematic Innovation and Cross-Border Networks -- Transcending Markets and Hierarchies to Create a New Techno-Economic System", paper presented at Seminar on "Science Technology and Economic Growth", Paris, 5th-8th June.

JO, S-H. (1988), "Foreign direct investment and industrial growth in South Korea", Research Project on "Foreign direct investment and industrialisation in developing countries", Paris, OECD Development Centre, first revision.

JONES, D.T. (1988), "Structural adjustment in the automobile industry", *STI Review*, No. 3, OECD, April.

KAY, N. (1984), *The Emergent Firm*, London, Macmillan.

KAYE, L. (1989), "Problem programme", *Far Eastern Economic Review*, 2nd March, p. 87.

KIERZKOWSKI, H.K. (ed.) (1984), *Monopolistic Competition and International Trade*, Oxford, Claredon Press.

KIM, L. (1988), "Technological transformation in Korea and its implications for other developing countries", *Development and South-South Cooperation*, December, VI:7, pp. 105-112.

LALKAKA, R. and Mingyu WU, eds., (1984), *Managing Science Policy and Technology Development: Strategies for China and a Changing World*, Dublin, Tycooly.

LANDES, D. (1969), *The Unbound Prometheus. Technological Change and Industrial Development in Western Europe from 1750 to the Present*, Cambridge, Cambridge University Press.

LEVIN, R.C., A.K. KLEVORICK, R. NELSON and S.G. WINTER (1987), "Appropriating the returns from industrial research and development", *Brookings Papers on Economic Activity*.

LANDES, D. (1965), "Japan and Europe: Contrasts in Industrialisation", in Lockwood, W.W. (ed.) "The State and Economic Enterprise in Japan", Princeton.

LIM, L. (1978), "Multinational firms and manufacturing for export in less-developed countries: The case of the electronics industry in Malaysia and Singapore", unpublished PhD dissertation, Ann Arbor, University of Michigan.

LIM, L. (1988), "The electronics industry in Southeast Asia: Confounding the critics", paper presented at the Association for Asian Studies annual meeting, San Francisco, 25th-27th March.

LITTLE, J.S. (1986), "Intra-firm trade and US protectionism -- Thoughts based on a small survey", *New England Economic Review*, January/February.

LITTLE, J.S. (1987), "Intra-firm trade: An update", *New England Economic Review*, May/June.

LOONEY, R.E. (1982), *Trade, Employment and Industrialisation in Mexico*, International Division of Labour Programme, Geneva, ILO, (WEP 2-36/WP-20).

LUNDVALL, B-A. (1988), "Innovation as an interactive process: From user-producer interaction to the national system of innovation", in G. Dosi, *et al., op. cit.*, pp. 349-69.

MERHAV, M. (1969), *Technological Dependence, Monopoly and Growth*, Oxford, Pergamon.

MISTRAL, J. (1983), "Competitiveness of the production system and international specialisation", mimeo, Paris.

MOWERY, D. (ed) (1988), *International Collaborative Ventures in US Manufacturing*, Cambridge, Mass., Ballinger.

MOWERY, D. and N. ROSENBERG (1989), "New developments in U.S. technology policy -- implications for competitiveness and international trade policy", mimeo, January.

MURALIDHARAN, S. (1988), "Electronics: Liberalisation reconsidered", *Economic and Political Weekly*, 13th August, pp. 1661-7.

NAU, H. (ed) (1989), *Domestic Trade Politics and the Uruguay Round*, New York, Columbia University Press.

NIETO PONTES, Mauricio (1988), "Renovacion del crecimiento, politica industrial y ortodoxia economica: Elementos para un analysis critico", *Desarrollo y Sociedad*, September, 22, pp. 77-106.

O'CONNOR, David (1986), "Transnational corporations in the international semiconductor industry", study prepared for the United Nations Center on Transnational Corporations, New York.

OECD (1987), *Structural Adjustment and Economic Performance*, Paris.

OECD (1988a), *The Newly Industrialising Countries: Challenges and Opportunities for OECD Industries*, Paris.

OECD (1988b), *Technology, Flexibility of Manufacturing and Industrial Relations*, Paris, 18th October.

OECD (1988), *OECD Science and Technology Policy Outlook 1988*, Paris.

OFFICE OF TECHNOLOGY ASSESSMENT (1988), *Paying the Bill. Manufacturing and America's Trade Deficit*, Congress of the United States, Washington, D.C.

PARK, Y.C. (1989), "Structural change and development in Pacific Asia", paper presented at the OECD Development Centre 25th Anniversary Symposium on "The Next Decade: Interdependence in a Multipolar and Two-Track World Economy", 6th-8th February 1989.

PARTHASARATHI, A. (1970), "Some Aspects of the Development of Poor Countries and the Role of International Scientific Co-operation in that Process", paper prepared for Pugwash Symposium on "What Can Scientists Do for Development", Stanford University, August.

PEREZ, C. and L. SOETE (1988), "Catching up in technology: Entry barriers and windows of opportunity", in G. Dosi, *et al.* (eds.), 1988 pp. 458-79.

PIORE, M. and C.F. SABEL (1984), *The Second Industrial Divide. Possibilities for Prosperity*, New York, Basic Books.

PRESTOWITZ, Jr., C.V. (1988), *Trading Places. How We Allowed Japan to Take the Lead*, New York, Basic Books.

PUGEL, T.A. and R.G. HAWKINS (eds.) (1986), *Fragile Interdependence. Economic Issues in US-Japanese Trade and Investment*, Lexington, Mass., and Toronto, Lexington Books.

ROSENBERG, N. (1982), *Inside the Black Box: Technology and Economics*, Cambridge, Cambridge University Press.

SIMON, D.F. (1989), "Technological change in the electronics sector -- perspectives, and policy options for China", paper prepared for OECD Development Centre Project on "Technological Change and the Electronics Sector...".

SOETE, L. (1985), "International diffusion of technology, industrial development and technological leapfrogging", *World Development*, March, 13:3, pp. 409-22.

STRANGE, Susan (1985), "Protectionism and world politics", *International Organisation*, Vol. 39, pp. 233-59.

TEECE, D.J. (1977), "Technology transfer by multinational firms: The resource cost of transferring technological know-how", *Economic Journal*, 87 (346), pp. 242-61.

TEECE, D.J. (1986), "Capturing value from technological innovation: Integration, strategic partnering, and licensing decisions", Center for Research Management, University of California, Berkeley, manuscript, March.

THUROW, L. and L.D. TYSON (1987), "The economic black hole", *Foreign Policy*, June.

TYSON, L.D. (1988), "Making policy for national competitivenss in a changing world" in A. Furino (ed.), *Cooperation and Competition in the Global Economy*, Cambridge, Mass., Ballinger.

UNCTAD (1987), *Trade and Development Report 1987*, Geneva.

UNCTAD (1988), *Technology-Related Policies and Legislation in a Changing Economic and Technological Environment*, 8th August, TD/B/C.6/146.

UNCTC (1986) (United Nations Centre on Transnational Corporations), *Transnational Corporations in the International Semiconductor Industry*, New York, ST/CTC/39.

UNCTC (1988), *Transnational Corporations in World Development: Trends and Prospects*, New York, ST/CTC/89.

UNESCO (1986), *Statistical Yearbook*, Paris.

VEBLEN, T. (1915), *Imperial Germany and the Industrial Revolution*, London, The Macmillan Company.

VICKERY, G. (1986), "International flows of technology -- Recent trends and developments", *STI Review*, Paris, OECD, No. 1, Autumn.

VILLALOBOS, F. (1986), "Las politicad de ajuste y el proceso de industrializacion -- Uruguay, 1980-1985", *Cuadernos de CLAEH*, October, 38, pp. 85-105.

VILLARREAL, René P. (1988), "La Reconversion en la siderurgia paraetatal en Mexico", *Comercio Exterior* 33(3), pp. 191-201.

WAKASUGI, Ryuhei (1988), "Technological Innovation and Diffusion in Japan and Asian NIEs", paper presented at the Third International Technical Innovation and Entrepreneurship Symposium held at the Gold Coast, Australia, 5th-8th September.

WALSH, Vivien (1987), "Technology, Competitiveness and the Special Problems of Small Countries", *STI Review*, No. 2, pp. 81-129.

WESTLAKE, M. (1989), "Seeds of a Bitter Harvest", *South*, February.

WIENERT, H. and J. SLATER (1986), *East-West Technology Transfer: The Trade and Economic Aspects*, Paris, OECD.

WILLIAMSON, O.E. (1985), *The Economic Institutions of Capitalism*, New York and London, Free Press.

WOODARD, Thomas M. (1987), "The Prospects for the World Electronics Industry", *The Financial Times World Electronics Conference*, London, 13th-14th May, Speakers' Papers.

*Appendix*

# LIST OF PARTICIPANTS

Expert Group Meeting
"New Technologies, Global Competition and Latecomer Industrialisation:
Implications for International Trade and Structural Adjustment"
Hostellerie Blanche de Castille, Place des Halles, 91410 Dourdan, France
20th to 24th February 1989

Professor Manuel CASTELLS
Director
Seminario de Sociologia de Nuevas Tecnologias
Facultad de Ciencias Economicas
Universidad Autonoma de Madrid
MADRID
Spain

Dr. Carlos CORREA
Senior Research Fellow
Centro de Economica Internacional
BUENOS AIRES
Argentine

Dr. Michel DELAPIERRE
CAREA-CEREM
Université Paris-X
NANTERRE
France

Professor Dennis ENCARNATION
Harvard Business School
CAMBRIDGE, Massachusetts
United States

Professor Fabio ERBER
Deputy Secretary General
Ministry of Science and Technology
BRASÍLIA DF
Brazil

Dr. Michel FOUQUIN
CEPII
PARIS
France

Professor Chris FREEMAN
Science Policy Research Unit (SPRU)
University of Sussex
Falmer, BRIGHTON
United Kingdom

Professor Kotaro HORISAKA
Faculty of Foreign Languages and Studies
Sophia University
TOKYO
Japan

Mrs. Maria Elena HURTADO
Editor, Science and Technology
South Magazine
LONDON
United Kingdom

Dr. Henry KELLY
Project Director
Office of Technology Assessment
Congress of the United States
WASHINGTON, DC
United States

Mr. Masayuki KONDO
Deputy Director
Information Processing Administration Division
Ministry of International Trade & Industry (MITI)
TOKYO
Japan

Professor David MOWERY
Associate Professor of Business & Public Policy
University of California at Berkeley
School of Business
BERKELEY, California
United States

Professor Lynn MYTELKA
Carleton University
OTTAWA
Canada

Professor David O'CONNOR
Department of Economics
Ateneo de Manila University
QUEZON CIT
Philippines

Dr. Ashok PARATHASARATHI
Additional Secretary
Department of Scientific & Industrial Research
Ministry of Science and Technology
NEW DELHI
India

Professor Hak PYO
Chairman
Department of International Economics
Seoul National University
SEOUL
Korea

Dr. Gee SAN
Research Fellow
Chung-Hua Institution for Economic Research
TAPEI
Taiwan

Dr. Francisco SERCOVICH
Centre de Recherche en Développement et Technologie
Université du Quebec à Montréal
MONTREAL, Quebec
Canada

Professor Jon SIGURDSON
Director
Research Policy Institute
LUND
Sweden

Professor Denis SIMON
Fletcher School of Law & Diplomacy
Tufts University
MEDFORD, Massachusetts
United States

Dr. Louis TURNER
Royal Institute of International Affairs
LONDON
United Kingdom

\#　\#　\#　\#　\#　\#　\#

OECD STAFF

Mr. F. CHESNAIS, DSTI/SPT
Mr. Graham VICKERY, DSTI/IPD

Development Centre

Mr. Dieter ERNST
Mr. Charles OMAN
Mr. Richard CONROY
Mr. Antonio BOTELHO
Ms. Maud BRUCE
Mr. Halvor NAFSTAD

# WHERE TO OBTAIN OECD PUBLICATIONS
# OÙ OBTENIR LES PUBLICATIONS DE L'OCDE

**ARGENTINA – ARGENTINE**
Carlos Hirsch S.R.L.,
Galería Guemes, Florida 165, 4° Piso,
1333 Buenos Aires
    Tel. 30.7122, 331.1787 y 331.2391
Telegram.: Hirsch-Baires

**AUSTRALIA – AUSTRALIE**
D.A. Book (Aust.) Pty. Ltd.
11-13 Station Street (P.O. Box 163)
Mitcham, Vic. 3132    Tel. (03) 873 4411
Telex: AA37911 DA BOOK    Telefax: (03)873.5679

**AUSTRIA – AUTRICHE**
OECD Publications and Information Centre,
4 Simrockstrasse,
5300 Bonn (Germany)    Tel. (0228) 21.60.45
Telex: 8 86300 Bonn    Telefax: (0228)26.11.04
Gerold & Co., Graben 31, Wien 1    Tel. (1)533.50.14

**BELGIUM – BELGIQUE**
Jean de Lannoy, Avenue du Roi 202
B-1060 Bruxelles    Tel. (02) 538.51.69/538.08.41
Telex: 63220

**CANADA**
Renouf Publishing Company Ltd
1294 Algoma Road, Ottawa, Ont. K1B 3W8
    Tel: (613) 741-4333
Telex: 053-4783    Telefax: (613)741.5439
Stores:
61 Sparks St., Ottawa, Ont. K1P 5R1
    Tel: (613) 238-8985
211 rue Yonge St., Toronto, Ont. M5B 1M4
    Tel: (416) 363-3171
Federal Publications Inc.,
165 University Avenue,
Toronto, ON M5H 3B9    Tel. (416)581-1552
Telefax: (416)581.1743
Les Publications Fédérales
1185 rue de l'Université
Montréal, PQ H3B 1R7    Tel.(514)954.1633
Les Éditions la Liberté Inc.,
3020 Chemin Sainte-Foy,
Sainte-Foy, P.Q. G1X 3V6,    Tel. (418)658-3763
Telefax: (418)658.3763

**DENMARK – DANEMARK**
Munksgaard Export and Subscription Service
35, Nørre Søgade, P.O. Box 212148
DK-1016 København K    Tel. (45 1)12.85.70
Telex: 19431 MUNKS DK    Telefax: (45 1)12.93.87

**FINLAND – FINLANDE**
Akateeminen Kirjakauppa,
Keskuskatu 1, P.O. Box 128
00100 Helsinki    Tel. (358 0)12141
Telex: 125080    Telefax: (358 0)121.4441

**FRANCE**
OCDE/OECD
Mail Orders/Commandes par correspondance :
2, rue André-Pascal,
75775 Paris Cedex 16    Tel. (1) 45.24.82.00
Bookshop/Librairie : 33, rue Octave-Feuillet
75016 Paris
    Tel. (1) 45.24.81.67 or/ou (1) 45.24.81.81
Telex: 620 160 OCDE    Telefax: (33-1)45.24.85.00
Librairie de l'Université,
12a, rue Nazareth,
13602 Aix-en-Provence    Tel. 42.26.18.08

**GERMANY – ALLEMAGNE**
OECD Publications and Information Centre,
4 Simrockstrasse,
5300 Bonn    Tel. (0228) 21.60.45
Telex: 8 86300 Bonn    Telefax: (0228)26.11.04

**GREECE – GRÈCE**
Librairie Kauffmann,
28, rue du Stade, 105 64 Athens    Tel. 322.21.60
Telex: 218187 LIKA Gr

**HONG KONG**
Government Information Services,
Publications (Sales) Office,
Information Services Department
No. 1, Battery Path, Central
Tel.(5)23.31.91    Telex: 802.61190

**ICELAND – ISLANDE**
Mál Mog Menning
Laugavegi 18, Pósthólf 392
121 Reykjavik    Tel. 15199/24240

**INDIA – INDE**
Oxford Book and Stationery Co.,
Scindia House,
New Delhi 110001    Tel. 331.5896/5308
Telex: 31 61990 AM IN    Telefax: (11) 332.5993
17 Park St., Calcutta 700016    Tel. 240832

**INDONESIA – INDONÉSIE**
Pdii-Lipi, P.O. Box 3065/JKT.
Jakarta    Tel. 583467
Telex: 73 45875

**IRELAND – IRLANDE**
TDC Publishers - Library Suppliers,
12 North Frederick Street,
Dublin 1    Tel. 744835-749677
Telex: 33530TDCP EI Telefax: 748416

**ITALY – ITALIE**
Libreria Commissionaria Sansoni,
Via Benedetto Fortini 120/10,
Casella Post. 552
50125 Firenze    Tel. (055)645415
Telex: 570466    Telefax: (39.55)641257
Via Bartolini 29, 20155 Milano    Tel. 365083
La diffusione delle pubblicazioni OCSE viene assicurata
dalle principali librerie ed anche da :
Editrice e Libreria Herder,
Piazza Montecitorio 120, 00186 Roma
Tel. 6794628    Telex: NATEL I 621427
Libreria Hœpli,
Via Hœpli 5, 20121 Milano    Tel. 865446
Telex:31.33.95    Telefax: (39.2)805.2886
Libreria Scientifica
Dott. Lucio de Biasio "Aeiou"
Via Meravigli 16, 20123 Milano    Tel. 807679
Telefax: 800175

**JAPAN – JAPON**
OECD Publications and Information Centre,
Landic Akasaka Building, 2-3-4 Akasaka,
Minato-ku, Tokyo 107    Tel. 586.2016
    Telefax: (81.3) 584.7929

**KOREA – CORÉE**
Kyobo Book Centre Co. Ltd.
P.O.Box 1658, Kwang Hwa Moon
Seoul    Tel. (REP) 730.78.91
Telefax: 735.0030

**MALAYSIA/SINGAPORE – MALAISIE/SINGAPOUR**
University of Malaya Co-operative Bookshop Ltd.,
P.O. Box 1127, Jalan Pantai Baru 59100
Kuala Lumpur, Malaysia/Malaisie
Tel. 756.5000/756.5425    Telefax: 757.3661
Information Publications Pte Ltd
Pei-Fu Industrial Building,
24 New Industrial Road No. 02-06
Singapore/Singapour 1953    Tel. 283.1786/283.1798
Telefax: 284.8875

**NETHERLANDS – PAYS-BAS**
SDU Uitgeverij
Christoffel Plantijnstraat 2
Postbus 20014
2500 EA's-Gravenhage    Tel. (070)78.99.11
Voor bestellingen:    Tel. (070)78.98.80
Telex: 32486 stdru    Telefax: (070)47.63.51

**NEW ZEALAND – NOUVELLE-ZÉLANDE**
Government Printing Office Bookshops:
Auckland: Retail Bookshop, 25 Rutland Street,
Mail Orders, 85 Beach Road
Private Bag C.P.O.
Hamilton: Retail: Ward Street,
Mail Orders, P.O. Box 857
Wellington: Retail, Mulgrave Street, (Head Office)
Telex: COVPRNT NZ 31370    Telefax: (04)734943
Cubacade World Trade Centre,
Mail Orders, Private Bag
Christchurch: Retail, 159 Hereford Street,
Mail Orders, Private Bag
Dunedin: Retail, Princes Street,
Mail Orders, P.O. Box 1104

**NORWAY – NORVÈGE**
Narvesen Info Center – NIC,
Bertrand Narvesens vei 2,
P.O.B 6125 Etterstad, 0602 Oslo 6
    Tel. (02)67.83.10/(02)68.40.20
Telex: 79668 NIC N    Telefax: (47 2)68.53.47

**PAKISTAN**
Mirza Book Agency
65 Shahrah Quaid-E-Azam, Lahore 3    Tel. 66839
Telegram: "Knowledge"

**PORTUGAL**
Livraria Portugal, Rua do Carmo 70-74,
1117 Lisboa Codex    Tel. 347.49.82/3/4/5

**SINGAPORE/MALAYSIA – SINGAPOUR/MALAISIE**
See "Malaysia/Singapore". Voir «Malaisie/Singapour»

**SPAIN – ESPAGNE**
Mundi-Prensa Libros, S.A.,
Castelló 37, Apartado 1223,
Madrid-28001    Tel. 431.33.99
Telex: 49370 MPLI    Telefax: 275.39.98
Libreria Bosch, Ronda Universidad 11,
Barcelona 7    Tel. 317.53.08/317.53.58

**SWEDEN – SUÈDE**
Fritzes Fackboksföretaget
Box 16356, S 103 27 STH,
Regeringsgatan 12,
DS Stockholm    Tel. (08)23.89.00
Telex: 12387    Telefax: (08)20.50.21
Subscription Agency/Abonnements:
Wennergren-Williams AB,
Box 30004, S104 25 Stockholm    Tel. (08)54.12.00
Telex: 19937    Telefax: (08)50.82.86

**SWITZERLAND – SUISSE**
OECD Publications and Information Centre,
4 Simrockstrasse,
5300 Bonn (Germany)    Tel. (0228) 21.60.45
Telex: 8 86300 Bonn    Telefax: (0228)26.11.04
Librairie Payot,
6 rue Grenus, 1211 Genève 11    Tel. (022)731.89.50
Telex: 28356
Maditec S.A.
Ch. des Palettes 4
1020 – Renens/Lausanne    Tel. (021)635.08.65
Telefax: (021)635.07.80
United Nations Bookshop/Librairie des Nations-Unies
Palais des Nations, 1211 – Geneva 10
    Tel. (022)734.60.11 (ext. 48.72)
Telex: 289696 (Attn: Sales)    Telefax: (022)733.98.79

**TAIWAN – FORMOSE**
Good Faith Worldwide Int'l Co., Ltd.
9th floor, No. 118, Sec.2, Chung Hsiao E. Road
Taipei    Tel. 391.7396/391.7397
Telefax: 394.9176

**THAILAND – THAILANDE**
Suksit Siam Co., Ltd., 1715 Rama IV Rd.,
Samyam, Bangkok 5    Tel. 2511630

**TURKEY – TURQUIE**
Kültur Yayinlari Is-Türk Ltd. Sti.
Atatürk Bulvari No. 191/Kat. 21
Kavaklidere/Ankara    Tel. 25.07.60
Dolmabahce Cad. No. 29
Besiktas/Istanbul    Tel. 160.71.88
Telex: 43482B

**UNITED KINGDOM – ROYAUME-UNI**
H.M. Stationery Office    (01)873-8483
Postal orders only:
P.O.B. 276, London SW8 5DT
Telephone orders:    (01) 873-9090, or
Personal callers:
49 High Holborn, London WC1V 6HB
Telex:297138    Telefax: 873.8463
Branches at: Belfast, Birmingham, Bristol, Edinburgh,
Manchester

**UNITED STATES – ÉTATS-UNIS**
OECD Publications and Information Centre,
2001 L Street, N.W., Suite 700,
Washington, D.C. 20036-4095    Tel. (202)785.6323
Telex:440245 WASHINGTON D.C.
Telefax: (202)785.0350

**VENEZUELA**
Libreria del Este,
Avda F. Miranda 52, Aptdo. 60337,
Edificio Galipan, Caracas 106
    Tel. 951.1705/951.2307/951.1297
Telegram: Libreste Caracas

**YUGOSLAVIA – YOUGOSLAVIE**
Jugoslovenska Knjiga, Knez Mihajlova 2,
P.O.B. 36, Beograd    Tel. 621.992
Telex: 12466 jk bgd

Orders and inquiries from countries where Distributors
have not yet been appointed should be sent to: OECD,
Publications Service, 2, rue André-Pascal, 75775 PARIS
CEDEX 16.

Les commandes provenant de pays où l'OCDE n'a pas
encore désigné de distributeur devraient être adressées à :
OCDE, Service des Publications, 2, rue André-Pascal,
75775 PARIS CEDEX 16.

72547-6-1989

OECD PUBLICATIONS, 2, rue André-Pascal, 75775 PARIS CEDEX 16 - No. 44925 1989
PRINTED IN FRANCE
(41 89 07 1) ISBN 92-64-13279-1